"The way Steven lives, the honest, real stories he has shared, and the encouragement he has given me has had a profound impact on my life. I know that will be how everyone who reads this book will feel too."

—**Hillary Scott**, lead singer of Lady Antebellum

"We loved Steven Curtis Chapman's deeply personal book, *Between Heaven and the Real World*! Each story he tells and each life circumstance he shares is an illustration of the 'glorious unfolding' of God's plan for him, Mary Beth, and their incredible children. We've been fans from almost the beginning, as Steven's songs have mirrored each stage in our own family and ministry, including grieving the loss of a dearly beloved child. When I list the most helpful things that have helped us grieve our son, *Beauty Will Rise* is always in the top three. Thank you, Steven, for allowing so many of us to grow closer to Jesus through the stories your music tells."

—**Pastor Rick and Kay Warren**

"My heart resonates whenever I connect with someone who understands suffering—not in theory but in the gut and heart. Through decades of quadriplegia, I've learned that when you are hemorrhaging human strength, sometimes answers—even though good, right, and true—can sting like salt in a wound. It's what I love about Steven Curtis Chapman. He doesn't give pat, one-size-fits-all answers to the big questions about life. It's because he has suffered . . . and suffered long. If you do not know this about our friend Steven, then you are in for an enlightening surprise as you turn the pages of *Between Heaven and the Real World*. It is indeed real, pointing the reader to the only Answer that suffices—Jesus, the One who wrote the book on suffering. Steven Curtis Chapman knows Him well. And Lord willing, you'll know Him better too, for having heard Steven's heart in this remarkable book."

—**Joni Eareckson Tada**

"To me, SCC has always been the gold standard of Christian music. His influence on me and my music has been more that I could ever say in words. No doubt Steven is a phenomenal songwriter, musician, and artist. However, as I have gotten to know him more, I have come to realize that the power and impact of his music comes from a place of deep humility. I am honored to call Steven a friend and so happy to recommend his story to you in *Between Heaven and the Real World*."

—Chris Tomlin

"Millions have been inspired by the music of my friend Steven Curtis Chapman—his words and melodies have found their way into countless hearts, ushering in the life-giving truth of Jesus. I believe this book will do the very same thing—for the 'up close' Steven is just as inspiring as the one we find on stage. As he tells his personal story of faith through this book, many will find hope, strength, and inspiration for their own journey."

—Matt Redman

"When Steven wrote the song 'The Great Adventure,' I wonder if he had any idea how adventurous his life would be. While no one can anticipate the highest highs and the lowest lows of their journey, Steven has invited us to experience all of it with him through his honest music and storytelling. We are all changed for the better as a result of it."

—Amy Grant

"We all have a story. But few of us have a story as dramatic and redemptive as the one of Steven Curtis Chapman. His music has touched millions of hearts. May his story touch even more."

—Max Lucado

"I have had the great honor of knowing, sharing the stage with, and making music with my good friend Steven Curtis Chapman. This book is an amazing insight into the heart and spirit of a living legend in Christian music.

One who not only has given us incredible music and messages in the past but also continues to create great music now that inspires and encourages."

—Mac Powell

"By any measure, Steven Curtis Chapman has left his mark on the music industry. Not only has he been recognized with countless awards and accolades, he is loved by people all over the world. How amazing that with all his success, his legacy will be bigger and longer-lasting than any of the trophies. What Steven and Mary Beth have accomplished in the world of adoption is unparalleled. Caring for the widows and the orphans is a great command, and I don't know anyone who has answered that call with greater passion than my friend Steven Curtis Chapman."

—Michael W. Smith

"I cannot express to you the impact Steven Curtis Chapman's music has had on my life. You know how when you hear a song and it immediately takes you back to a specific moment in your life? Well . . . Steven was there when I came to know Christ. He was there when my father passed away. He was there when I surrendered to ministry. He was there when I got married. He was there when my first child was born. I could go on, but then you'd be reading two books. Needless to say, this man is very important to me, and I'm proud to call him my friend."

—Bart Millard

"Steven Curtis Chapman is one of those men who raise the bar for all of us. I have admired him for as long as I can remember. He has always been a role model of humility and gentleness to me. At the same time a man in the trenches, putting action to his heart for the orphan—building Show Hope—forever expanding the hearts of thousands of families who have welcomed a child into their lives. Steven truly inspires me as a husband, father, songwriter, and artist."

—Toby McKeehan

"It's been my privilege over the last eighteen years to call Steven Curtis Chapman a friend. But you don't have to know him personally to know his heart or know his story. His music and lyrics have spoken to millions. He's the Michael Jordan of Christian music. When you read *Between Heaven and the Real World* you will come to know a man who has walked the walk with an incredible grace and a rock-solid faith. If you like his songs, wait till you read this book!"

—**Ernie Johnson Jr.**, studio host, *Inside the NBA* on TNT

Between Heaven & the Real World

My Story

STEVEN CURTIS CHAPMAN

WITH KEN ABRAHAM

Revell
a division of Baker Publishing Group
Grand Rapids, Michigan

Published by Revell
a division of Baker Publishing Group
P.O. Box 6287, Grand Rapids, MI 49516-6287
www.revellbooks.com

Printed in the United States of America

Library of Congress Cataloging-in-Publication Data
Names: Chapman, Steven Curtis, author.
Title: Between heaven and the real world : my story / Steven Curtis Chapman with Ken Abraham.
Description: Grand Rapids : Revell, 2016. | Includes bibliographical references.
Identifiers: LCCN 2016045647 | ISBN 9780800726881 (cloth) | ISBN 9780800727642 (ITPE)
Subjects: LCSH: Chapman, Steven Curtis. | Contemporary Christian musicians—United States—Biography. | Christian biography—United States.
Classification: LCC ML420.C4537 A3 2016 | DDC 782.42164092 [B] —dc23
LC record available at https://lccn.loc.gov/2016045647

Published in association with Creative Trust, Inc., 210 Jamestown Park Drive, Suite 200, Brentwood, TN 37027, www.creativetrust.com.

17 18 19 20 21 22 23 7 6 5 4 3 2 1

In keeping with biblical principles of creation stewardship, Baker Publishing Group advocates the responsible use of our natural resources. As a member of the Green Press Initiative, our company uses recycled paper when possible. The text paper of this book is composed in part of post-consumer waste.

To the one who has journeyed
faithfully and fiercely at my side
on this amazing adventure . . . so far . . .
my bride, Mary Beth.
I love you, always and forever.

Contents

Prologue

The Wild Mouse

When I was a little blond-haired boy, my older brother, Herbie, and I loved to go to Noble Park, a 135-acre picturesque public property that includes a five-acre lake in my hometown of Paducah, Kentucky. It was a great place where families could take young children, play on the playgrounds, have a picnic, feed the fish, maybe get chased by a goose, and just enjoy the beauty of nature.

Years later, in the gazebo of that same park, I would kneel down before a beautiful young lady named Mary Beth, who'd stolen my heart, and ask her to be my wife.

As a boy, one of my favorite things about the park was the section called Funland, a small amusement park that was home to cotton candy and popcorn stands as well as several kids' thrill rides, like the ones you'd find at a county fair, that operated all summer long. Herbie was especially fond of the helicopter ride. Each helicopter held two passengers and had a control bar that you pulled back and forth to cause the helicopter to rise or drop as it circled around a large stationary pole. If you pulled the bar toward you, the helicopter soared higher, and if you pushed the bar away from you, the helicopter eased down lower, similar to the Dumbo ride at Disney World.

As soon as Herbie and I climbed inside the helicopter, my brother pulled on the bar and the helicopter zoomed straight up as high as it could go. The attendant punched the start button, and the helicopter began going round and round. I screamed the whole time, terrified of heights, and tried to push the bar away as Herbie, always the thrill seeker, pulled it back, laughing the whole time with that evil big brother laugh.

I got off the helicopter, took several deep breaths to calm myself down, and searched out the little train that slowly chugged around the park. That was more my speed. We'd chug past the Haunted House and the Tilt-a-Whirl, and I'd reaffirm my commitment never again to step foot on that crazy spinning death trap. If you can't tell, I was a bit of a safety-conscious young fella—a condition my brother found great joy in exploiting when given the opportunity.

Then life changed for all of us in Paducah the day the Wild Mouse arrived at Noble Park. It was our town's first roller coaster. I hadn't ridden the Wild Mouse yet and had no intention of doing so—even Herbie wasn't sure about this one—but all my friends were talking about it. As I listened to their stories, I could only imagine the horror of that speeding coaster. "Man, that thing is terrifying . . . you drop down this hill, and you twist and turn, and I thought I was gonna fall out for sure!"

I'd never been to an actual amusement park, where real roller coasters ripped and roared around the track, so I didn't know the difference. I had never experienced a "grown-up" roller coaster. All I knew from the stories I'd heard was if I valued my life, I should stay completely clear of the Wild Mouse . . . so I did . . . for a while.

In actuality, the Wild Mouse was a little roller coaster car that could carry four kids, followed by a few other cars, going around on a short track that had some small dips, bumps, and slight inclines. The cars weren't even connected but ran in sequence.

I should have known better. After all, the ride was named the Wild *Mouse*, not the Wild Dragon or the Wild Lion. It was the Wild *Mouse*, for cryin' out loud.

Finally, the day came to face my deepest fears and stare death in the face of the Wild Mouse. I boarded with a prayer, and the ride began. I twisted and turned and dipped and bumped, screaming and laughing the whole time . . . and lived to tell about it! And if you had asked me back then, "Steven, have you ever ridden on a roller coaster?" I would have pumped my chest and replied, "Oh yeah. I've ridden on the Wild Mouse!"

Fast-forward a few years later to when our uncle Barry took Herbie and me to St. Louis on Uniform Day at Busch Stadium. Once a year on that special day, kids could get in free to the St. Louis Cardinals Major League Baseball game if they wore their Little League uniforms, so Herbie and I packed up our Concord Lions uniforms and our ball gloves with hopes of catching a foul ball and headed to the big city of St. Louis. Uncle Barry did it up big-time. We stayed overnight at a fancy downtown hotel, went up in the St. Louis Arch, went to the ballgame in our uniforms, and ate hot dogs. Then the next day we went to a huge theme park, Six Flags Over Mid-America, known today as Six Flags Over St. Louis.

We rode a lot of the rides and were having a great time. Then we got in line for the Screamin' Eagle—a real roller coaster, and not just *any* roller coaster. Oh no. When the Screamin' Eagle opened in time for America's bicentennial celebration in 1976, the three-minute thrill ride was billed as the highest roller coaster in the world—with peaks up to 110 feet high—and the fastest coaster—with speeds of 62 miles per hour. Located at the back of the park on a bit of a hill, the white wooden track was even more awe inspiring thanks to the cars decorated in red, white, and blue.

I was ready for it. After all, I'd ridden the Wild Mouse!

Herbie, Uncle Barry, and I squeezed into one of the cars after the Screamin' Eagle idled into the station . . . this didn't look so scary. I was perfectly fine . . . until the roller coaster starting moving. Like most coasters, the Screamin' Eagle chugged slowly out of the station, then began inching up the incline, up and up, higher and higher, with the clackity-clack of the wheels on the wooden track sounding more ominous every moment.

Herbie and me all suited up and ready for a St. Louis Cardinals game.

The view was fantastic, but the higher we ascended, the more my mind screamed, *What have I gotten myself into!*

We finally reached the top, and our car seemed to teeter there precariously for a second, or at least long enough for me to gasp for one last breath, and then whoosh! The Screamin' Eagle lived up to its name, whisking us around a U-turn and then straight down, jolting, twisting, and turning as it went! I heard sounds of screaming all right, but it wasn't the eagle that was screaming. It was *me* . . . screaming like a little girl. It was downright embarrassing, but I didn't care because I was sure this was the end.

The coaster careened around another turn and down another drop, and then another, and kept on going, tossing us first one way and then the next, with the wheels screeching loudly through every turn. The coaster track ran close to a forest with trees right alongside the railing, and at one point, it looked as though we were going to smack right into a couple of branches dangling out over the track. But just a second or two before we became "one" with the branches, the coaster dove down a hill, causing us to miss the limbs, but my stomach was still hanging up there in the trees! The Screamin' Eagle kept right on screaming. My heart was pounding, and my face was red. My body lurching one way and then another, I was holding on for dear life. I was sure I was gonna fly right out of my seat at any moment.

Herbie was going crazy, whoopin' and hollerin' (a thing we do in Kentucky when we're having the time of our life), his hands in the sky, lovin' every minute of it! And Uncle Barry was laughing all the way. Just about the time I thought I was going to lose my breakfast, as well as everything I'd eaten for the past few days, the coaster raced down several more hills, slowed slightly, and then slammed on the brakes, coming to an abrupt stop, pitching all three of us forward in our seat and then slamming us back again with a thud.

Dazed, I climbed out of the roller coaster car and staggered off the station platform, trying to catch my balance and look strong in front of all the other kids watching in wonder, waiting to get on the ride.

I felt pretty good about myself. After all, I had survived the Screamin' Eagle!

The Screamin' Eagle was behind me, and I had conquered it. It was awesome! And best of all, it was over. I wasn't about to get back in line for that ride! But you can bet all my buddies back home were gonna hear about how I took the Screamin' Eagle by the tail feathers and showed it who was boss!

Before my Screamin' Eagle experience, I thought I had been on a roller coaster, but this was a whole different journey. Yeah, I'd been on a roller coaster—I'd been on the Wild Mouse. Life is like that . . . I know mine certainly has been. You live through "wild ride" experiences with some tremendous highs, some horrible lows, some hand-raising moments of exultation, and some gut-wrenching twists and turns . . . the cheers and the tears, like the experiences, are very real and valid. But then things or *some thing* happens that takes you far higher and much deeper than you could've ever imagined. And you realize that your Wild Mouse journey has suddenly jumped the tracks onto the Screamin' Eagle.

A songwriter once wrote these words: "We'll travel over mountains so high, we'll go through valleys so low. Still through it all we'll find that this is the greatest journey the human heart will ever see. The love of God will take us far beyond our wildest dreams." Okay, I confess that songwriter was me and the song was "The Great Adventure." Even as I wrote those words, I had already experienced higher mountains and deeper valleys than I could've ever imagined as a boy riding those roller coasters. And I certainly had no idea how much higher and deeper the journey was going to take me. I'd love to take you on some of that journey with me, if you'd like to come along.

I'm humbled and grateful that you'd take the time to pick up this book, and I have to confess that even as I was writing it, I wrestled with whether my story is something I would want to ask people to take time to listen to or read. After all, my story isn't any more important or worthwhile than anyone else's just because I've had my picture on album covers and I've won a few music awards. It is my story, however, and maybe by reading it you might be reminded of the importance of your own story.

While I've woven my life and my story into the songs I've written all these years, my desire has always been to tell the bigger story of God's grace and His faithfulness. With my prayer being, "God, I want to know You and I want to make You known with the gifts You've given me and the life I live," my songs have always come from the places in my journey where I've seen more of who God is and more of my need for Him. I want to tell honest stories and sing songs about how God shows up in our "real world." So that's what my hope and prayer is for this book as well, that as I share with you my journey over the mountains and through the valleys, you might find encouragement for your own journey and be reminded of what's *most* true as we travel this journey together . . . between heaven and the real world.

Enjoying a "heavenly experience" on the stage of Carnegie Hall.

Chapter One

Carnegie Hall Y'all

The sun was turning the freshly fallen snow to slush under my feet as I walked the familiar sidewalks of New York City on a clear February day. As a boy running through cow pastures to my favorite fishing spot, I never imagined I'd stroll the streets of the Big Apple someday, much less have so many memories come flooding back as I did.

"There's the intersection at Times Square where we did an outdoor photo shoot for *The Great Adventure* album" . . . "There's Radio City Music Hall, where I won my first Grammy" . . . "There's the famous deli where one of my musical heroes, Ricky Skaggs, introduced me to another musical hero, Michael McDonald of the Doobie Brothers" . . . "There's that Italian restaurant that doesn't take credit cards where I had to leave my wife, Mary Beth, waiting alone as collateral while I went to get cash to pay for our meal" . . .

Then I turned the corner and saw something I'd never seen, and never in my wildest dreams thought I would.

"Tonight in Concert . . . Steven Curtis Chapman on Stage at Carnegie Hall."

Carnegie Hall! Are you serious? I'm really playing Carnegie Hall tonight? This is crazy!

A few minutes later, I stepped onto one of the most prestigious stages in the world for a sound check prior to my performance later that evening. I walked over to the edge of the stage to get a feel for the room and gazed in awe at the five tiers of red-velvet seats in front of me. The main floor was surrounded on three sides by four ornate, golden balconies. Each balcony was lined with decorative lights, with a rotunda-style ceiling illuminated in a circle of lights shining like stars inside the theater. The iconic concert hall was somewhat smaller and more "intimate" than I had anticipated, but everything about it felt majestic.

I took a deep breath and thought, *Pavarotti has sung here! What in the world am I doing standing on this stage?* How does a boy from Paducah find himself playing his music at Carnegie Hall, in the legendary Isaac Stern Auditorium, where incredible artists such as Frank Sinatra, the Beatles, Stevie Wonder, Bob Dylan, and Liza Minnelli have performed? The first person to conduct an orchestra at Carnegie Hall, way back in 1891, was none other than the world's greatest composer at the time, Pyotr Ilich Tchaikovsky!

Although I was far from a Tchaikovsky, I wasn't exactly a newbie either. By the time I walked onto that famous platform in February 2014, I had been working in the music business for more than thirty years. I'd been singing professionally from my solo debut at a gathering around a swimming pool, to sold-out concerts in arenas around America and on stages around the world, giant music festivals with tens of thousands of people out under the stars, and even performances on platforms with Reverend Billy Graham before massive crowds. I had performed thousands of concerts. Yet despite my years of experience, performing in Carnegie Hall was certainly a pinnacle in my career and an experience I would remember for the rest of my life. I was very excited . . . and very nervous!

Part of the reason for my nervous excitement was the fact that not only would most of the twenty-eight hundred seats in the venue be filled that night but the stage would also be filled with a fifty-piece orchestra and a three-hundred-voice choir behind me. Over the years of my career, I had occasionally performed a song or two live with an orchestra, but my band and I had never done an entire concert accompanied by a full symphony and a choir, the orchestra playing my songs with arrangements I had never performed in public before. The whole idea was a bit intimidating.

I had rehearsed with the choir the day before, so I knew what that felt like. I was scheduled to rehearse with the orchestra later that afternoon; then it would be lights up and let's go!

As a performer, playing a major venue in New York City always produces added tension because of the many stipulations strictly enforced by the theaters. If ever there was a place where "time is money," it would be a concert hall in the Big Apple. Our show was scheduled to run no longer than 120 minutes . . . not even *one minute* longer. If I happened to talk too much—as I've been known to do on occasion—or play a few minutes overtime—which I'm somewhat famous for—an additional few thousand dollars would be added to the cost of the night. Still, I knew that staying within my preestablished, ironclad time frame was going to be a challenge for me. This was bound to be a very emotional evening, with my set list full of songs that had special meaning to me and an opportunity to perform them live in a way I never had before. Added to that, my wife, Mary Beth, and my entire family would be sitting in the audience cheering me on for this milestone performance.

Most major New York auditoriums are staffed by professional stagehands, sound and lighting staff, and crew members whom artists are required to use to cart their equipment and merchandise in and out of the venue. All of these pros are union workers who tenaciously guard their areas of responsibility, and may God help the naïve musician who decides to move his own microphone or amplifier!

"Hey, put that down! That's my job," a hard-nosed union hand will shout forcefully.

"Um, yes, sir," is the only correct response.

Dressed entirely in black, the union guys are typically not too concerned with trying to be our buddies. Their attitude is, "We'll do our job, and you do yours, and we'll all get along fine and make this work." Some of them can be downright scary as they hover around offstage, checking cables, resetting lights, or otherwise setting up for the show.

My band members and I began our sound check before the orchestra arrived, and I started to play and sing "Spring Is Coming," a song that wasn't typically in the set list for my normal concerts but one I was particularly excited about performing that night. Already the emotions started to well up inside me as I blinked back the tears, partly because I was singing onstage at Carnegie Hall and could imagine what it was going to sound like with three hundred voices and fifty orchestral instruments joining me in just a few hours, but mostly because of the significance of the song and what it meant to be standing on this stage singing it.

> We planted the seed while the tears of our grief soaked the ground
> The sky lost its sun and the world lost its green to lifeless brown
> Now the chill in the wind has turned the earth as hard as stone
> And silent the seed lies beneath ice and snow
> And my heart's heavy now but I'm not letting go
> Of this hope I have that tells me
> Spring is coming, Spring is coming
> And all we've been hoping and longing for soon will appear
> Spring is coming, Spring is coming
> It won't be long now, it's just about here.

Almost six years had passed since the events took place that had led me to write that song.

It was May 24 of 2008, three days after our youngest daughter, Maria, had passed away as the result of a tragic accident in our driveway. My family and I had arrived at Williamson Memorial Gardens in Franklin, Tennessee, and walked to the spot Mary Beth and I had selected just two days earlier to be the place where the body of our little girl was to be buried. You could smell the fresh dirt as we took our seats. Our hearts were so heavy that we could hardly breathe.

Many of our friends gathered around, and our pastor, Scotty Smith, began to speak. He talked about this day being a day of planting . . . planting a seed that was the body of Maria. He read 1 Corinthians 15, verses 42 through 44.

> What is sown is perishable; what is raised is imperishable. It is sown in dishonor; it is raised in glory. It is sown in weakness; it is raised in power. It is sown a natural body; it is raised a spiritual body.

He talked about how a seed first falls to the ground and dies in order to come back to life . . . how we must plant a seed and wait. He reminded us that because of Jesus's resurrection from the dead and His promise of our coming resurrection, this *perishable* seed of Maria's body that we were planting is going to be raised *imperishable*. He talked about the promised "Spring" that is coming when all things will be made new according to God's own promise. He reminded us of the hopeful words of Revelation 21 and the coming day when God will wipe every tear from our eyes.

Somehow we were able to grasp God's promise not fully—not even close to *fully*—but just enough that we were able to drop handfuls of dirt on the casket that day believing that the story of Maria's life was far from over . . . that there is in fact a Spring that is coming when we really will see her again . . . more alive than ever. That day we were able to catch a glimpse of heaven in our very real world, a glimpse we desperately needed, and the hope it gave me inspired the song "Spring Is Coming."

Now during the sound check at Carnegie Hall, after singing through an emotional verse and chorus of that song, I noticed a commotion on the side of the stage. Several big, burly stage crew guys were gathered around a man who was down on one knee on the floor. They had their hands on the back and shoulders of the man who had knelt down, and he appeared to be crying.

We cut short the sound check, and I went over to the men, thinking that perhaps somebody was hurt or something else was wrong. "Is everything okay?" I asked. I looked at the man on his knees, his face still wet with tears. "Are you all right?"

He looked up at me and quietly said, "I have one of those stories." He slowly stood to his feet. "My wife and I lost a little girl too," he explained.

Right in front of his fellow crew members, he and I hugged.

His name was Scooter, and he was the main house sound guy at Carnegie Hall. He began to tell me about the hard struggle he and his wife had endured since they had lost their daughter several years earlier. Even with their strong faith as Christians, the hurt and grief had been agonizing. I knew all too well what he was talking about.

"My wife and I went to your concert at Nokia Theater in Times Square a few years ago," Scooter said, "when you did the tour with your wife speaking and your sons playing in your band. That night your wife shared how she was afraid to let go of the grief because, if she did, she would lose that connection with Maria. Hearing another grieving mother share that was a real breakthrough for my wife, and that concert had a profound effect on us."

He explained how at the Nokia concert they bought Mary Beth's book, *Choosing to SEE*, and my album, *Beauty Will Rise*, which they listened to on their way home that night. When they heard "Spring Is Coming," they were moved to tears. That song in particular, Scooter told me, was instrumental in helping to bring some deep healing to their hearts. Later, his wife read Mary Beth's book, and that too was a huge step toward helping them heal. He said he felt like God had orchestrated this concert at Carnegie Hall as a gift to encourage him and to help him continue the healing process.

I put my arm around Scooter, prayed with him, and thanked him for sharing his story with me. Then both of us went back to work.

A few minutes before 7:00 p.m. I took my place on the side of the stage and listened as the orchestra began its preconcert tuning ritual. My heart was racing, and I peeked out to see a full house as well as a full stage of singers and musicians. *This is really getting ready to happen!* While the orchestra was filled with professional musicians who had been hired for the concert, the

choir consisted of singers who were fans of my music and had come from all over the country to be a part of this night. They were *almost* as thrilled as I was to be there, which only added to the excitement!

I took my place at center stage to an enthusiastic ovation from the crowd and the choir, and with a small wave of the conductor's baton, the orchestra launched into the prologue from "The Great Adventure." *Here we go!*

The concert that evening was amazing. Maybe it was the adrenaline rush, or maybe talking to Scooter had put me at ease and reminded me of what really mattered, but for some reason, despite the emotional moments and all the artistic tensions, I was like a little boy filled with wonder and joy onstage. The sound in the room was incredible, and I easily understood why the impeccable acoustics of Carnegie Hall are legendary. I had never imagined hearing my songs with a live orchestra and choir—on recordings, maybe, but never onstage like that. Mary Beth said later that I looked like a twelve-year-old Steven having the time of his life—probably because that's what I felt like.

We performed a "greatest hits" type of concert as well as a few songs I had seldom, if ever, performed live. One such song called "Savior" was particularly powerful because of the beautiful orchestral and choral arrangement. I was overcome with emotion several times but was somehow able to hold it together and resist the urge to have a full-on breakdown.

One of the most emotional points in the show for me was when I got to sit down on the piano bench at center stage and just listen. I didn't play or sing. I simply sat and listened along with the audience as the orchestra and the choir filled Carnegie Hall with the melodies and lyrics of two of my best-known songs, "His Strength Is Perfect" and "Be Still and Know." It was truly a "taste and see that the Lord is good" moment to get to hear my own songs like that. Many of the people in the choir had been singing my songs for years. They had journeyed with my family and me through good times and hard times, mountaintops and valleys. It was like a gift from them to me as they sang their hearts out to show me how much the music had meant to them.

I sat in the middle of the stage and listened in awe. It was as though the choir singers and the members of the audience were saying, "This is a celebration of your life and your music and the impact they have had on our lives." It was a heavenly moment for me, and the best was yet to come.

Near the close of the concert, as I often did, I performed the song "Cinderella" and then followed it with "Spring Is Coming." As I began to sing that song, I looked back at the sound-mixing console and saw my new friend Scooter standing with his head back and both of his hands raised high in the air, singing along on every word and worshiping God.

Just above where Scooter was standing, in the front row of the first balcony, I could see my family. Mary Beth, Shaoey, Stevey Joy, Will Franklin, Caleb, Emily, and her husband, Tanner, were all there to celebrate this moment with me, and as incredible as this whole Carnegie Hall experience had been, nothing could compare with seeing them there . . . *together.* It was a beautiful picture of hope and a powerful reminder to me that God had carried us through the cold, hard winter of our grief. Even though our hearts still ached for the little girl who wasn't there with us, the healing had begun and we were beginning to feel joy again and experience the first signs of what we knew to be true: Spring really *is* coming.

The concert ended with an emotional standing ovation, and I took a bow and looked around the room one last time, trying my best to take it all in. After the concert, several people asked me if playing at Carnegie Hall was a dream come true. I had to answer honestly, "No, a boy from Paducah doesn't think to dream that big."

Dad, Mom, and me on Christmas Day, 1966.

Chapter Two

Unresolved Chords

When I'm writing a song, my natural tendency has always been to resolve the last chord . . . to bring it back to "the 1 chord," as we say in Music City. There have been a few occasions when I got a little adventurous and decided to leave the last chord unresolved, but for the most part, I think resolution is just in my DNA.

The musical concept of resolution basically means bringing a song to its natural and most obvious conclusion, that place where it seems to most naturally want to return, bringing the tension to an end. Music is like life in many ways; there are fast songs for when we're happy and slow songs for when we're sad or feeling introspective or maybe even romantic. And those songs are made up of chords, a collection of individual notes arranged in such a way that they bring order and give a sense of movement and direction to the music. It's as if the song is a journey, full of twists and turns, hills and valleys, all leading to a final destination.

The resolution is crossing the line that says, "This is done, I'm coming back home" and feeling the release that comes with it. The resolution is the answer to the question, the period at the end of the sentence. I like resolution in my life—a lot! And I strongly dislike things I can't resolve or fix, and for good reason.

As I share about my childhood, it's important for me to say how grateful I am for my parents and how important it is that I honor them in telling my story. I've asked their permission to share some of the details of our family's story that I know they wish they could change. I'm proud of them and thankful for many of the choices they made that helped shape me into the person I am. They are both amazing people, and I'm grateful for their willingness to let me share honestly. I know it's their hope and prayer that God might be able to use their story—the good, the bad, and even the ugly—to encourage others on their own journeys. One of the many amazing things about our God is how He can take even the broken parts of our stories and bring about something beautiful as we trust Him with them.

I was born to bring resolution, to tie up loose ends, to help, and if at all possible, to single-handedly *fix* whatever was broken in my world. From conception, it seems like my life was to be defined by fixing broken things, broken situations, and broken people.

Prior to my birth, my mom and my dad found themselves at a crossroads and had to make a tough decision. Judy Rudd was a beautiful, bright-eyed country girl who was barely sixteen years old when she met Herb Chapman, who was nineteen, handsome, played a guitar, and drove a cool car. Herb knew this girl was different from the ones he'd dated before, and he used to tell me the story of how one night after a date he knelt down under a tree in his backyard and prayed, "God, would you please let me marry that girl?" With the same engagement ring his dad gave his mom years earlier, Herb asked Judy to be his wife a few months after they met. She said yes, but soon began to question if she was ready to make the commitment of a lifetime. As the two young people were still in the process of trying to figure out where their relationship was headed, Judy discovered she was pregnant.

Thankfully, they made the frightening but brave decision to get married and raise the little boy that would come along eight months after the wedding.

Herb Chapman Jr. was born on June 2, 1960. Probably to more easily differentiate between father and son, Judy and Herb called their baby boy

Herbie, and most people have done the same ever since. The young couple tried to figure out life together. It was a rocky beginning, to say the least.

After about a year and a half of intense struggle in their marriage, Judy and Herb came to another crossroads: should they divorce and go their separate ways? Somewhere in the discussion, Herb (my dad) suggested that maybe they should try having another child, "on purpose" this time, to see if that might make a difference and help save their marriage.

They chose the latter course of action . . . thankfully.

Judy got pregnant again, and on November 21, 1962, Steven Curtis Chapman came riding in on a white horse to save the day. I was literally conceived to help fix my parents' marriage. Obviously, I had no idea of all that was going on between Mom and Dad at the time. As crazy as this sounds, Herbie and I didn't even know that he was conceived before my parents were married until we were in our thirties. We had never even given it a thought or "done the math."

But years later, learning the backdrop to my arrival on the Chapman family scene helped me connect the dots in many ways. I was the Fix-it Kid. And for most of my early life, I filled that bill relatively well. I was the compliant and happy child who was always smiling with my mouth wide open.

I grew up in Paducah, Kentucky, a river town of around twenty-five thousand people located just off Interstate 24 in the southwestern corner of Kentucky. It was the home of a US uranium enrichment facility and a hub for the Illinois Central Railroad.

Right after high school, my dad had gone to work for the railroad, where his mother and many of my relatives worked. His real love, however, was music, and a few years after I was born, he was able to fulfill his dream of owning a music store. After injuring his back at work, he quit his railroad job, rented space in an old office building for $35 a month, and opened Chapman Music in Mayfield, a small town about thirty miles from where we lived. With no business education or training, but lots of hard work and determination, his small business began to grow.

Self-taught with his own style, Dad was a great guitar player and a great singer. But his real forte was teaching guitar. Since he had no other employees at the store, he opened late, usually around 2:00 p.m., and stayed open late to accommodate his clientele. The unusual hours were mostly due to Dad's teaching business. Sometimes he wouldn't go in to work until noon, because most of his students came after school or work, and then he stayed at the store until after nine or ten o'clock every night. Dad often got home long after I'd already gone to bed. Consequently, Mom, Herbie, and I saw Dad mostly on the weekends.

Mom and Dad's relationship had been rocky from the start, and the fact that Dad's work schedule left Mom alone much of the time to raise two young boys probably created even more tension. Dad's upbringing didn't help either. He was determined to be a good dad, and he was, but his father had abandoned their family when my dad was just a boy, leaving him without a strong example to follow when it came to knowing how to love and lead a family well. Money was sometimes tight, and family vacations were nonexistent other than an occasional Saturday fishing trip. Dad worked hard to provide for our family, and Mom helped to make ends meet by working outside the home at Curtis and Mays Photography Studio.

My earliest memories are of a relatively happy home. When we were all together, however, it often seemed like Dad had a lot on his mind and it didn't take much to light his short fuse. He had undergone surgery on his back after his injury at the railroad. Unfortunately, the surgery had not rectified the problem entirely, so Dad lived with the added stress of chronic back problems.

Fights between Mom and Dad were fierce and flared quickly. Dad sometimes punctuated his statements by slamming the door in a rage. Mom would usually end up in tears. The arguments never got physical, although I recall seeing my dad throw a bowl of coleslaw across the room. It wasn't thrown *at* anyone so much as thrown out of frustration. Still, that sort of outburst can have an effect on young boys, and it did on Herbie and me. We were really sad and really scared and felt like we were walking on eggshells any time Mom and Dad started arguing.

A few times the arguments increased in intensity to the point where Dad stormed out of the house, slammed the door, climbed in his car, and drove off. Mom was crying, Herbie was crying, and I stood at the kitchen door crying and thinking, *Dad, please don't go! Please don't go.* I had no idea whether Dad would ever return. Thankfully, each time he came back. In fact, usually he wouldn't go far, but sometimes he'd be gone for several hours and wouldn't come back home until after Herbie and I were in bed.

Meanwhile, Mom tried to calm Herbie and me with her reassuring words. "Your dad is a good man. And your dad loves you. We're struggling right now, but it is not because of you. Both Mom and Dad love you." Mom's words were meant to soothe our anxious minds, but nothing really helped until we saw or heard Dad coming back through the door.

Dad was not a mean man, far from it, but he carried a heavy load of shame and anger, much of which stemmed from his own hard childhood, and he had few emotional or psychological tools to help him deal with it. His own dad was an alcoholic and had left the family when Dad was only three years old. His mom worked hard, trying to support the family, so she was not home much either. Apparently, when Dad and my uncle Barry were young, some people suggested to their single mother that they should be sent away to a boys home or an orphanage, a fact Dad didn't share with me until recently. My determined grandmother would have nothing to do with that idea. Eventually, Dad's grandparents moved in with his mom, and together they raised my dad and my uncle, but Dad never lost the sense of shame and embarrassment he felt about being abandoned by his own father.

Because Mom and Dad both worked outside the home, Herbie and I sometimes were cared for by babysitters. When Herbie started attending elementary school during the day, I had to spend a few days a week at a local day care center. There I encountered my own first traumatic experience of shame, and it left an indelible impression on my heart and mind. To this day, when I see a child being shamed in public by an angry parent or hear a child crying and see a parent responding with frustration instead of kindness, it can reduce me to tears. I think it has something to do with what I experienced at Kiddie Kamp (not the real name).

Kiddie Kamp day care center had a cute name, but for a little boy, the place seemed more like a prison camp. If a child was lying in a crib or on a mat and his or her leg happened to hang off the mattress, an attendant would come by and whack the child with a paddle. "Git your leg back on the bed," the warden would growl.

The food was awful too, but the rule was that we had to clean our plates completely or we'd be disciplined—usually with the paddle. I can still taste the flavor of the sticky, candied yams—yucky sweet potatoes—they served. I hated those yams, but if I didn't eat them, I knew I'd be paddled. So one day when nobody was looking, I took my yams and stashed them under the table by pressing them against the underside of the tabletop. For a moment, I worried about being caught. *What am I gonna do if the yams don't stick? How am I gonna explain dropping my yams under the table?* But the yams were so sticky that they bonded firmly to the underside of the table. They may still be under the table for all I know.

One day it was discovered that a little boy named Aaron had not washed his hands before eating his lunch. A staff person pulled down the little boy's pants right there in front of everybody and spanked him on his bare behind. Aaron stood in the middle of the big room bawling his eyes out, possibly from pain or embarrassment or both. I looked on in *terror.* I felt so sorry for him. Then the worst part came.

"Look at Aaron's red butt," the attendant warned. "And if you don't do the right thing, you're going to end up with a red butt too." Embarrassed, I stared sheepishly at Aaron's behind, and sure enough, it was beet red.

I thought to myself, *Oh no! I do* not *want to get in trouble.* The message was clear to me: Don't screw up.

It was one of the first times I felt a fierce commitment to stay safely between the lines and to please everyone as much as possible. I certainly didn't want to be that embarrassed and ashamed, so I was going to find out what was expected and what the rules were, and I was going to be good—even better than good. I was going to be Mr. Perfect!

Even though I wasn't the boy who received the paddling, the impact of that shame was so powerful that I kept the incident to myself for years. When I finally told my mom years later, she was appalled and heartbroken. "Why didn't you tell me this earlier?" she asked.

"I don't know, I guess because I thought that's the way bad kids were treated," I said.

When I was old enough to attend school, Mom continued working at the photography studio, so most days Herbie and I came home to an empty house. I suppose we were "latchkey kids," but since we rarely locked the doors where we lived, we weren't too worried about being locked out. Our house was located on three acres of our own property outside Paducah, with large fifty- to one-hundred-acre farms and fields all around us. A field planted with soybeans backed up right to our backyard. It was a young boy's dream being able to play outside, go fishing in one of a couple ponds around our property, or ride a bike every afternoon until Mom came home from work.

After school one day, Herbie and I were playing outside when we saw something that scared the daylights out of us. An airplane flying overhead suddenly dove right toward the roof of our house! It came so close that Herbie and I could see the propellers whirling. We raced toward the back door just as the plane streaked over our yard. "Watch out, Herbie! It's gonna hit us!" We dove onto the ground and covered our heads to avoid being hit by the plane, or so we thought.

The plane pulled up and then circled around in the sky. Before we could even get up, the plane was diving toward our rooftop again. "He's tryin' to kill us!" I screamed.

My big brother Herbie and me going for a dip in the pool.

The next time the plane pulled up, Herbie and I made a beeline for the back door and ran inside the house. We called Mom, terrified.

"Mom, there's an airplane . . . we don't know what's going on . . . but he's aiming right at our house and he's tryin' to kill us!"

"What? Wait, wait," Mom calmly said. "Crawl over to the window, look out, and tell me if something is coming out of the bottom of the plane when he flies over the field."

"Yeah, it looks like water or white smoke or something.'"

Mom chuckled. "He's not going to kill you. That's a crop duster, and he is spraying insecticide on the fields around our house."

Reassured that the Russians were not invading Paducah, Herbie and I went out in the backyard and watched the plane repeatedly fly right over our house, now thinking it was the coolest thing we'd ever seen.

As a little boy, I believed wholeheartedly anything my big brother told me. Herbie is two and a half years older than me, so when he spoke, it had to be true, and it usually was, although at times he was prone to exaggeration.

Herbie has always been a great actor with a flair for the dramatic, even at a young age. One day while chopping down an old, dead tree using a hatchet that Dad had just sharpened, Herbie took a swing and missed the tree but hit himself in his knee, slicing all the way to the bone. His leg was immediately covered with blood. When Herbie saw the blood, he cried out, "I'm dying! I'm dying!"

Mom came running and carted Herbie off to the emergency room, but as they drove off in a rush, I thought for sure I'd never see my brother again because, after all, Herbie—my big brother—had told me, "I'm dying."

Of course, he didn't die, and the doctors patched him up. After a few days, he was back outside playing with me.

Mom and Dad were strict with Herbie and me, but they didn't go overboard on discipline. Dad often simply cautioned us, "No goofing off, no foolishness, no horseplay." He never defined what that meant, but he didn't have to . . . we knew that included almost everything.

As a kid, I felt afraid any time I sensed Dad's anger. I loved him and I wanted to please him. I wanted to be around him—I wanted to be like him—but his anger was something that scared me.

Like most country kids our age, Herbie and I didn't grow up with video games or five hundred television stations to watch. We had three good stations if the weather was just right and the antenna was pointed in precisely the right direction. As a result, we used our imaginations and made our own games and entertainment outside. A lot of our creativity involved our bicycles. Like most other boys in the neighborhood, we practically lived on our Schwinn bikes.

One of my best friends, Tom Lindsay, got a new bike for Christmas every year, and one of our favorite things to do was to set up some wooden planks on top of cinder blocks and then get a running start by pedaling like mad the length of the driveway, hit the ramp at full speed, and launch off the ramp Evel Knievel daredevil style. Hey, we had seen Evel riding a motorcycle and jumping over nineteen cars, so a bike jump was nothin'. This was in the 1970s, long before BMX bike competitions existed in which similar jumps and much more difficult biker feats were commonplace. We were just jumping with regular two-wheelers and pedaling as fast as our short legs would take us.

The trick, of course, was to get up to full speed and hit the plank in the center. Most importantly, the rider had to yank the front wheel up off the board at just the right moment to get the perfect launch as well as a good landing.

Tom was the best ramp-jumper around, and he had taught me how to do it. When Herbie came out and saw Tom make it look easy, he said, "Hey, I want to try that!"

Herbie hadn't done much ramp-jumping, but he got a good running start down the driveway. He hit the plank just right and flew up the board, but he failed to pull the front wheel of his bike upward.

From there, it was as though time stopped and everything that happened next looked like a slow-motion movie. I saw Herbie fly off the ramp . . .

and then the bike came down with its full weight on the front wheel . . . catapulting Herbie forward and over the handlebars. He landed hard on the ground, with the bike bouncing off the front tire and back up into the air like a basketball, seemingly hanging in the air above him. Herbie tried to push himself up and scramble out of the way, but the slow-motion movie was still running, and the bike came crashing down right on top of Herbie's shoulder, pinning him back to the ground with a thud and a crunch.

Herbie lay on the ground crying in a crumpled heap, holding his shoulder with the bike on top of him.

He seemed to be alive, so I wasn't too worried about him. But I was real worried about me. *Oh no!* I thought. *This is definitely going to qualify as foolishness and horseplay. If my big brother is hurt, I'm in trouble. Dad is going to find out that I set up the ramp and this whole thing was my fault.*

Tom and I helped Herbie get up, and for the next few minutes, I did my best to convince my brother that he was okay and wasn't hurt. I knew Herbie could be dramatic. Besides, he wasn't bleeding as far as I could see, and he could walk, so I figured he'd survive. "You're okay, Herbie. You're not hurt. Shake it off." I tried everything I could to pump up my brother. "You're fine. Man, that was a great jump! You shoulda seen it . . . and that was a really cool fall."

Herbie wasn't buying it. He grimaced in pain and held his shoulder. Tom and I helped Herbie shuffle into the house and eased him down onto his bed. "You're fine, Herbie," I reassured him. "Can I get you some aspirin?"

"Oh, it hurts so bad," Herbie said, raising his hand to his shoulder, milking the situation for all the sympathy he could get.

"No, it doesn't hurt," I assured him. "It will feel better in a little while."

"Nooo!" Herbie wailed. "It hurts."

I knew this was not going to work out well.

When Mom came home, Herbie was still writhing in pain. "Oh my," she said. "We better go to the emergency room."

Uh-oh, I thought. *I'm dead.*

Mom hustled Herbie and me off to the hospital, where the doctors discovered that Herbie had dislocated his shoulder. They sent him home wearing a sling, so I knew there was no way we were going to be able to hide Herbie's injury from Dad.

Sure enough, when Dad got home late that night, he came looking for me. I knew he was mad because when Dad got upset, he clenched his teeth together as he spoke. "Did you set up that ramp, boy?" he asked through his locked teeth.

"Yes, sir," I said quietly, my eyes focused on the floor.

"What'd I tell you about setting up those ramps?"

"Not to . . ."

"Go out in the kitchen and wait for me there," Dad ordered. I knew I was in trouble.

One of the reasons Dad was so strict with us was because he was so rambunctious as a boy himself. He was a rascal. He rode motorcycles when he was just a kid of thirteen and did all sorts of reckless, crazy things. He once was towed along by a car with a rope because his motorcycle wouldn't run. He fell off the motorcycle and was dragged along on the highway, leaving him with a deep scar on his side to give weight to his story. It's a wonder he survived. He sometimes skipped school to go squirrel hunting and barely graduated.

Because of his own mischievous childhood, Dad had a tendency to overreact with Herbie and me. He understood that boys will be boys and that most will sometimes do stupid things, but he worried constantly that we would do something foolish and get hurt badly. Consequently, he was always warning us about horseplay. I never knew horses to be such troublemakers, but I didn't question him.

I've always had a great relationship with my dad, despite the fact that he was still trying to process issues from his own childhood. In fact, as we got a little older, he would often say that Herbie and I were two of his best friends.

During my childhood, if Dad was doing a project, I wanted to be right beside him, helping him any way I could, learning from him, but most of all just being with him. I loved being around my dad.

As a boy, my dad gravitated toward music and hot rods. He always had a love for old cars and was a great mechanic in the days when cars had motors under the hood instead of computerized propulsion systems. To this day, he loves tinkering around in his garage.

Dad had always wanted a jeep when he was a kid, so when I was about seven years old, he found an old 1947 Willys jeep, similar to an army jeep, in a junkyard. The vehicle was in such bad shape that the wheels wobbled as he towed it up the driveway.

Dad began a year-and-a-half ordeal to restore that jeep, working on it in any spare time he had, taking parts off and repairing or replacing them until the jeep looked and ran like new. Throughout the process, I "worked" with Dad as often as I could, lying on my back under the jeep while Dad did the actual work. My main job was trying to keep Dad from getting angry and frustrated.

"I need a nine-sixteenth-inch wrench," Dad might say.

I'd quickly slide out from under the jeep and run to the toolshed, where I'd scour through the toolbox drawers until I found just the right wrench. Then I'd run back and slide back under the vehicle while holding the wrench out for Dad. "Here ya go, Dad."

"Oh, just lay it there," he might say. "I don't need it anymore."

The happy smile on my face would quickly fade as I realized he had fixed something without my help.

"I could use a Phillips screwdriver," he'd say a few minutes later.

Again, I'd race to the toolshed and return with the right screwdriver only to have Dad say, "Oh, I got it. Never mind."

Time after time I'd run to the toolbox as fast as I could, find a tool, and run back only to have him say, "Never mind, I don't need it now." I was so bummed. I wanted so badly to be a help to my dad, but I couldn't seem to get it right. Once in a while, he would actually use the tool I brought him, and I'd feel a sense of great accomplishment.

At times, Dad would ask me to hold the flashlight, which I would do, but after a while I'd get bored and my concentration would lapse and I'd shine the bright light right in Dad's eyes. That was never a good thing!

Only as an adult and a father myself did I become suspicious that maybe Dad had sent me for tools only to give me something to do and to keep my little energetic self busy!

Nevertheless, a few years ago while watching a movie with my two boys called *The Kid*, starring Bruce Willis, I was undone by a scene in which the little boy finds the missing screw in his pocket that his dad had been looking for and his dad becomes angry with him. The scene reminded me of how hard I had tried to help my dad, how I had wanted him to acknowledge me, and yet how often I had felt like I was just a frustration to him. I sobbed so hard in the movie theater during that scene that my son Caleb reached over and patted me on the back, trying to console me and minimize his embarrassment that his dad was crying his eyes out at a Disney movie!

One of the most defining moments of my childhood took place one summer when I was helping Dad set up an above-ground swimming pool. It was only a four-foot-high circular pool, but this was a big deal, and our entire family was excited about it—we were going to have a swimming pool right there in our backyard! We all pitched in to help. We had to clear the grass from a large spot, level out the ground with shovels, then lay a large piece of heavy plastic on the ground so the grass wouldn't grow up through the bottom of the pool. It took several days of work to get everything just right before Dad assembled the pool and we watched excitedly as the water began to fill the blue plastic liner.

While Dad was bent over and fiddling with the pool filter, I was playing with the pool skimmer, a basket at the end of an eight-foot-long aluminum shaft used to clean bugs and leaves off the surface of the water. I dipped the basket into the water and pulled it up quickly and was fascinated by the way the water flew out of the basket, the spray glistening brightly in the sunlight.

Dad wasn't paying attention to my antics, so I kept plunging the basket deeper and deeper, playing in the water from over the edge of the pool wall, splashing the basket over and over.

On one stab of the skimmer into the water I pushed down too hard and hit the bottom, and the light aluminum shaft bent in half! Dad wasn't watching, so I quickly brought the shaft up out of the water and tried to bend it back so it would be straight again. But as soon as I bent the shaft back, the light aluminum pole snapped, breaking completely.

"Oh no!" I whispered to myself. There was no way I could fix that aluminum pole.

"Dad," I said, barely breathing as I held up the skimmer to show him.

Dad raised up from where he was working. As soon as he saw the skimmer, his face stiffened, his jaw locked, his mouth pursed, and he spoke tersely through his clenched teeth.

Dad's words devastated me. He said some things I'd never heard him say. What he basically said, or at least what I heard, was, "What an idiot. How dumb can you be? Use your head! Think. Any numbskull would know better than to do something like that." The shame associated with his words seared into my memory. Although I didn't fully realize it at the time, I think I resolved at that moment, *If you can't do something well and do it right, then don't even attempt it, because you don't ever want to hear those words again, and you don't ever want that feeling again.* It was as though I wrote a mental note to myself: *Be very careful. Don't mess up.* The ramifications of that boyhood experience have haunted me throughout my life.

Years later, I was part of a men's group called "The Stories We Live By" along with a friend, Al Andrews. Al led the discussion and asked a poignant question: When do you first remember tragedy entering your story? Some of the guys told stories about losing a parent, incidents of child abuse, drunken parents, and all sorts of other horrendous things experienced in their childhoods. As I listened, I said to myself, *Maybe I should give up my spot to somebody who has experienced something hard. I don't have anything like that in my past.* I was glad for that, but after our group met one morning, I was sitting in my car rehashing what I had just heard. I wondered, *What am I gonna talk about when it's my turn to tell my story?* I remembered the incident with the pool skimmer, and I suddenly started sobbing uncontrollably. There I was, as a full-grown adult, weeping over that childhood experience. I've come to realize over the years that my early experiences shaped me more than I ever imagined. Or maybe I've come to understand a lot more about how profoundly early experiences shape us into the people we become. It's certainly proven true for me.

I love my dad and honor him to this day. He was and is a great man in my eyes. He did his best, and I know he never wanted to hurt me. Just the opposite; he was always trying to teach me how to be a man—although what that meant to him might be different from what it means to many people today—and I learned many important truths from him. My dad, Herb Chapman Sr., influenced me more than anyone in the world in my love for music as well as what it means to live as a man who desires to honor God with his life.

So nearly forty years later, I asked him about that pool skimmer incident and, more specifically, his response. Ironically, he barely remembered, so I reminded him of his words and told him I'd come to realize how deeply they had affected me.

He was truly sorry to know his words had hurt me. He went on to talk about the heavy burden of latent anger and shame that he carried around through much of his life. He apologized to me for allowing that anger to influence some of his words and actions during my early years. He loved his family and really tried to be a good dad to his boys. He took us hunting and fishing, and in many ways, he was breaking the chains that had been wrapped around him since his own childhood. He was, after all, working hard to put in a swimming pool for us when that incident occurred. The pool wasn't for him; it was for us.

I understood that Dad wasn't being malicious by what he had said or done, but his actions had a profound impact on me that I still deal with to this day. Even as I'm typing this and remembering the power of shame in my life and in my dad's life, I have tears in my eyes. Maybe I always will—until the day I first step into heaven and God fixes what I've never been able to fix.

One of the few public appearances of the Chapman Family.

Chapter Three

A Transformed Family

It seemed that nearly everyone in Paducah went to church when I was a boy—everyone, that is, except Herb Chapman, our dad. Both Mom and Dad had taken steps of faith years earlier in their lives, making public professions of their faith in Jesus Christ. Every good Southern Baptist knew Billy Graham's invitation practically from memory. Billy always spoke emphatically as he extended the invitation: "Every person that Jesus called He called *publicly.*" So anyone who claimed to be a Christian was required to make a public confession of faith in Christ. Both Mom and Dad had done that years ago, and even before he and Mom were married, when they had first discovered that Mom was pregnant, Dad had knelt out by a tree and asked God for forgiveness and the courage to do the right thing. That's why he had decided to marry Mom. So although Dad had a Christian background, for most of my early life, he rarely attended church services.

Mom, on the other hand, took Herbie and me to church every Sunday at Olivet Baptist Church. She wanted her boys to grow up going to "the Lord's house" on Sundays. Dad, however, usually slept in late on Sunday morning, his one day off from working at the music store.

Just about every Saturday night when the weather allowed it, Dad and his best buddy, Jack Martin, took his redbone hound dog Douglas out to the woods to chase raccoons. Dad loved coon huntin' with his buddies and often didn't get home till late Saturday night. He wasn't about to get out of bed early on Sunday morning.

The pastor of Olivet Baptist Church was Brother David McMichael, and he and his family lived down the street from us. Some ministers believed in door-to-door evangelism. Brother David believed in window-to-window evangelism! Brother David knew where my mom and dad's bedroom window was located, so he'd often come by on Sunday morning, knock on the window, and call out, "Herb Chapman! Get out of bed and come to church with your family. I want to see you in church, Herb."

Dad would roll over, put the pillow over his head, and go back to sleep.

About the time I was seven years of age, Brother David announced that we were going to have a layman's revival at Olivet Baptist Church. We'd had plenty of revival services in Paducah before. Usually in the spring or the fall of the year, the church would put up a sign announcing a revival, bring in a special speaker as the evangelist, and hold a series of nightly services, each one culminating with an invitation to trust Jesus as your Savior or to rededicate your life to the Lord. I was familiar with revivals. But I had never before heard of a *layman's* revival.

It turned out that a layman's revival did not feature a "professional evangelist" but centered around the personal stories presented by a group of "lay witnesses," men and women who were not members of the clergy but businessmen, nurses, doctors, building contractors, and men and women from other professions. The laymen simply shared their own experiences of putting their faith in Jesus Christ and then stayed around to talk, answer questions, and pray with anyone wishing to trust Christ with his or her life. It was a deeply spiritual yet very natural, low-key presentation, with no pressure or arm-twisting or singing of ten verses of "Just As I Am."

Because many of the "witnesses" were visiting our congregation from out of town, a number of families in the church freely opened their homes to provide food and lodging for our guests. One of the laymen, Dr. Findlay

Baird from Louisville, Kentucky, stayed with us. Dr. Baird was not a theologian or a preacher; he was a dentist.

That Mom and Dad invited the dentist to stay with us was, in itself, nothing short of a miracle. We *never* had overnight guests in our home during my early years. Herbie and I never invited our friends to our house for sleepovers. But for some reason, Mom felt strongly that we needed to open our home to help house the laymen. Mom approached Dad and said, "I want to have one of these people stay with us. They need someplace to stay, and it will be good for us too."

When I heard Mom asking Dad, I thought, *That ain't gonna happen!* I'd heard that some people have a "gift of hospitality." That wasn't *us*.

But Dad shocked me by saying, "Okay. Tell the preacher someone can stay with us."

Looking back, I can see how God's hand was at work in all of this, especially in the selection of Dr. Baird as our houseguest. Dr. Baird was such a winsome, kind, gentle spirit, yet he was also a highly successful businessman. He was somebody to whom my dad could relate but also someone whose work ethic and business success Dad could respect.

Besides being a dentist, Dr. Baird was an airplane pilot and owned nice cars and other accoutrements that accompany financial success, yet he was quick to emphasize that those things had not made him happy; they didn't satisfy. "I had all the stuff, but I was still miserable. The only thing that gave me peace," he told us, "was a relationship with Jesus." Dr. Baird wasn't preaching at us; he wasn't pointing a finger and saying, "Herb Chapman, get your life straightened out and act right." Dad had never really heard about a God who wanted to have a relationship with him. Neither my mom nor my dad had ever really heard that kind of gospel message—the gospel of peace.

Dad didn't say much at the time, but I could tell he was pondering Dr. Baird's story and resonating with it. When it came time to go to church each evening, Dad shut down the music store and went along with us. The night Dr. Baird shared his story with the congregation, my mom and dad were some of the first people to walk down to the front of the church and kneel at the altar area to rededicate their lives to God. Herbie walked forward that week too, praying for the first time to ask Jesus to come into his heart and be his Lord and Savior. At that point, I didn't feel any inclination to join them. I stayed back and watched.

Dr. Baird and Brother David gathered around Mom, Dad, and Herbie—who all had tears trickling down their faces—and they prayed together.

I didn't understand everything that was happening, but I saw my parents crying, and I heard them say they wanted to be better people. I saw my brother crying too. "I don't want to go to hell," Herbie said. "I want to go to heaven."

Over the next months, I witnessed a real transformation in my family members, especially in Mom and Dad. The arguments didn't disappear completely, but there was definitely a different spirit in our home. After a fight, our parents modeled genuine repentance. "I don't know how to do this," Dad would say with tears in his eyes. "But I believe God can give me the wisdom to be a good father. I wanna be a good husband and a good dad, so let's get on our knees and ask God to help us." The four of us would kneel on the floor beside the couch and pray together. For my mom, prayer and Bible study became an important part of her life, and our conversations began to be laced with Bible verses.

Years later, when my wife, Mary Beth, and I were struggling and dealing with our own issues, we'd do much the same thing that my parents had modeled for me. We'd gather our kids around us, get on our knees together, and attempt to honestly express what was happening. "Guys, I love your mom," I'd say.

Mary Beth would say, "And I love your dad."

I'd continue, ". . . even though it's obvious we aren't real happy with each other right now." We'd look at each other and say, "I'm sorry, please forgive me," and then we'd pray.

When Dr. Findlay Baird left our home, he placed three dollars on my pillow and three dollars on Herbie's pillow, along with a note saying, "Thank you, boys, for taking care of me this week." It wasn't the money—although we thought we were rich with a few dollars in our pockets—but Dr. Baird's kindness that impressed my brother and me.

Following the layman's revival, the Chapman family attended church services together every Sunday morning and evening and often on Wednesday night too. A few months later, not long after I had turned eight years of age, I was sitting in church on a Sunday morning along with my family as Brother David preached a sermon based on Revelation 3:20: "Behold, I stand at the door, and knock: if any man hear my voice, and open the door, I will come in to him, and will sup with him, and he with me." (He was a King James Version guy for sure!)

Brother David explained the meaning of "sup" in a way that even a child could understand. "That means the Lord will come in and have supper with you," he said. "He wants to be involved in your life and guide you through your life. He's knocking at the door of your heart because He wants to have a relationship with you."

As powerfully as I've ever felt anything in my life, my heart started beating faster and louder, and I thought, *I hear Jesus knocking at the door of my heart, saying, "Will you let Me in? Now is your time. It's not about your family. It's not about doing what everybody else did . . . your buddies or your brother. This is between you and Me. I'm knocking at the door of* your *heart."*

I could hardly wait until Brother David quit preaching and announced the invitational hymn. I felt as though my heart was about to explode. Scared, and with my knees knocking, I stepped out of the row where my family was standing and singing, and I walked down the aisle to the front of the church. I told Brother David, "Jesus has been knocking at the door of my heart."

The pastor understood immediately.

"I want to open the door," I continued. "I can hear Him knocking, and I want Him to come into my life."

I knelt down at the front of the church and prayed while the congregation continued singing. Brother David knelt and prayed with me.

I remembered Herbie cried when he prayed to ask Jesus to come into his heart, but I was happy just to know I was on my way to heaven. I didn't have a lot of deep, dark sins to confess, so my conversion experience wasn't as dramatic as some. "Am I supposed to cry?" I wondered aloud. "I don't feel like crying. I feel like smiling!"

It wasn't a fear of hell or even a strong desire to go to heaven that motivated me to respond. It was the reality of having a relationship with Jesus that meant the most to me. *This is a good day*, I thought.

Our entire family began to grow spiritually. Mom made sure we prayed together every morning before we ran out the door to catch the school bus, which we were often late for. We had a long walk/run to get to the bus while it honked the horn for us to hurry up, and she had just enough time to quote her favorite Scripture passage to us as we ran out the door. "Trust in the LORD with all your heart, and do not lean on your own understanding." (Honk, honk!) "In all your ways acknowledge him, and he will make straight your paths" (Prov. 3:5–6). (Swish! The bus door would close behind us.) My mom was deeply committed to praying for my brother and me and helping us "hide God's Word in our hearts." I know that much of my music and ministry through the years has come as a result of her commitment, and I'm very grateful for the seeds of truth that she planted in my life of faith as a young man.

Brother David invited our family to sing in church, so we gathered around the kitchen table and practiced some songs that we could sing together as a family. Prior to that, when he wasn't working or coon hunting, Dad would go out and play music on the weekends with a group called the Village Singers. It was a fairly well-known folk-style music group in our area, and Dad was the lead singer. Dad had even made a few recordings with the Village Singers and was beginning to get some attention from people in the music business in Nashville. However, it wasn't very long after the change began to take place in our family that he left the group so he could spend more time with us. Now, Dad and our family were singing in church together!

When Olivet Baptist Church's minister of music left for another ministry, Brother David asked Dad if he would be the minister of music and lead the singing in our church services. Dad had never formally studied music, but he consented and became the choir director too. Mom, Herbie, and I sang in the church choir, and Dad served as the minister of music alongside Brother David, the man who had come pounding on Dad's window on Sunday mornings. Brother David would become one of Dad's dearest friends; he was the minister who baptized Herbie and me.

Mom and Dad sometimes spoke at layman's revivals at other churches, telling their story of what God had done in their lives. In addition, we sang more often as a family. Herbie played an upright bass and Mom shook a tambourine while Dad and I played guitar, and we all sang.

Besides singing together in church, we sang at various functions in the surrounding area. Herbie and I wore matching blue denim outfits, and we all crammed into our little Volkswagen Beetle. With Herbie's upright bass sticking out the window as we drove to the program, we hoped it didn't rain before we arrived at our destination.

Although Dad and I played guitar together, worked on old cars, and occasionally went hunting or fishing, he didn't care much for sports such as football, basketball, or baseball. To make matters worse, I had asthma as a kid, so no matter how much I wanted to play sports, I was always somewhat limited. The kid with the Primatine Mist inhaler is usually the last to be picked when boys are dividing up teams. My two attempts at making my mark in the world of athletics came by way of church league basketball, where I spent most of my time warming the bench and trying to convince the coach to put me in, and Little League baseball. Even with asthma, I was one of the fastest runners in school, so being able to get around the bases in a hurry seemed to make baseball the sport for me.

Showing off my new Concord Lions baseball uniform.
(It's better to look good than to play good.)

When Little League started, I was pretty doggone excited to be wearing a baseball uniform! One of my first lessons in Little League, however, was learning what *not* to do: specifically, never eat bacon and drink milk before running the bases.

Even though I was fast and my coaches had identified me as a great base stealer, I didn't often get to run the bases during games because I usually struck out. (Fortunately, in my early years, when most pitchers couldn't throw strikes, there were a lot of walks.) For some reason, I just couldn't hit the ball.

My coach was patient with me and tried to encourage me. "Hey, it's okay, Steve. You'll get it next time." Even a few of my buddies in the dugout said, "Don't worry about it; everybody strikes out once in a while. You took a cut at it. You had a good swing. Good try." While I appreciated their kind comments, what I heard in my impressionable, nine-year-old mind was my own voice taunting, "What a loser!"

Then one day a miracle happened on the Little League field. Late in the game, our team was three runs behind and the bases were loaded when I stepped up to the plate. No doubt, some of the parents and maybe even some of my teammates were whispering under their breath, "Oh no. We might as well pack up and go home. Chapman is up to bat. And he always strikes out."

And they would have been right.

But on that day the winds of change were blowing, and the pitcher put the ball right in my sweet spot, whatever that was. I took a swing, and to everyone's surprise, including my own, I heard the crack of the bat connecting with the ball. The baseball zoomed past the second baseman and into right field! I took off running for first as fast as my legs would take me. Fortunately, I had learned my lesson, so there was no bacon in my system to slow me down this time.

As I approached first base, I got the sign from my coach to head to second. I continued running for all I was worth. As I stepped on the bag and rounded second base, I looked over at my coach along the third baseline, and I saw him waving me on to third. Amazingly, before I got halfway to third base, the coach was already doing the "windmill," swinging his arm in a circular motion, which meant only one thing to me—keep running toward home! I stepped on third and rounded the corner at full speed. I raced down the third baseline and stomped on home plate to a deafening roar from the crowd of about seventeen spectators in the stands as well as from my buddies in the dugout.

I had done it—I had hit a grand-slam home run! Okay, so it was actually a legitimate single followed by a multitude of overthrows and errors on the part of the opposing team that resulted in an inside-the-park home run. But it gave our team the win.

Suddenly, I was a hero. A few innings earlier, I had tasted my tears after striking out again, feeling the agony of defeat, the shame, and the embarrassment . . . wanting to disappear. Now, I was welcomed into the dugout with backslaps and "Atta boy" and "Way to go, Steve!" Not to mention the approving roar of the crowd. I really liked that sound.

I thought, *I know what it feels like to fail . . . and now I know what it feels like to succeed. I don't ever want to step up to the plate again if I can't hit a home run.*

As the pitchers became bigger and the baseballs came faster, I became more reluctant to stay in the box. And then it happened. The pitcher on the mound was short and stocky, but he could throw hard, and to make matters even worse, he was a lefty. I stepped into the batter's box with the bat on my shoulder and watched the short but solid Goliath. After glaring at me, leaning toward me, and shaking off a few suggested pitches from the catcher, he decided on one he liked. He scrunched up his face, wound up his left arm, and threw the ball with lightning speed—right at me! I tried to jump out of the way, but my reflexes were no match for the speed of his arm, and the ball hit me in the side, about five inches above my waist, right in my rib cage.

I probably should have charged the mound like they do in the Majors when someone gets hit, but I was too busy lying on the ground, trying to breathe, and wondering how many of my ribs were broken. Turns out, my ribs were all fine and I got to proceed to first base.

My reception in the dugout at the end of the inning was that of a wounded hero returning from war. Unfortunately, even with all of that affirmation for a job well done, what little courage and confidence I had in the batter's box disappeared. From that time on, I was fearful of getting hit again.

I never got another hit. I swung a few times, but I struck out and was called out over and over, so I let the bat stay on my shoulder. I was afraid to even try.

It was another moment in my young life when I made a subconscious decision to do only those things at which I could succeed; I'd choose only things that would make the crowd cheer. Throughout my early years, for instance, I'd raise my hand in class only if I was certain I knew the answer. I never asked a girl out on a date unless several friends confirmed to me that she would not only accept my invitation but also be excited about saying yes.

Maybe that explains why, when people seemed to like my music and it was something I enjoyed, I thought, *I can do this! Not only that, I can re-create this performance and hopefully those euphoric feelings will follow again and again. I can succeed.* Of course, at the time, I had little idea of the reality of the life of a musician—or how many ways I could fail.

My first live musical performance was with my brother, Herbie, at the Concord Elementary School talent show when I was in first grade. Herbie was the singer, and I accompanied him on guitar. We rehearsed the Donny Osmond hit "Go Away Little Girl," but the night of the show I developed a fever and felt nauseous.

Herbie and I were in a back room when I heard one of the teachers express her disappointment onstage. "Well, we were supposed to have a song by the Chapman brothers next," she said, "but they can't perform because Steve is sick."

The audience responded sympathetically, "Aw, that's too bad."

As I languished in the back room, the crowd's response roused me from my misery and motivated me to go out onstage. In my young mind, I heard ten thousand screaming fans expressing their disappointment.

Something rose up inside of me, besides what I had eaten earlier, and I knew we had to give the crowd what they wanted. I figured I had about ten good minutes before another wave of nausea hit, so I told Herbie to let the teacher know we could go on next.

Herbie and I went onstage and sang and played our hearts out. The audience applauded appreciatively, probably partly for our performance and partly because I didn't puke on the stage. Regardless, I wanted to hear that sound again. People applauding, cheering, and saying, "I like you; what you did made me happy" was a powerful force in my life.

When I was twelve years old, I won a double album (vinyl!) and two tickets to attend an Andraé Crouch and the Disciples concert. It would be no overstatement to say that what I experienced at that concert changed my life. The arena pulsated with passion, soul, and spirit, and the worship and watching and listening to Andraé had a powerful effect on me. His song lyrics were straightforward messages about Jesus, but they were presented in an engaging and exciting way that I had never experienced before. Perhaps for the first time, I began to understand how God could use music to reach deep into the hearts of people who otherwise might not be open to the message. I'm not sure I even dared to dream that night that God could use *me* in such a way, but the thought was certainly implanted somewhere deep within me.

Because Herbie was such a good singer, sometimes I'd get intimidated and frustrated that I was not. In fact, I was a pretty weak singer; my voice was small and my range was limited.

"Sing! Take a big breath and just belt it out," Dad and my brother would try to encourage me. "Sing out." But somehow their encouragement felt more like intimidation to me, and I became even less confident in my singing.

Instead, I began to find my voice through songwriting. As he had done with the guitar, Herbie had dabbled with writing songs, but he hadn't really followed through. I found some of the ideas he had written down and decided to try my hand at finishing them. It felt natural; writing songs seemed like something I might be good at. I had been fascinated with the whole idea of songwriting for as long as I could remember. My dad and some of his music buddies would get together on Saturday night in our kitchen, shut the door to keep the kids out, set up some microphones, and write and record songs on an old reel-to-reel tape recorder. I would press my ear up to the door and listen. There was a mystique about what was happening on the other side of that door, and I wanted to be a part of it.

My first attempt at writing a complete song was simply titled "Well Done." I was about fifteen years old, and the song was sort of a mission statement—long before I even knew what a mission statement was or had ever heard that phrase. The lyrics were based on Jesus's parable of the talents found in the Bible. In the story, Jesus told about a master going away on a trip, but before leaving, he entrusted three servants with three different amounts of money to care for while he was gone. In the version I first heard, based on the King James Version of the Bible, the word describing the money was *talents.* The master gave one servant five talents, another servant three talents, and the last servant one talent.

In the story, the servant who had been given the most, five talents, invested them well and doubled them. When the master came back, he was rewarded. "Well done, good and faithful servant," the master said.

The second servant did something similar, using and increasing his talents.

But the third servant had buried his talent. He had hidden it away, perhaps thinking, *I don't want to screw this up; I need to be careful with this; I don't want to squander what the master has given me, so I'll hide it.*

When the master returned, the servant gave him back the one talent, but the master was not pleased. In fact, he was angry with the servant for not doing something more productive with the talent he had given him.

As a teenager with a bit of talent that I knew God had given me, this story resonated with me. People had often told me, "Steve, you really have a talent." Or "God's given you a lot of talent." I was as restless and rascally as any teenager, but I had a heart's desire to please God. I prayed, "God, I want to use the gifts and talent You have given me in a way so that when Jesus comes back, He can say to me, 'Well done, good and faithful servant.'"

My dad remembers that I was out on the tractor mowing the three-acre field in front of our house when he saw me come flying up to the house in fourth gear. His first thought was that I'd mowed over a nest of wasps and had been stung, but it turns out I'd been stung with a song idea and had to get it written down before it got away from me. I sat down on the cinder block steps in the back of our old country house with my guitar and wrote the lyrics and guitar chords on a sheet of notebook paper. The pencil kept poking holes in the paper because of the rough texture of the cinder blocks, but I couldn't stop to find a smoother surface. I was lost in the creative flow for the first time in my life! The message was simple:

> Before He left this earth for heaven
> Jesus commanded us to go
> And bring all people to Him
> By letting His love through us show.
> When Christ comes, I just want to hear Him say, "Well done."
> He said He'd come back for His children
> And His coming is not too far away
> I pray that when I stand before Him
> Well done is what I'll hear Him say . . .
> When Christ comes, I just want to hear Him say . . .

I didn't record it at the time, and I certainly had a long way to go as a songwriter, but my musical journey began with that song and my desire to hear Jesus say, "Well done." Since then I've wanted that desire to direct not only the musical gifts He's entrusted to me but also how I live all of my life.

So I began writing more songs, and I discovered that when I put my own heart into the lyrics, people tended to listen. In school, I'd play a few popular songs of the day, and my friends would think it was cool and would listen politely, but when I said, "I wrote this song," people seemed to lean in and listen more intently to what I had to say. I didn't try to preach at anyone; I just told my stories and shared through my songs what I believed and what was most important in my life. After all, if I had been entrusted with a talent from the Master, I certainly wanted to use it in a way that would allow Him to say, "Well done" when He returned.

Another of my early Christian musical influences was Dallas Holm, a solo artist who traveled with David Wilkerson, the evangelist and author of the book *The Cross and the Switchblade.*

When the Wilkerson team came to Paducah for a crusade, I attended and heard Dallas Holm sing "Rise Again," his own version of the resurrection story. As I listened to him, I thought, *I would love to do that, to be able to stand onstage and sing about Jesus.*

I had a Dallas Holm *Peace, Joy, and Love* eight-track tape that my brother and I wore out listening to whenever we rode in the family jeep. Hearing the way Dallas wrote honestly about his own journey as a follower of Jesus in songs such as "If I Had It to Do All Over Again" made me feel like I was listening to a friend tell me his story and the story of God's love in a way I could relate to.

For as long as I could remember, I was drawn to the singer/songwriters that my dad liked. They included James Taylor, Jim Croce, John Denver, and Carol King. I remember listening to their albums as a little boy, and their songs were some of the first I learned to play on the guitar. So when Dallas Holm came along as a singer/songwriter singing about what was most important in his life and in my life, the love of God and faith in Jesus, I was deeply affected. More than anyone other than my dad, Dallas Holm was the musician I most wanted to emulate and who had the greatest impact on my early career.

Oddly enough, it wasn't my guitar playing or my singing that led to my first experience on a tour bus or in a recording studio—it was my drum playing. I started playing drums in the band at Concord Elementary School and continued drumming all the way through junior high and high school in both concert and marching band. I convinced my dad and mom somewhere along the way that I needed a drum set as well. I would put on a pair of headphones and beat my drums to smithereens, practicing to songs such as "The Banana Splits," which boasted such profound lyrics as, "One banana, two banana, three banana, four!" I wasn't great, but what I lacked in skill I made up for in volume! My poor parents tolerated the relentless pounding, so I guess it is divine justice that one of my sons grew up to be an incredible (and loud!) drummer.

One of my best buddies in school, Denny Alvey, and his family performed in a part-time gospel singing group known as the Alveys. They sang mostly on weekends and during school vacations, and they traveled in an old 1946 Flxible tour bus.

Over Christmas break one year, Denny called me and said, "We're leaving for Mobile, Alabama, tonight and will be gone for a few days to do some concerts, but our drummer, Eddie Bell, is really sick and can't make the trip. You wanna go along and fill in on the drums?"

"Are you kidding? You want me to go *on tour,* in a tour bus, with one of my best buds?"

I knew Eddie's playing—he was a good, solid drummer who later left Paducah to play professionally in Nashville with the Hemphills and then with the Whites, Ricky Skaggs's wife and in-laws. Denny played bass guitar, and his dad, Densel Alvey, played acoustic guitar and sang. The band also had a steel guitar player and a piano player. Densel's wife, Joy, and Denny's sister, Lisa, did most of the lead vocals. Lisa was a great singer who went on to work in country music with the group Dave and Sugar and then sang background vocals with the legendary Roy Orbison until he passed away. Lisa also sang "Peace," one of the first songs I ever wrote. Other than Herbie and me, Lisa was the first person to sing one of my songs.

I went along that weekend and played the drums. I knew most of the songs, and the arrangements were relatively simple, so with a bit of preconcert rehearsal, I was able to follow Denny well enough to keep the beat.

From then on, whenever the Alveys needed a fill-in musician, Denny would give me a call. Sometimes I played guitar, and once I even played piano, but mostly I played the drums. I learned a lot in those days about playing live music, connecting with an audience, and surviving on an old tour bus with a heater that didn't work in the winter and brakes that were prone to fail. I learned a lot about prayer too! Occasionally, in the middle of a concert, Densel would call on Denny, Lisa, and me to step to the microphone. "Come on up here, young'uns, and give 'em a little of that new song you learned."

Denny, Lisa, and I sang the Imperials' song "Oh, Buddha," as recorded by the incredible singer Russ Taff. The song wasn't really about Buddha so much as it pointed to Jesus as the only way to heaven.

Densel Alvey had a good buddy, Jerry Crutchfield, another Paducah native who had gone to Nashville and made a name for himself as an artist, songwriter, producer, and eventually the head of MCA Music. When the Alveys decided to record an album, Mr. Crutchfield allowed them to work in the state-of-the-art studio at MCA on Nashville's famous Music Row. The Alveys wanted to record "Oh, Buddha" and my song "Peace," so I went along.

Walking into the studio, I was in awe. I was fascinated by all the buttons and knobs on the sound console and the huge recorder that was about the size of a kitchen stove with two-inch-wide recording tape. I had never seen anything like it. I was most amazed at the Nashville studio musicians who listened to the Alveys' songs and then played them as though they had been performing them for years. I had listened to my dad talk about the recording studios of Nashville and particularly the studio musicians who were some of the best pickers in the world. As a kid, I had dreamed of being a studio session guitar player, and here I was in an actual recording studio surrounded by studio musicians playing better than I'd ever heard anyone play, and I was a part of it. This was heaven!

If that wasn't enough, the Alveys recorded my song "Peace" using studio players. Just hearing world-class musicians play something I had written was inspiring. We also recorded "Oh, Buddha," and I got to sing the second verse, so technically, my first professionally recorded performance was on the Alveys' album. Thankfully, those recordings live only in my memory now, because they probably sound a lot better there.

In junior high and high school, I continued to fill my role as best I could as Mr. Do the Right Thing. I ate my vegetables (except for candied yams, which aren't technically a vegetable anyway), did my homework (mostly), colored inside the lines, and tried to do as I was told. As a result, I didn't get invited to the weekend parties with the cool kids, which was just as well. After all, it had been ingrained in me to avoid any form of horseplay, and one could assume that most of what went on at those parties would certainly qualify. That isn't to say I didn't have any fun. I had a great time with my buddies listening to music (real vinyl records on a real turntable), playing music, and working on my '71 Camaro with my dad or the old '67 Pontiac GTO that Denny and I tinkered around with.

My senior year I was voted Mr. Heath High School by the teachers and Mr. Senior by the students. The only reason these were significant is that I had made a conscious decision to try to be nice to everybody, even the guys and girls who were on the outside. It was not the kind of thing that typically put someone on the popular list, but somehow it seemed to make people respect me. Of course, there were always a few kids who felt it was their job to make sure I knew I wasn't cool. Not being on the football team and playing in the marching band were kind of an uncool double whammy! But I had my guitar and my blond feathered hair working for me, so at least a few girls thought I was cute.

Years later, at class reunions, some former classmates told me, "We always knew where you stood as a Christian, and that made you kind of uncool, but we respected you." Another classmate said, "You never tried to force your faith on anybody, but you weren't ashamed of your beliefs either. When I became a Christian a few years ago, you were one of the first people I wanted to tell because even though you never knew it, I saw how you lived out your faith. You were real, and you had an influence on me, so I knew you would understand."

I smiled and remembered the second verse of that first song I'd written back in high school:

> Before He left this earth for heaven
> Jesus commanded us to go
> And bring all people to Him
> By letting His love through us show.

The Chapman Brothers.

Chapter Four

Showtime!

When I was growing up, my brother, Herbie, was actually the best singer in the Chapman family. Herbie was "the voice," "the golden throat"—when Herbie sang, the church ladies cried. His voice had a big sound and a pure tone with a strong vibrato, like that of a trained singer, although he hadn't taken formal vocal lessons. Singing just came naturally to him.

When we began performing together as the Chapman Brothers, Herbie sang the lead parts, and with his friendly, gregarious personality, Herbie enjoyed doing the emcee work, introducing the songs. I played guitar behind him, more comfortable in the shadows. I'd sing harmony with Herbie on the choruses of songs, and every once in a while I'd take a lead line or two, but mostly I stayed in the background.

Herbie was the singer, and I was the musician. My first guitar was a hand-me-down from Herbie, and although it was pretty much a toy with a picture of Roy Rogers on it, I loved that guitar. Herbie had learned a chord or two, but he wasn't interested in playing. Once I picked it up, though, I had that instrument in my hands all the time, and I really wanted to learn how to play well. It sure helped that Dad was a guitar teacher.

Then when I was around eight years of age, for Christmas I received a Lotus, an off-brand guitar that probably sold for about $80, if that much. But to me, it was the greatest guitar ever made, and it was mine! It was unusual to find me without that guitar on my lap in those days. I couldn't get enough of music and that guitar. In the first photos of Herbie and me as the Chapman Brothers, I held that Lotus guitar and Herbie had a tambourine. Eventually, Herbie learned to play bass guitar. Later, at sixteen, I got an Ovation Legend from Dad's music shop. The Ovation was similar to the one Glen Campbell played, with the deep contour cutaway shape, the shiny black glass-composite top face, and the pearl diamond-shaped position inlays. It was a great guitar, and I loved playing it onstage behind Herbie.

The Chapman Brothers performed a few sad songs such as "Go Away Little Girl," but mostly we did uplifting numbers with a positive message. Our set list always included Glen Campbell's "Try a Little Kindness," Mac Davis's "I Believe in Music," and Johnny Cash's "A Thing Called Love." Herbie was famous around our neck of the woods for his rendition of "My Tribute" by Andraé Crouch. People always responded, "Wow, Herbie is a really great singer." When I sang, they usually said something like, "Wow, Herbie is a *really* great singer."

After Herbie went off to college, he took a summer job touring with a patriotic music group called the Young Americans. I had convinced Herbie to audition for the Young Americans, and I was really excited for him, but I was sad too, because he was going to leave and take our duo with him.

One day I received a phone call from somebody in Paducah wanting the Chapman Brothers to sing at a private luau.

"Ah, okay . . . " I said tentatively. "What exactly *is* a luau?"

"It's a Hawaiian-themed party, and it will be held at our swimming pool."

"Well, my brother has gone away to college, so unfortunately, there are no Chapman Brothers currently."

"That's okay. Would you come do it yourself?"

I nearly said no. *Gosh, I've never sung anywhere by myself,* I thought. *And I've never played at a full-blown luau, for cryin' out loud . . .*

Feathered hair, a shiny shirt, and an Ovation guitar . . . a dangerous combination! Me performing at my high school variety show.

"We'll pay you twenty dollars."

Twenty bucks! That would put a lot of gas in my car. I had been working at Dad's music store and another job at a tree-farm nursery, where I barely made twenty dollars for a day's work, so twenty bucks in one evening was a lot of money to me.

"Okay, yeah, I'll do it," I said.

I had sung by myself occasionally in school, although not often, but I figured I could muddle my way through a pool party. So I learned the melody lines to all of Herbie's and my songs. I dressed in the closest thing I could find in my closet to a silky Hawaiian shirt with a flower print, combed my feathered hair back, and packed up my guitar.

I performed for about twenty people around the swimming pool, most of whom didn't pay much attention to me. By the time I was done, though, my voice was shaking and my knees were knocking. I was so terrified being the front guy. I thought, *I don't think I ever want to do that again!*

Nevertheless, that was my first paid public performance as a solo artist, and I felt good to have done it, even though it had scared me half to death. Time went by, and I received another invitation from someone who had heard about my debut at the luau. I think it was the Hawaiian shirt. But I wasn't sure I could perform again by myself.

Why am I so fearful about playing in public? I wondered. Part of it might have been because I wasn't used to being the front man, the one who had to be the performer. I was a musician who loved playing music. I loved playing guitar, and I enjoyed being in the background, but being out front terrified me. My dad had similar qualms about performing by himself and actually developed panic attacks related to singing in public, so much so that he stopped performing for the most part and resigned himself to teaching guitar lessons.

Years later, when I did an exclusive bluegrass album for Cracker Barrel Old Country Store, I invited Dad and Herbie to perform with me on the *Grand Ole Opry*. It was one of the most special performances of my life, having two of the guys who had inspired and influenced me most as a musician and as a Christian standing on either side of me on the Grand Ole Opry House stage. At seventy-two years of age, Dad said that he had to muster everything within him just to walk out on that storied stage, but it was an incredibly special experience for him and for me. I also had the opportunity to have my dad and brother sing with me on another of Nashville's most notable stages, that of the historic Ryman Auditorium. Dad told a story onstage about how he used to come to Nashville when he was trying to make it in the music business. He'd drive by the Ryman Auditorium and wonder if he'd ever get to sing on that famous stage someday. After he gave up pursuing a career in music to be with his family, he was sure that dream would never be realized. Years later, however, partly because of the choices he made, he got to sing on that stage . . . with his two sons.

Speaking of the *Opry*, performing on the *Grand Ole Opry* was a major milestone in my music career, and it really happened thanks to my brother, Herbie.

During the summer following my luau debut, Herbie wanted to audition for a singing job at Opryland, a music-oriented theme park in Nashville, so I went along with him as his background musician. Opryland held separate auditions for musicians, and I planned to try out for a guitar-playing position in one of the theme park's bands. At the musicians' auditions, I quickly realized I was out of my league. While I played guitar fairly well, most of the pickers at the audition were college-trained musicians who could play by note, following the sheet music placed in front of them. I knew music, but I mostly played by ear. I wasn't at the same level as the other musicians and didn't really think I'd get the job.

So after I finished my audition, I hurried over to the I Hear America Singing stage at the American Music Theater, a show theater near the Grand Ole Opry House where Herbie was waiting for me. For Herbie's audition, he performed "I Write the Songs" by Barry Manilow, and I played guitar for him and sang background on the choruses. Herbie did a fantastic job during his audition and was pretty much a shoo-in for the job.

"How 'bout you, Steve?" the talent coordinator asked. "Do you do any solo work? Do you sing any songs by yourself?"

"Ah . . ." I looked at Herbie, and he motioned for me to step up. "Sure . . . yeah . . . okay," I said, inching closer to the microphone.

In a shaky, nervous voice that sounded like a Dolly Parton–style vibrato, I sang one of Kenny Rogers's many hits, "You Decorated My Life," as my audition for the Opryland vocal group. When I finished, I thought, *There's no way they're going to hire me*, and that was okay. I didn't consider myself a soloist; I was part of a duo. So a few weeks later, when I received a call from Opryland Entertainment, I was amazed. The Opryland group must have liked the "brother element," because they hired both Herbie and me!

Joe Jerles was the piano player and music director for the show groups. Bob Whittaker headed up the staff. His wife, Jean, the dance instructor, taught me how to clog. I was timid about singing, so actually *moving* onstage was a far greater stretch for me! When the director at Opryland said, "Come on, Steve. We're going to teach you to dance," I wanted to say, "Okay, you can just fire me now and save us both a lot of time and embarrassment." But of course, I didn't. I practiced hard, and Jean was patient with me. "Don't worry," she said. "I've had guys with two left feet before, and every one of them learned to dance. You'll get it . . . eventually."

Oh yeah? What about a guy with forty-seven left feet? I thought.

But I did get it. Jean Whittaker taught me how to clog. Every once in a while, even to this day, I'll be onstage and I'll get the notion to stomp a number. The audiences are always surprised and respond with cheers.

Herbie and I rehearsed with the show's cast for several weeks before the directors sent all of us—three guys and three girls, along with a four-piece band—to Gatlinburg, Tennessee, where we spent the summer performing live every night of the week in one of the Opryland shows in the Smoky

Mountains resort community. The show was called "Today's Country Roads." It was a country music revue tracing the history of classic country music up to the current, popular country hits. The entire show was one big medley of hit songs.

Recently, somebody sent me a recording of our show along with a note saying, "You might enjoy hearing this." When I listened to it, I thought, *How in the world did I ever get a recording deal? Who would ever think, "That guy needs to be on an album"?* But back then, I thought I sounded okay.

As much as I loved music and hoped it would always be a part of my life, I was headed off to college after that summer. I was enrolled at Georgetown College, a small Christian college located north of Lexington, Kentucky, and known for its excellent premed program, which is what I listed as my major. Although I loved music, I didn't see myself as a band director or a music teacher, and because I had made all As on a few report cards, my dad had strongly encouraged me to "use the brain God had given me" to go to school and get a "real job."

That certainly seemed like the right thing to do, so being the compliant son, I turned my eye toward pursuing the most real job I could think of—becoming a doctor or maybe a dentist.

A few weeks into the semester, however, I discovered that college-level chemistry and calculus were entirely different from Heath High School chemistry (of which I was president of the Chemistry Club, thank you very much!) and calculus. I was quickly coming to the realization that I was not premed material and that the world would be a much happier and safer place if I stuck to practicing guitar rather than practicing medicine! Fortunately, at the same time I realized what direction I shouldn't be going, an amazing door opened in a very exciting direction.

While performing during the summer before I started college, Herbie and I had met a college student, Danny Daniels, after one of our shows. Danny was attending college in Indiana at what later became Anderson University. As he, Herbie, and I talked, we discovered a mutual interest in Christian music, and he said he'd love to hear some of the songs I had written.

Herbie and I sat down and played some songs for Danny, and he loved them. Other than Herbie and my mom and dad, Danny Daniels was the first person who really saw my potential as a songwriter.

"These songs are pretty good," he said. "I should take them to my friend who does gospel music and let him hear them."

"Your friend?"

"Yeah, I have some family friends—Bill and Gloria Gaither," he said. "My family has known them for years."

"You *know* Bill and Gloria Gaither?" I asked in awe. The Gaithers were icons in Christian music. They had set new standards for concert performances with the Bill Gaither Trio, and their songs "He Touched Me," "Because He Lives," "The King Is Coming," and so many others were already being sung around the world. Many of the songs my family first sang together in church were Gaither songs. To even think they might listen to my songs seemed like a crazy dream. But Danny had high hopes; he also had a small recording studio in Alexandria, Indiana.

Danny said, "Hey, you should come to Alexandria, and you and Herbie and I can sing your songs and put them down on tape."

That sounded good to us, so the three of us recorded some demos of my songs in Danny's studio. Danny was a great piano player, and we had such a good time recording that we decided to form a band, which we called Chapman Daniels. Herbie played bass and sang most of the lead vocals, while Danny played piano, I played guitar, and the two of us sang background vocals.

Danny then took some of my songs to Bill Gaither and his partner, Gary McSpadden. Incredibly, Bill liked what he heard, and I was offered my first publishing deal with Bill and Gary's company, 19th Street Music, a branch of the Paragon publishing family in Nashville. Billy Smiley, of the band White Heart, was writing for the company, and Michael W. Smith had written for them as well before moving on to Meadowgreen Music. I didn't get paid for writing, nor did I receive a stipend or any money as a draw against future royalties, but the publisher promised to pitch the songs, trying to get recording artists to cut them.

Meanwhile, Danny told Herbie and me more about Anderson University. Danny explained that, thanks to the Gaithers' help, Anderson had pioneered a music business program. "You can study music, but even more than that, you can learn recording techniques and take songwriting classes, copyright and publishing courses, and music business classes."

"Really? I can go to school for that?"

"You sure can," Danny said. "You guys ought to think about transferring out here."

He also told us about one of his good friends—a girl with two first names—who had just graduated from Anderson. "She has one of the most amazing voices I've ever heard," Danny said, "and she's going to transform Christian music."

Later, Danny played some of my songs for this new female artist and reported back to me. "She liked a couple of your songs," Danny said. "She wants her producer to hear them, and she might want to record one."

"Really?"

"Yeah, but you might want to wait," Danny said. "Nobody has heard your songs yet, so you might want to shoot for a more established artist to record one first."

I thought that made a lot of sense. I agreed with Danny and told him, "Maybe we should let some other artists who are already known and successful hear my songs just to see if they might be interested in recording one of them."

Two days later, I was listening to the radio in my dorm room at Georgetown College when I heard a station spinning Christian music. A song was playing that stopped me in my tracks. I had never heard a song or a singer quite like what I was hearing coming through that little radio speaker.

When the song concluded, the deejay said, "And that's a newcomer, Sandi Patty, singing "We Shall Behold Him."

I ran to the phone and dialed Danny's number. "Danny, who was that girl with two first names you were telling me about who was interested in my songs?"

He responded, "Her name is Sandi Patty. Why?"

"Well, I just heard her on the radio, and if she wants to record one of my songs, you tell her she can record any of them, because she is gonna change the world with that voice!" Sandi's producer didn't include any of my initial songs on her album, but I was encouraged nonetheless. The fact that she and her producer liked them was like gas on my creative fire, and I started writing more songs. I walked into my dorm room one afternoon after class in a creative flow and noticed the words "Built to Last" engraved on a basketball that belonged to my roommate. I ran to the piano in the lobby of a building next door and sat down and started writing a song by the same title. That song would eventually become the first song of mine recorded by another artist and in many ways the official launch of my songwriting career.

An interest in my songs, a publishing deal offer, a great new friend, and a college course of study in an area of music I was interested in proved to be too much to resist. So in the spring semester of my freshman year, I joyfully bade farewell to college chemistry forever and transferred, along with Herbie, to Anderson University in Indiana. I spent that spring semester studying in the music business program while writing, recording, and performing more songs with my brother and Danny between classes. I also began to spend some time with "the master," Bill Gaither himself, talking about the craft of songwriting. As he has done for so many artists over the years, he encouraged, inspired, and instructed me in ways I could never have dreamed possible. I even had the opportunity along with Herbie and Danny to be the opening act for a Sandi Patty homecoming concert at Anderson during that semester. Things were definitely looking up!

"Ladies and gentlemen, the incomparable George (Steven Curtis) Jones!" Ready for the Opry.

Chapter Five

A Little Tribute to George

The summer after my freshman year, with wide-eyed wonder about all the creative doors that were opening before me, I headed back to Nashville and to Opryland again. I threw myself into writing and spent as much time as I could in the writers' rooms and the recording studio at my publisher's offices in Nashville. I couldn't believe I was getting these opportunities, making money playing music, and getting to work on Music Row as a songwriter. It wasn't all fun and games, though. They don't call it the music *business* for nothing.

I had many meetings with the head of publishing, Ron Griffin, in which I'd play my latest songs for him. These were my newest babies, so I would come in excited to show them off, sure he was going to be impressed. But after listening to my songs, Ron would critique and basically shred my songs to pieces, or at least that's how it felt to me. It was not uncommon to leave his office fighting back tears, thinking, *Maybe I don't have what it takes after all.* I later realized that much of what I learned about the craft of songwriting and the task of working hard to make every word and every line count came from those painful meetings, and I'm grateful for it.

I was also getting the chance to hone my skills as a performer while Herbie and I worked at Opryland, this time at the theme park in a show called "Country Music USA."

Herbie and me going to work at Opryland USA.

We performed at an outdoor theater boasting a large working waterwheel. The show was similar to the one we'd done in Gatlinburg, only it was a ramped-up version with a larger cast and a bigger band. We also dressed up as the stars we were imitating—everyone from Porter Wagoner to Lester Flatt and Earl Scruggs to the Oak Ridge Boys. One of the solo parts for which I had auditioned was that of country music legend George Jones. When I had first seen the show, before I had ever performed in it, to me, the George Jones imitation had been one of the coolest moments in the show. Everything stopped and a low-toned announcer's voice came over the sound system: "The incomparable George Jones." At that, a guy stepped out onstage wearing a long black-velvet coat and sang in an equally velvet voice, "He said, 'I'll love you till I die.' She told him, 'You'll forget in time.'" As the crowd recognized George's greatest hit, "He Stopped Loving Her Today," they erupted in applause.

I wanted that part. So when I became a member of the troupe, I auditioned for the George Jones gig and got it! I sang the first verse and chorus to "He Stopped Loving Her Today" six days a week, five shows a day. It was a special feature during each performance.

That summer I was invited to sing on the matinee show of the *Grand Ole Opry*. When I was asked, I thought at first they had made a mistake. "Are you sure you got the right Chapman? Herbie is the real singer in our family." Yet when the invitation came for me to sing on the *Opry*—rather than Herbie—he still encouraged me, even though we both knew Herbie was a far better singer than I was. In a real way, right from the beginning of my career, Herbie was my biggest cheerleader, and everything I have achieved can be traced back to his unselfish attitude. Of the many amazing blessings God has granted me on my journey in this life, my big brother, Herbie, is one of the greatest.

Apparently, the George Jones imitation had established me as a country singer of note—well, kinda. Still, the invitation to perform on the *Opry* was real. The director said, "You can sing anything you want. What would you like to do?"

That was an easy decision for me. I chose to sing one of the greatest country songs ever written, the George Jones classic "He Stopped Loving Her Today."

I called my dad right away. "Dad, you aren't going to believe this," I said. "I'm going to sing on the *Grand Ole Opry*!"

Dad was never one to gush or get overly excited, but I could tell he was thrilled for me. "Son, that's great. Your mom and I, we're gonna come. When is it? We'll be there." Throughout my early years, any time Herbie or I achieved some goal or received an award, Dad always said, "I'm so proud of my sons, but I'm not surprised. I always knew they were going to do great things." So when I told him about the *Opry*, he said, "I always knew they'd discover what we've always known. I'm proud of you, son."

One of my dad's many endearing qualities as a guitar teacher is his fun, lighthearted way of encouraging even the most average of his students. He usually begins every lesson with, "Grab your geetar and git on back here. I'm gonna make you a big star!" This time maybe he felt like he'd really done it for once. For my part, I was pretty excited to think I had finally pleased my dad. I had seemingly helped "fix" my parents' marriage, and I had tried to help him fix cars and mow the grass and weed the garden like I was told. I had started out in college as a premed student because I had made good grades in school and Dad had said I should get a "real job" since the music business wasn't a stable career path as far as he could tell. I had lasted only one semester thanks to college chemistry . . . and calculus . . . and most of my other premed courses. But now I was singing on the *Grand Ole Opry*!

I appreciated that Dad was proud of Herbie's and my musical abilities, but he had rarely attended any of our performances. Mom was always there in the front row cheering us on, but Dad was always working at his music store or giving lessons. He had no other employees, so if he didn't open the store and stay there all day to operate it, the business had to close. If Herbie and I won a music contest or received accolades of some sort for one of our performances, Mom would tell Dad, and he'd write us little notes the next morning. "Congratulations, boys!" He'd draw smiley faces on a piece of paper he'd torn out of our notebooks or on a napkin. "I heard you did great last night." Those little notes were a treasure to me, worth far more than any trophy or monetary prize we'd received.

I was grateful for how hard Dad worked, so at the time, I didn't give it much thought that he never attended our performances. But when I told him I'd be singing on the *Opry*, that was special. Our dad was a big fan of country music and had grown up listening to WSM radio in Nashville. When Dad was a young man, his best friend was Jack Curtis Martin, a Dobro player who went on to achieve his childhood dream of playing professionally with Lester Flatt and Earl Scruggs. Mom and Dad gave me my middle name in honor of Dad's best friend. Dad himself had once had a songwriting deal with Glaser Brothers Music Publishers in Nashville, and occasionally, he'd drive to Music City to record some demo tapes of his songs. So for Herbie and me, Nashville held a powerful mystique.

In Paducah, Kentucky, located about a two-and-a-half-hour drive from Nashville, if the planets were lined up perfectly and the weather was just right, we could receive WSM radio on our car's AM radio. Ordinarily, Dad liked everyone to be quiet when he was driving, but occasionally, he'd set the radio dial to 650 AM hoping to hear WSM as we traveled. Although WSM boomed all over North America, the station was often difficult to pull in until the sun went down, especially in Paducah. But then suddenly, through the static, we'd hear the signature guitar riffs leading into the show's introductions.

"Boys, that's the *Grand Ole Opry*," Dad would say with a mixture of excitement and reverence obvious in his voice. "That's the ultimate music experience right there, where the magic happens, in Nashville."

So when I told Dad I'd be singing on the *Grand Ole Opry*, he thought that was the best thing ever. He drove from Paducah to Nashville to be in the audience, along with Herbie, my mom, and even my grandmother, who had always encouraged me in my music and was my biggest fan.

For my performance, I dressed in my favorite "country-looking" outfit—jeans, a sports coat, and my Opryland-show-issued two-tone cowboy boots. I was so excited I could barely stand it and paced nervously prior to the show. There's no feeling in the world quite like standing backstage at the Grand Ole Opry House and peering out at the stage where music superstars such as Johnny Cash, Loretta Lynn, Charlie Pride, Willie Nelson, Charlie Daniels, and a host of others have performed. To a young musician like me, the stage looked majestic, replete with the white encased microphone stands bearing the WSM logo, the famous barn set, and church pews right on the stage where special guests could sit and watch the show up close. The *Opry* musicians were already in place as I stood in the dimly lit offstage area awaiting my introduction.

As if I wasn't nervous enough, out from one of the dressing rooms walked country music legend Roy Acuff—not a Roy Acuff imitator (I'd been singing Mr. Acuff's music in our show five times a day all summer long!) but the real Roy Acuff! When I saw Mr. Acuff getting ready to take the stage, I was both awed and petrified. Roy Acuff was going to hear me—Steve Chapman, guitar player from Paducah—sing onstage. *I am so in over my head,* I thought.

I had grown comfortable with my performance in the Opryland show because I knew the material well. Dad had taught me to always be prepared. We'd sit around our kitchen table for hours practicing a song we were going to sing in church on Sunday. "We have to practice. Always be prepared. Git it good," Dad insisted. One of my dad's favorites among many of his famous sayings was, "If it's worth doing, it's worth doing right!" And the fact that we were just singing on Sunday morning in our little church was never a reason for anything less than a stellar performance. "If we're gonna do something for the Lord, it needs to be done with excellence. 'Study to show yourselves approved,' like the Bible says," Dad emphasized.

I've reflected over the years how grateful I am for those character lessons I received from my dad as well as the guitar lessons. As a result, I didn't like (and still don't) winging it anytime I was performing in front of people. If I didn't practice a song dozens of times before performing it, I felt unprepared and got really nervous.

But that's not the *Opry* way of doing things. The *Grand Ole Opry* employs some of Nashville's finest musicians. They rarely even rehearse with an artist before the show. They have arrangement charts, and someone asks, "What key is this in?" and they go out and play live in front of thousands of people in the audience and millions of radio listeners, an audience spanning as many as thirty to forty states across America. Not a great approach for Mr. Do It Right or Don't Do It at All.

So I was nervous already, and now Mr. Roy Acuff was going to introduce me!

To make matters worse, although I sang "He Stopped Loving Her Today" twenty-five times a week or more, it was part of a medley in the Opryland show, so I sang only the first verse and chorus every day. For the *Grand Ole Opry*, I had practiced repeatedly and prepared to sing the entire song.

Roy Acuff walked onto the stage as though it were second nature to him. "Well, we have a special treat for you this afternoon," he told the audience. "We've got a young performer from our park out here . . . and I encourage you to go out after the show and enjoy Opryland park. We have all kinds of great performers throughout the park doing live music . . . you'll enjoy it. And here's one of the performers you can hear in the 'Country Music USA' show. Here he is . . . Steve Chapman!"

I stepped onto the famous stage, and the band hit the first chord as though we had rehearsed it a thousand times. *Wow, this really is the big-time!* I thought. I stepped up to the microphone and launched into my best imitation of George Jones. "He said, 'I'll love you till I die,'" I sang perfectly. "She told him, 'You'll forget in time.'" I finished the first verse, then sang the chorus, nailing them both. I went on to the second verse, and my mind raced as the words came to me. I finished by hitting and holding the high note in the chorus: "He stopped loving *herrr* . . . today."

Maybe the audience members were just being kind or cheering on the new kid, or maybe they really liked me; I'll never know. But I do know that the crowd responded with a tremendous standing ovation! I looked down into the smiling faces in the audience and saw my mom smiling; my beaming dad, who had taught me how to hold a guitar; my brother, who had made all this possible; and my grandmother, who had supported me from the time I sang my first note. They were all on their feet applauding. I could hardly believe my eyes and ears . . . a standing ovation for my first song ever on the *Grand Ole Opry*. I had hit the grand-slam home run . . . again! Only this time it was even better—I was in the music big leagues.

Roy Acuff walked out onto the stage and clasped his famous fiddle-playing fingers onto my arm. Mr. Acuff was elderly at this point in his life and a bit frail, so I could feel him stabilizing himself as he held onto my arm and spoke into his microphone. "Steve! Ya did good. I think the folks liked ya!" I nodded in sincere, humble appreciation to the master musician. But Mr. Acuff wasn't done. He was the quintessential showman. He knew that if a crowd enjoyed something once, ya give it to 'em again. So still holding my arm, he said, "I think you need to give 'em a little more of that. Give 'em another chorus of that song!"

There I was basking in the glow of accomplishment when suddenly a curveball was thrown directly at me! My fluster meter instantly banged into the red zone. *Wait! Another chorus? We didn't practice that! I don't know the arrangement!*

Too late. The *Opry* band hit the first chord, and I sang, "He stopped loving her today . . ." And then I stopped.

My mind went totally blank

I saw the panicked expression on Dad's face. I saw Mom. I saw Herbie trying to draw the words out of me. I saw my grandma praying for me . . . and I saw my future going up in flames.

It was as though time stood still. To my stark terror, I suddenly realized I could not remember the words to the next line of the chorus! Not the second verse of the song but the same chorus I had sung five times a day, six days a week. In that moment, I was completely and utterly lost. I couldn't come up with the next line to the song. Right then, I could not have told anyone my name or what planet I was living on, much less the lyrics to the George Jones classic. Meanwhile, the band was vamping behind me, playing the same few chords over and over, waiting for me to remember the words.

After a few measures, the guys in the band started trying to feed the words to me: "They placed a wreath upon his door," one of the musicians called out as they continued playing.

"Huh?" I turned around partially, trying to figure out what they were saying. "Wha . . . They placed a wha . . . ?"

My mind was racing. *I'm nineteen years old. I'm onstage at the Grand Ole Opry. My family is here. Roy Acuff is standing onstage twenty feet away watching and listening to me. And my world has just completely ended. My only hope is for the stage to open up and swallow me so I can completely disappear from this moment!*

The band was still playing the chorus over and over, so one of the musicians hollered to me, "They placed a wreath upon his door!"

"Huh? Oh, yeah, yeah, yeah." I had to wait for the band to come around to the top of the chorus again, and then I picked up with them after the first line, "They placed a wreath upon his door . . ." and then finished out the chorus. The audience applauded politely this time, their enthusiasm tempered with pity. I waved at them and thanked them.

I looked over toward Mr. Acuff, who was walking across the stage in my direction. I thought, *Well, that's the end of my career on this stage and probably any other stage.* I knew the king of country music had to say something about my gaffe because it was so obvious. Everyone in the forty-four-hundred-seat venue had witnessed it.

Mr. Acuff attempted to smooth over the situation in a nice way. "Well, Steve, it looked like you forgot the words or something. What happened there?"

Standing on the Grand Ole Opry House stage at a pivotal moment in my fledgling career, I remembered that during that season of his life George Jones had a troublesome drinking problem. He was at the peak of his career, but sometimes due to the alcohol he would literally slip and fall off a stage in the middle of a concert. His drinking had grown so chronic that he often failed to show up for concerts or performances on the *Grand Ole Opry*, and promoters and fellow musicians sometimes whimsically referred to George as No-Show Jones.

While there was nothing funny about George's drinking problems, if you've ever wondered whether God has a sense of humor, let me assure you He does. I know. Because whether it was the Lord or just quick thinking, when Mr. Acuff asked me what had happened, I replied with the first thought that came into my mind. "Oh, I just wanted to do it like George does it these days . . . just a little tribute to George."

The crowd howled with laughter, and they began applauding again. Roy Acuff cracked up too, as did the band members and all the people watching in the wings of the stage. It was a hilarious moment to everyone else, but I was still just trying to get my heart rate back down into the safe zone!

Afterward, Roy said to me, "Boy, you got somethin' special. If you can think on your feet and pull that off, you're gonna be okay. You can sing it perfectly a hundred times, and the crowd will clap their hands and forget it, but the audience is going to remember that performance!"

"Well, thank you, sir," I replied. I whispered a quick prayer, "Okay, God. Thank you for that. I thought I was over and done!" Once again, even though I had messed up, I'd been able to "fix" it in a way, and I felt grateful.

As it turned out, that was not my last appearance onstage at the Grand Ole Opry, but it was certainly one of my most memorable. (As a side note, the next time I was asked to perform on the *Opry* I tried to learn a song the night before and forgot the words . . . *again*! For some strange reason, I didn't get asked back until years later, when I was singing my own songs as Steven Curtis Chapman. I remembered the words that time!)

I began to realize after my initial *Opry* performance that as much as I was intent on not messing up and doing things right, maybe God had given me an ability that was more important than always doing things right. I felt like I'd started to discover a kind of unique gift for taking even those embarrassingly awkward, stumbling moments and connecting with the audience in a way that drew them in a little closer and made us feel more like friends.

Chapman/Henderson
(Mark Apple, me, Brent Henderson, and Herbie).

Chapter Six

The Call

Following my "successful" albeit harrowing appearance on the *Grand Ole Opry*, Dad and I had a conversation about whether I should consider performing country music. I enjoyed writing songs and playing guitar as part of somebody else's band, but at that point, I certainly did not see myself as an artist. Dad, however, saw potential in his boy, but he was also trying to be a realist, knowing a bit from his own experience as well as relationships with other career musicians how difficult it was to make a living as a musician, especially as a Christian artist, at the time. "If you're going to pursue music, country music is much bigger than gospel," Dad reminded me.

Dad wasn't suggesting I compromise my Christian convictions. He simply saw the opportunities. So he asked, "Son, why don't you consider doing country music? You've been on the *Grand Ole Opry*, and ya did good. And they liked ya."

At the time, Ricky Skaggs's career was soaring. A fantastic musician, known as a top-tier country and bluegrass artist, Ricky is also a dedicated Christian. Dad mentioned Ricky as an example of someone who worked in mainstream music without compromising his faith.

"Dad, I love performing. I enjoyed performing at Opryland, and I was really thrilled to play on the *Grand Ole Opry*," I said. "But I really feel like God has made me to write music about my faith. That's what is most natural for me. When I do country music, it's like putting on a costume, but when I sing about my faith, it feels right."

Dad looked at me respectfully. "If that's what you really believe, okay. But just keep your heart open and pray about it."

Dad had always told me, "Son, if you please God, you're going to please me." Whether I was doing a job or going out on a date, Dad reminded me of that adage. It was another one of his famous sayings. I knew he felt the same way about my music.

Although my heart seemed most alive when I wrote and sang gospel music, I did as Dad asked and considered "going country" if that could help me have conversations about God in secular venues. Amy Grant was doing some shows that went beyond the Christian music venues and had found a receptive audience both in and out of churches. Maybe I could too.

Some of my fellow musicians at Opryland that summer eventually became the platinum-album-selling, award-winning country band Diamond Rio. Marty Roe and Jimmy Olander were in the Opryland group originally known as the Grizzly River Boys, named after one of the theme park's attractions. Marty and I were Lester Flatt and Earl Scruggs together in the Opryland show.

During our breaks, Marty and I had discussions backstage about Christians in country music and potentially having a larger influence. Marty posed the possibility of me being a Christian who performed country music.

"You need to do country music," Marty encouraged me, "because we need Christians in country music too. You can have a big influence with the country music audience."

"I hear you, Marty, but the songs I write and what I love to sing most are songs that talk pretty honestly and openly about my faith and my relationship with God. That just seems like what God made me to do," I said.

Even though I hadn't had any success getting one of my songs recorded by an artist, I felt it was right around the corner, and leaving Nashville at this point to go back to school seemed like a bad idea. So I stayed on at Opryland through the fall of 1982 and set my sights on getting my career started as a songwriter—and maybe as a George Jones impersonator on the side! I had several songs put on hold by artists (which means they were strongly considering recording them), but each time the artist or album producer would pass at the last minute. As Thanksgiving approached, I grew more and more discouraged. Maybe I didn't have what it took.

During this time, my mom and dad came to Nashville for a visit, and we discussed the possibility of me going back to Anderson University to get more education and leaving all this music career stuff in God's hands. I prayed hard about it and decided that at nineteen years old maybe I didn't need to have it all figured out just yet. I made plans along with Herbie to return to Anderson in the spring of 1983.

I was attending classes at Anderson and writing songs in my spare time when I received a phone call from my publisher, 19th Street Music, that changed everything. Herbie had taken the call and came looking for me to tell me that "a certain artist" had put a song of mine on hold, and it really looked like it was going to happen this time. He asked me the question, "If you could pick any artist we've been big fans of for years to record your first cut, who would you pick?" At this point, I was so excited that someone might record a song of mine that I was thinking, *It really doesn't matter.* So when he said, "How about the Imperials?" I just about passed out!

The Imperials had been singing gospel music professionally almost as long as I'd been alive. As kids, Herbie and I had gotten to see them perform at First Baptist Church in Paducah, one of the first live bands I'd ever experienced. I had studied every note of their *Priority* album. And now they wanted to record a song I'd written!

I thought back to the frustrations only a few months earlier and the decision to leave behind my diligent pursuit of a career as a songwriter. I sensed God whispering to my heart, "Why don't you trust Me with this? I've got some great plans for you, in My time."

By the time the Imperials recorded one of my songs, the members were David Will, Armond Morales, Jim Murray, and Paul Smith. Their *Side by Side* project was a unique double-album set on which each of the four singers had his own "side." Tenor Jim Murray sang my song "Built to Last."

Shortly after the Imperials recorded "Built to Last," I got my second cut, a song called "Carried Away," which I had written with Billy Smiley and Mark Gersmehl for their second White Heart album. I was on a roll! Maybe I really *could* make a living as a songwriter.

Danny Daniels had graduated by this time, so my brother and I joined forces with another Anderson student named Brent Henderson to form a group called Chapman Henderson. Herbie played bass guitar and sang, Brent sang and played piano, and of course, I played guitar. We picked up right where we'd left off with Chapman Daniels and even had satin jackets with our band name and logo imprinted on the back.

Anderson University sent Chapman Henderson out on the road that summer to promote the university to potential students and donors around the country. We invited a drummer, my longtime friend Craig Klope, to play with us as well as an auxiliary keyboard guy, a college buddy named Mark Apple. Occasionally, a friend from Paducah named Eric Horner would join us to play banjo or guitar. Eric had been one of my first guitar students when I had started teaching as a thirteen-year-old kid. He would go on to play for Lee Greenwood years later.

Brent, Herbie, and I were the core of the band. About 75 percent of the songs we performed were our own original compositions. We also sang songs by artists such as the Imperials and Dallas Holm. We played primarily at Anderson-affiliated Churches of God around the country, youth camps and conventions, and anywhere else we could promote Anderson. We spent the summer of 1983 putting about eighteen thousand miles on the college van, sleeping on the floor in people's homes and sometimes in the van, and some nights playing a concert for five people with their fingers in their ears (we had a drummer!) in a tiny church in the middle of a town that time forgot. But we were on tour and having the time of our lives, and learning a lot too!

We returned from touring just in time for the beginning of the fall semester in 1983. Anderson boasted a lot of music groups on campus, and several touring groups went out on weekends and in the summer to represent the school. For entertainment, and also to provide fledgling artists with showcase opportunities, Anderson frequently held campus variety shows. At least once a month, we had a "Cheap Thrills" show, a full evening of performances by student performers for only a five-dollar ticket. It was a great place to showcase new songs and talent.

Chapman Henderson was a fairly well-known band at "Cheap Thrills," so not surprisingly, we were asked to perform at Anderson's 1983 freshman orientation concert to help welcome the new incoming Anderson students.

Fresh off the summer tour, I wore my cool two-tone cowboy boots with light leather uppers and dark toes, which I had worn in the show at Opryland. I played a green electric guitar and had my hair styled in a bit of a mullet, nicely feathered in the front and a little longer down my neck in the back. I thought I looked pretty good.

Although I didn't know it at the time, in the audience that evening was an attractive young woman from Ohio. Her name was Mary Beth Chapman—yep, same last name as mine.

Mary Beth and her best friend, Dondeena Bradley, her roommate at Anderson, were in the back of the audience making fun of the hillbillies onstage and laughing especially at me with my thick Paducah accent.

Mary Beth and Dondeena were so busy giggling that they barely paid attention to our music. Mary Beth later admitted that I was kinda cute in a silly country sort of way. Of course, that's before I really turned on my charm!

When the concert concluded, the guys in the band hung around to talk to the incoming freshmen and friends in the audience. Mary Beth was not among the adoring fans. She and Dondeena were long gone.

A boy in love with a girl in denim. Me and Mary Beth shortly after we started dating.

Chapter Seven

Red Lobster and a Blue Speedo

I didn't meet Mary Beth at that event, but a few days later, while walking toward the cafeteria with my buddy Greg Kroeker, I saw a beautiful girl come out of the cafeteria and head in our direction. She had long, wavy hair that curled around her shoulders, and she was dressed in a blue denim skirt and a denim jacket decked out with several large, round buttons bearing slogans, similar to the kind of buttons a fan of a rock band might wear. The prevailing look for women at Anderson at the time was a conservative skirt, blouse, and sweater combination, so this young woman caught my attention. In her blue denim decked out with buttons, she stood out from the crowd and looked a little like a cool "rock 'n' roll chick." But even more than her look, there was something about her that was different—something that made me want to stare at her.

As we got closer, I saw that the buttons on her jacket were not promoting AC/DC, Metallica, or Guns N' Roses; they were all Precious Moments buttons with pictures of porcelain collectible figurines on them. One of the buttons pictured a little girl looking eye to eye with a goose and included the slogan, "Honk if you love Jesus." Another button read, "Please be patient. God isn't finished with me yet." Now I was really intrigued!

As we passed each other on the sidewalk, Greg spoke to her. "Hey, Mary Beth."

"Hi, Greg," she replied as she walked on by.

"Wait a minute." I looked at Greg in shock. "Who was that? Do you *know* her? What's her name?"

"Yeah, I know her," Greg answered nonchalantly. "That's Mary Beth Chapman."

"Chapman? The same last name as mine?"

"Yeah, but you wouldn't like her. She's an alcoholic."

"*What!* How do you know that?" I asked Greg. I recognized immediately that Greg was trying to derail my interest in the denim girl. Greg knew I wasn't into the party scene, so if a girl was a partier, I wouldn't be interested.

Later, I learned that while Mary Beth had dabbled in the typical high school party scene for a while, she was far from being an alcoholic. In fact, she had experienced a profound spiritual revival in her life during the summer before coming to Anderson University and was more serious about her faith than ever. She had come to college with a new attitude, a new determination, and she was committed to growing closer to Jesus at Anderson.

When Greg told me the girl's name, it piqued my interest. *Hmm, Mary Beth Chapman. Wait a minute. That's the girl I'm sharing a mailbox with. This is good!*

At Anderson, the US mail wasn't delivered to the dorms; students picked up both letters and packages at a central post office located in Decker Hall, where every two students shared a mailbox.

The first time I saw her mail I actually thought, *In college, sometimes you meet the person you will marry. How weird would it be to meet and fall in love with a girl in college who has the same last name as mine?* Even thinking such a thought was new territory for me. I had never seriously considered marriage, much less thought about it that specifically. Ever!

I wanted to meet Mary Beth. We had crossed paths on campus a few times, but we had never been formally introduced. I had a friend, though, who knew of my interest in her.

After attending church services one Sunday morning, I returned to campus and had barely kicked off my shoes when my buddy came running into my dorm room. "She's coming."

"Who's coming?"

"Mary Beth. Mary Beth Chapman is walking toward her dorm and is coming down the sidewalk in this direction right now!"

I looked out my window, and sure enough, there she was, walking all by herself toward my dorm. *This is my chance*, I thought. I didn't even take the time to put my shoes back on. I raced out the door and tried to pretend I had just gone out to get some air . . . still in my Sunday go-to-meetin' clothes, including my polyester dress socks. That detail matters because it was fall and there were lots of leaves on the ground, and polyester dress socks have a magnetic attraction to leaves, it turns out. So by the time I walked from the door of my dorm to where Mary Beth was, I had accumulated a small tree's worth of dead leaves on each of my feet. It looked as though I was wearing some type of organic leaf slippers. Not exactly the first impression I was hoping to make on this fair maiden.

Mary Beth was just a short distance away, though, so I went for it. "Hi, I'm Steve Chapman," I volunteered. "I think we share a mailbox."

The pretty girl smiled at me but didn't let on that she recognized me. "Yeah, I think we do. I noticed your name on some mail."

I shuffled nervously on the sidewalk as I tried to pick some of the leaves off my socks. "Would you wanna eat lunch together sometime? Same last name, maybe we're related, or maybe we have some long-lost cousins in common or something."

Mary Beth smiled again, probably guessing (or hoping) that we were nowhere near related, especially considering my country-boy accent.

"What time do you usually eat lunch?" I pressed. "How about tomorrow?"

Mary Beth looked at me as though analyzing whether I was for real, but she finally flashed her pretty smile and agreed to meet me for lunch.

We had lunch together the following day. I knew she had a couple of guys pursuing her, so after lunch I asked as casually as possible, "What time do you eat dinner?"

She told me, and I made sure I showed up at the cafeteria at the same time. From that point on, I contrived every opportunity I could to see her. It was more like, *How many times can I run into her on campus today?* We had all sorts of "chance meetings" that I purposely arranged.

I was really fascinated by and taken with this girl, but I wouldn't dare risk asking out a young woman who might say no. So in keeping with my strong commitment not to do something that would make me feel shame or embarrassment, I had a general rule. Before I asked out a girl, I needed at least two or three confirmations that she would not only say yes but also be very excited about it, as opposed to merely being nice.

So I had several friends check with her friends and give me reports. "Yes, she's *very* interested."

Finally, I mustered my courage and asked Mary Beth to go out to dinner with me. But this would not be just any dinner date . . . I had to sweep her off her feet. I needed to impress her and let her know right out of the gate what sort of guy she was dealing with, a man with great taste and a big spender . . . so I chose the obvious option—Red Lobster! How could I miss with those cheese biscuits?

Amazingly, she accepted!

About that time, I received a phone call asking if our band Chapman Henderson would provide music for a special event honoring World War II veterans in Anderson. It was scheduled for the same night I had asked Mary Beth to dinner. *No problem*, I thought. *The veterans event is at 6:00, and we'll be out of there by 7:00.* So I told Mary Beth I would pick her up around 7:00 p.m. or a few minutes later if things ran long with the veterans. She was fine with that.

When Brent, Herbie, and I arrived at the event, we soon discovered that the band was not first on the program. The veterans wanted to share war stories and then have some entertainment. I kept nervously staring at my watch as the soldiers reminisced. "Hey, that reminds me of the time when old Bill . . ." Sitting up front, I fidgeted in my chair as the vets told one story after another. It was their night, and I certainly didn't want to be disrespectful, so what was I to do? I knew there was no way for me to get back to Mary Beth's dorm on time.

We had no cell phones in those days, and there were no phones in the dorm rooms. Anderson dorms had only one phone on each floor. So there was no way for me to contact Mary Beth and let her know I was going to be more than a few minutes late. Finally, it was time for us to sing, and as soon as we finished our set and packed up our instruments, I hurried back to campus.

I showed up at Mary Beth's dorm two hours late. I was so nervous and very happy to find she was still there. My thoughts bounced in every direction. *I really like this girl, and I feel really bad, and I'm so excited to be going on a date with her!*

I ran in to her dorm room out of breath and, in what was a most uncharacteristic move for me on a first date, stepped right up to her and kissed her. I mean, I planted one right on her lips! I'm still not sure exactly what I was thinking other than, *I have one shot to try to redeem this situation, and I really hope this is a shot in the right direction.* And to be completely honest, I just really wanted to kiss the beautiful girl standing in front of me.

I stepped back and looked at Mary Beth, shocked at my own actions. But she seemed to have enjoyed the kiss and had even responded quite positively (as in, she had sort of kissed me back). Aw, yeah! This was definitely moving in the right direction.

She stood silently watching me as I tried to explain. "I'm so sorry, Mary Beth. Please forgive me. The veterans started telling their stories . . . and I'm really excited to be going on a date with you . . ."

"Okay," she said demurely, probably still stunned at my surprising forwardness. "It's okay," she said quietly. "I forgive you."

That was a defining moment for us. Years later when speaking at women's conferences, Mary Beth would quip, "He shows up two hours late and kisses me on our first date! I should have known what I was dealing with. For the rest of our life, he was going to walk in late many times and hope he could fix it all with a kiss."

We went out to Red Lobster and had a great time. Who knew popcorn shrimp and cheese biscuits were the perfect recipe for love? Hours flew by as we talked and talked long after the waitress had cleared our table.

From that time on, we were together as a couple. We couldn't get enough of each other and spent every free minute together. We discovered that we really enjoyed kissing each other too—a lot—despite Anderson's strict policy regarding inappropriate, premarital public displays of affection. For instance, Anderson guidelines said that if members of the opposite sex were together in a dorm room, the door had to remain open. And each member of the couple had to keep at least one foot on the floor at all times. Are you kidding me? That worked fine for us. You might be amazed at what "mischief" a young couple falling in love can get into while still keeping one foot on the floor!

Mary Beth and I walked to class together, studied together, ate our meals together, went to church together, and most importantly, prayed together. I wanted to be with Mary Beth every minute I could, and I wanted to know everything about her. I wanted to learn all about her family and what had brought her to Anderson. Mary Beth was a hard-working student and had even attended a community college part-time during her senior year of high school to get a head start on some college credits. I learned she had worked as a waitress at Friendly's Ice Cream in her hometown of Springfield, Ohio, to save money for school. She told me she had "wandered a bit" through some of her high school years but how God had drawn her back and how much she wanted to honor Him with her life. This was an amazing young woman, and the more I knew about her, the deeper in love I fell.

Ironically, both of us had enrolled at Anderson with the idea that we were not going to get involved in a serious dating relationship. In the past, I had become distracted by dating relationships, so I had come to school this semester with a new resolve to make my top relational priority growing closer to Jesus. I also had determined to stay focused on my schoolwork and my songwriting efforts. Mary Beth had come to school with a similar commitment to discover her future direction as well as to grow in her faith and deepen her relationship with Jesus after having had a personal revival just before starting school. We spent the first several weeks reminding each other that we didn't want to get serious, and then I'd ask, "But what are you doing later tonight?"

Mary Beth would say, "I want to go slow . . . let's not jump into this."

And I'd agree and ask, "But what time can I see you tomorrow?"

Within four to six weeks, I knew I was falling head over heels in love with Mary Beth. This relationship was totally different for me. Whenever I thought about the future, the picture in my mind always included Mary Beth. I wanted her to be with me. I had never before felt that way about anyone I had dated. And fortunately, she seemed to be feeling the same about me.

I was still traveling with Chapman Henderson most weekends, and every time I returned to campus I found my dorm room door covered with love notes from Mary Beth.

Sometimes she colored pictures with crayons or markers and included Scripture and other encouraging words for me. I kept them all and still have them to this day.

One of our early dates nearly killed me. At Anderson, we had an indoor, six-lane, twenty-five-yard swimming pool located in Bennett Natatorium. I'd never been in the pool. In fact, although this was my third year on campus, I didn't even know the pool existed.

Mary Beth, however, discovered the pool early in her college experience. She had grown up swimming, had been on a swim team, and had

Me in my dorm room at Anderson—decorated with notes from Mary Beth. (Notice the dress socks!)

spent a great deal of time at a pool every summer. Me? I was pretty good at dog-paddling. But when Mary Beth said, "I'm going to go swim some laps," all of my normal, nineteen-year-old, raging hormones kicked into gear, and I said, "You know, I've been wanting to check out the pool for a while now and just haven't gotten around to it. I think I'll go with you, if that's okay." Fortunately, she said yes.

Okay, I'm gonna go ahead and admit it, and if you need to go burn my CDs after reading this, I will understand, but I was pretty dang excited about the idea of seeing Mary Beth Chapman in a bathing suit. It was a high-necked, Anderson-required, one-piece, blue Speedo, but it was still a bathing suit—no way was I going to pass up that opportunity!

We went to our respective locker rooms, changed clothes, and headed to the pool. When I saw Mary Beth . . . I'm just gonna say I've never seen a Speedo look better. The moment Mary Beth hit the water she slipped into a lane and took off like a fish, so I followed behind her in the next lane. I wasn't a wimp, and I was in fairly good shape for a guitar player. Nevertheless, swimming exercises muscles musicians rarely use, so by the time I had swum twenty-five yards without any training and not even a warm-up, I was huffing and puffing and gasping for breath. But I was still excited because I was following Mary Beth.

When I reached the end of the lane, I popped my head up and grabbed onto the wall. "Whew, that was good," I said between gasps. I looked around for Mary Beth, but she had tucked her head, flipped, and reversed course without even stopping for a breath. She looked so smooth and sleek skimming through the water, so I gamely started swimming behind her again, flailing the water with all my might, trying desperately to catch up to her.

When I got back to the end of the lane, I was exhausted; my whole body was drained of energy. Mary Beth looked over at me and asked, "How are you doing?"

"Whew, you are a great swimmer, and I'm . . . not." I tried to sound as though this was just another day at the pool for me. "You keep going, and

I'll take a break. I'm going to run to the bathroom." I climbed out of the pool and attempted to keep Mary Beth from recognizing my condition while thinking, *I am about to die!* She waved and took off swimming again.

Meanwhile, I staggered to the locker room. My heart was pounding, and I felt lightheaded. *I know I'm going to throw up, and I'm pretty sure I'm having a heart attack*, I thought to myself. I stretched out on the cool tile of the locker room floor and tried to calm down and regain my composure. *This is terrible*, I worried. *I hope they don't find me in here dead!* But at least I could die a happy man with the vision of a beauty in a blue Speedo in my mind.

I lay there for about ten minutes before my heart rate returned to normal and I could breathe again. Finally, I got up and slowly walked back out to the pool, where Mary Beth was still swimming laps! She hadn't even been out of the pool yet.

I sat down on the pool's edge and waited for Mary Beth to come by. She saw me and swam up to me.

"I am *so* not a swimmer," I said.

"Oh, that's fine," she replied. "I've been swimming all my life, so I'm going to do a few more laps."

"You go right ahead," I said. "I'll just sit here and watch."

After my near-death experience, we continued to see each other, but we also continued to emphasize that we were not going to get serious. Mary Beth even went out on a few dates with other guys, but she decided there was nothing there. That solidified our relationship, and by the end of October, we were using the "love" word. On every level it seemed we connected so well; emotionally, spiritually, and physically. It was that physical part that started to cause some trouble.

During homecoming weekend, Mary Beth and I spent part of an afternoon at a local park lying on a blanket, looking up at the sky, talking, and kissing. I loved talking with Mary Beth, and I really loved kissing her. She is a great kisser. We talked and kissed . . . and before long we weren't talking anymore. We got carried away, and although we didn't have sex, our passionate kisses crossed some lines, and we both knew we were treading into dangerous territory if we were going to save ourselves for marriage.

I was upset with myself for letting things get that heated, and something was troubling me inside. That night when I pulled into the parking lot at the dorm, I didn't immediately get out of the car. I looked at Mary Beth and said, "We need to talk about something."

"Okay."

"I want to apologize to you, first of all, for this afternoon. I know I let things go too far, and if I made you feel uncomfortable, please forgive me. Kissing is one thing, but when it becomes too passionate . . . or too much . . . I want you to know I will never pressure you. I always want to honor you and respect you. We probably need to set some boundaries."

I looked at the young woman I loved and was thinking about spending the rest of my life with. "I'm really sorry for letting things get carried away," I said.

"Well, I wasn't pushing you away," Mary Beth said sweetly. "I was enjoying it too . . ."

"But I want to honor you." I took a deep breath. "Also, I want you to know that I made a decision early in my teens that I was not going to have sex until marriage. I know it may sound old-fashioned nowadays, but I'm saving myself for the girl I'm going to marry. That's where I've always been, and that's where I'm going to be until I get married. I want our wedding night to be special. That's a firm commitment I've made."

I'd never claimed sainthood, but maintaining my virginity until marriage was a big deal to me. I had remained true to that decision in all my previous dating relationships, although admittedly, I had occasionally pushed the limits. I had prayed often that God would help me stay strong in the face of temptation and that He would do the same for the woman I would eventually marry. I always knew that if a young woman did not have that same attitude, then she wasn't for me. To me, maintaining my virginity before marriage wasn't merely a physical matter; it was a spiritual commitment.

Mary Beth thanked me for sharing my feelings with her. I could tell by her response, though, that something wasn't right. So I asked her, "Do you feel the same way?"

Mary Beth turned her head away from me and stared out the window. "Absolutely, I do."

But she was sending me loud signals indicating that perhaps that had not always been the case. Had I been able to see her face in the darkness I would have noticed the tears welling in her eyes and trickling down her cheeks.

"Have you always had that conviction?" I pressed.

That's when I saw her tears. I heard sounds of sorrow in her voice as she quietly said, "I wanted to save myself for marriage, but I made some bad choices in high school . . . and some things happened."

My whole world crashed down around me. Her softly spoken words hit my heart with the force of a sledgehammer, smashing it into pieces. I thought, *This is the woman I want to spend my life with, and now I can't because of my own convictions.* I was broken, I was hurt, and I was mad—not at Mary Beth but at the whole situation, that this could be the end of something so incredible.

Mary Beth started openly crying, and I did too. "I can't deal with this," I said. "I don't know what to do with all of this. I need to go somewhere to think."

I left Mary Beth at her dorm, tears streaming down both of our faces. I quickly drove away and went back to the park, where I found a picnic table near where Mary Beth and I had been earlier in the day. I sat on the picnic table with my feet on the bench, my head in my hands. I was overwhelmed with sadness, and I cried harder than I'd ever cried in my life.

As I sat there wrestling with God, a million questions flooded my mind. Most of them centered around, *I love this woman, and I believe she loves me, but what can I do? Can I live with this?* Our relationship was so right. We had sought God's will from the beginning, often praying prayers like, "Lord, if this is right, let our relationship last, but if it isn't part of Your plan, please let us end it now. We want what You want."

That's why I had raised a concern about my actions in the first place, because I wanted our relationship to be right—right with each other and right before God. I felt convicted that we had carried the kissing too far. I wanted to honor God and honor Mary Beth. I wanted her to know I was committed to God but was also a guy who found her amazingly attractive and was struggling with that.

But her response had created an entirely new scenario I hadn't anticipated.

As God and I were having it out, the thought struck me, *Who do you think you are, Chapman? Are you sinless?* I knew what Jesus had said: "Let him who is without sin among you be the first to throw a stone at her" (John 8:7). I had to admit that my own thoughts and actions had been far from pure plenty of times. It was as though He was showing me, "The only things that have kept you on the right path were your circumstances and your accountability to others close to you. You are very far from perfect, young Mr. Chapman." God was pulling the curtain back a bit so I could see myself. And my self-righteousness was not a pretty sight.

At the same time, I really think it was the Holy Spirit who brought to my mind the verses in 2 Corinthians that say if someone is "in Christ," they are a new creation. "The old has passed away; behold, the new has come" (5:17). That included Mary Beth as well as me. Slowly but surely, God was revealing to me what I needed to do.

Meanwhile, Mary Beth, distraught as she was by my response, went and found Herbie at our dorm. "I'm worried," she said through her tears. "I've really hurt your brother. I'm afraid I've broken his heart, and I'm worried about him. Will you help me find him? I think I know where he went, but I'm not sure. Will you go and check on him?"

There weren't too many places to hide in Anderson, so Herbie easily found me. "How you doin', bro?" Herbie asked quietly. "You look pretty upset."

"Yeah, I don't know what to do . . . I'm really heartbroken."

Herbie may have thought my pain was the result of Mary Beth and me breaking up because of some sort of disagreement or couple's spat. He didn't ask, and I didn't offer any explanations. But I knew Herbie loved me and was concerned for me. He sat down with me on the picnic table, and we talked for a few minutes. I told him I was okay, but I wanted to talk to Mary Beth again. Herbie offered to get her and drive her back to me, which he did.

I sat in the car with Mary Beth and told her the things I felt the Holy Spirit had revealed to me on the picnic table in the park. "I'm so sorry I responded the way I did," I said. "God has given us a strong relationship. He's given you a new start. You've committed your life and your heart to Him. And if what the Bible says is true, then you are pure. That's what I see when I look at you. You have to know that."

We cried together, and Mary Beth told me how sorry she was that she had hurt me. Then we prayed together, asking for God's forgiveness and healing. When we parted late that night, we felt at peace.

We both knew this was another defining moment in our relationship. To Mary Beth, this incident confirmed that I was the man for her. I was totally convinced that she was God's woman for me.

What I didn't know at the time—and it would be years before I discovered—was that when Mary Beth told me she had made some bad choices in high school, she, like many women who have been mistreated, was really taking more responsibility and ownership than was appropriate. Yes, she may have made some wrong choices and allowed herself to get into some unwise relationships, but in her youthful vulnerability, she had been taken advantage of and deeply wounded by someone who knew exactly what he was doing. Only later in our journey would we come to understand the shame and pain she had carried alone for years that she never should have had to bear.

When I began to understand what a burden she carried, and later when I realized I had added to her sadness by turning away and saying, "I can't deal with this," adding shame on top of pain, it broke my heart profoundly. To this day, it grieves me that I added to Mary Beth's emotional turmoil by the way I responded to her when she bared her heart to me.

Even as young and foolish as I was, however, I recognized that going forward in our relationship required a serious commitment. Whatever that commitment might mean for us in the future, I knew there would be some struggles. I simply had no idea how difficult those struggles would be or where they would take us.

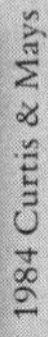

"Announcing the engagement of Steven Chapman and Mary Beth Chapman" . . . no, it's not a typo.

Chapter Eight

Fifty Dollars and a Green Ford Pinto

During our college spring break, I took Mary Beth to Noble Park in Paducah, to the gazebo not far from where I had taken my first thrilling ride on the Wild Mouse, to ask Mary Beth to be my wife. I had received $900 in royalties for my first song recorded by the Imperials, and I had gladly spent every penny of it on a tiny engagement ring I'd had custom-made for the love of my life. But for some reason, when I went to pick up the ring at the jeweler, I found myself walking around Kentucky Oaks Mall in Paducah for about an hour, pondering the life ahead of us. This was it! This felt like *the* defining moment of our life together. I knew once I gave her the ring, it was forever. I was scared and excited, but as I had noticed before, any picture of the future I could see in my mind's eye had Mary Beth Chapman right there beside me. So with my mind made up, I got the ring, picked up Mary Beth at my grandmother's house, where we were staying, and told her I wanted to show her a park I grew up going to.

I took her to the gazebo overlooking the lake and sat her up on a brick column about waist high so I could stand in front of her and look her straight in the eyes. We had played a little game a thousand times before this moment in which I would playfully ask her, "Will you marry me?" She would respond every time with a "yep" and a quick little kiss. This time when I asked her that question, she could tell something was very different. "No, really . . . I mean will you *really* marry me?" She would later tell me she could feel my heart pounding when she put her hand on my chest. I dropped to one knee and produced the little red-velvet jeweler's box from my pocket. She was completely surprised and proceeded to cry while holding the unopened box. Finally, she opened the box, threw her arms around me, and told me through her tears that she would happily be Mrs. Steven Curtis Chapman. That was a great day!

We returned to Anderson as an engaged couple and began making wedding plans. While we were still in school, Phil Johnson, a long-standing leader in the Christian record business who worked for the Benson Company in Nashville, came to Anderson to hear Herbie and me perform in Chapman Henderson. I was already a writer in the Paragon/Benson publishing group, so Phil was aware of me as a writer. He had apparently heard good things about our performances from people who had seen us in concert, and he wanted to check us out as potential recording artists. Phil had produced albums for numerous bestselling Christian artists, including some of my favorite albums by Dallas Holm and Andrus, Blackwood, and Company, so I was pretty much beside myself with excitement and nervousness at the thought that Phil Johnson might be involved in producing a record with me. Phil liked what he saw and heard and encouraged Herbie and me to relocate to Nashville to work more closely with him as potential artists and to further my songwriting career.

Mary Beth had sat with me in the music rooms at Anderson University as I had worked on songs, so she felt strongly I could make it in Nashville as a songwriter. She and I talked it over and decided we would move to Nashville after our wedding. She would leave her nursing education behind—which didn't bother her a great deal—and I would transfer to Belmont University, located just off Nashville's famous Music Row, so I could work with Phil. It seemed like a good plan at the time.

I enrolled in the music business program at Belmont, so I could be in a better position to pursue my songwriting career, and started classes there in September 1984. I auditioned and received a healthy scholarship from the university to play with the Belmont Reasons, the school's promotional band similar to the one Herbie and I had played in at Anderson. The six singers for the group had already been chosen, but they had an opening for a guitar player, which I gladly accepted.

Mary Beth generously took the money she'd saved for college and paid off my outstanding debt at Anderson so I could get my transcripts released to Belmont. Even though our wedding was a month away, she moved to Nashville and stayed with some friends so she could get acclimated while planning our wedding. She also took a job in the print publishing office at Benson, where I was now working as a writer. We knew finances would be tight, but we were sure the Lord would take care of us. We were livin' on faith and love and Mary Beth's meager salary of $250 per week. She often joked that she was working to support my "music habit."

On October 13, 1984, we were married in Mary Beth's home church in Springfield, Ohio. It was a simple ceremony, and Mary Beth looked breathtakingly beautiful in her long, flowing white wedding gown with flowery lace around the neckline and the hem. Her sister's wedding dress had been repurposed for our big day, but she looked perfect in it. I wore a black tuxedo with a black bow tie and sported a sorry excuse for a mustache that I had somehow convinced myself made me look suave and debonair.

The wedding and reception were simple and perfect in every way, except for the wedding photographer, who canceled at the last minute. So quality pictures of our big day are somewhat scarce. Mary Beth was nineteen, and I was twenty-one. We had $50 between us and Mary Beth's green Ford Pinto, but we were married!

We couldn't afford a fancy honeymoon, but I splurged so we could spend the first night of our marriage at the Clarion Hotel in Cincinnati,

Mary Beth's dad with our green Ford Pinto—that car and $50 were pretty much the sum total of our assets as newlyweds.

complete with a revolving restaurant overlooking the Ohio River. We had booked the honeymoon package, which meant we received a vase of red roses and a bottle of champagne in the room (which neither of us intended to drink, but we planned to keep as a souvenir). When we got to the room, however, there was no champagne, and my new wife was very intent on us getting our souvenir. I, on the other hand, was much more interested in "other things." So I called down to the front desk to make them aware of the problem. They said they would send our gift right up, so we sat on the edge of the bed for the longest fifteen minutes of my life waiting for the knock at the door. I've never been so happy to see a bottle of champagne!

The following day we went to the Cincinnati Zoo, and when the park staff saw our "Just Married" sign on the Pinto, they let us in for free. Unfortunately, the weather was gloomy and the skies poured down rain much of the day, so most of the animals were smart enough to stay inside out of the stormy weather. This was not the best way to start off our wonderful new life together.

I could tell Mary Beth was disappointed, and the cause went beyond the inclement weather. What had I done wrong? I felt she was upset with me. We had been so good for each other as a dating couple; everything had come so easily for us. We were in love, and we were perfect for each other. But now it seemed like a black cloud was hanging over us and neither of us could figure out what had changed. As we drove back to Nashville, my bride cried most of the way and I felt terrified. I was definitely going to have to figure out how to fix this.

We were pretty discouraged by our less-than-perfect start to married life, but we planned to go to Lake Barkley, a state park, for a "real honeymoon" in a week or so after we got settled into our tiny apartment in Nashville. Some friends of ours had offered to let us stay in their condominium as a wedding present. We went out on the lake in a small rental boat, had fishing contests and picnics, and took lots of pictures. At night, we'd cuddle up and dream about our future together . . . and that was our extravagant, four-day honeymoon.

With only $50 in our bank account when we moved to Music City, I had one goal in mind as I shopped for a place to live—to rent the least expensive apartment in Nashville. Certainly not the best goal for starting out a marriage. But I succeeded, for better and for worse. We found a tiny, one-bedroom place on Harding Road. The apartment had a kitchen, a bathroom, a living room, and a bedroom, all crammed into approximately three hundred square feet. It was drab and cruddy, but the price was right, about $290 a month, and it was our first home together, so we were excited! We signed the lease. Mary Beth bought some Clorox bleach and scrubbed every inch of the apartment—and some sections twice.

We realized fairly soon that our marriage was going to be a lot harder than we had thought. It wasn't that we didn't love each other; we were as much in love as ever. We were just beginning to discover how *different* we were. Mary Beth liked plans, routine, order, and structure. For most of Mary Beth's life, her dad, Jim Chapman, had worked at an International Harvester factory with a predictable schedule that had him home on time for dinner each evening. He changed the oil in the car every three thousand miles and mowed the grass every Saturday. Her mother, Phyllis, was a stay-at-home mom who poured herself into her children, cooking, doing laundry, and keeping the house. Schedules mattered. The calendar was set in stone.

On the other hand, I was cut from a creative cloth. A clock was an inconvenience, possibly imposed on humans by the devil. I didn't even wear a wristwatch. I attended classes during the week, wrote songs in between whenever I could, worked in the recording studio at night to make extra money, and on many weekends played with the Belmont Reasons. That meant Mary Beth was home alone most weekends. It was much the same schedule that I had kept when we were at Anderson, but with one big difference. We were married now.

We weren't married long before the struggles began to surface, but Mary Beth was not able to talk about what was bugging her. I could see she was unhappy, that she was stressed and worried, so I'd say, "What's going on? What are you thinking? Let's talk about it."

"I don't want to talk about it. I don't know how."

"Well, you gotta *talk* to me." We had always talked about everything. On our first trip home to Paducah to introduce her to my parents, I had actually run out of gas because we had been so caught up in talking to each other that I hadn't even noticed the gas gauge. I know, everybody rolls their eyes when I say I ran out of gas because we were "talking," but it's true!

Now we had to learn to talk about problems though. "I didn't come from a family that talked about problems," she said. "We brushed them under the rug. We held everything inside. We avoided unpleasant conversations. Your parents verbalized things, they'd yell and scream if they had to, they had arguments and fights, and they'd get everything out. I never saw my parents fight and argue like that, so I don't know how to do it."

"Well, we can't ignore things," I said. "We have to talk about this." Inside, I was screaming, *I have to fix this!* "If you have a problem, we gotta fix this because the Bible says not to let the sun go down on your anger. And that sun's going down. And I'm angry, and you're saying you're not angry, but I'm making you mad, so we gotta talk about this."

I was trying hard to be a good, Christian, head-of-the-house leader, to do the right thing, the right way, but without even realizing it, all too often I was coming across as a self-righteous bully. I'm ashamed to have to admit it, but sometimes after we argued, we'd semi make up and pray together, and I'd preach at Mary Beth during our prayer time. "Lord, please help my wife to understand that she needs to hear me in this, like the Scripture says . . ." Or I'd attempt to be the fourth member of the Trinity in my wife's life. My attitude was, "God, I know You've got this, but You probably need my help!"

We both agreed that our relationship was built on God's Word, so I assumed she'd be pleased when I quoted it to her. I didn't realize that Mary Beth needed her husband and friend, not simply another preacher. Of course, the more I quoted Scripture to her or urged her to open up to me, the more she clammed up.

One of Mary Beth's avoidance mechanisms was to simply lie down and fall asleep, sometimes right in the middle of an argument! Probably because she just didn't know what else to do with this relentless Mr. Fix-it she had married.

"Wait, wait," I'd plead with her. "We need to talk about this. We're not done here. We have unresolved conflict . . ."

Too late. Mary Beth was sound asleep.

After another argument in our bedroom that resulted in much the same, Mary Beth fell asleep again. I gritted my teeth, but that didn't help. "You gotta talk about this!" I growled through my clenched teeth, similar to how my dad had spoken to me as a boy. But my wife didn't move; she was done. A mixture of fear, desperation, and rage welled up inside me. *I have to fix this!* Finally, I got up from the bed to leave the room, and in my frustration, I swung my arm as hard as I could. Wham! My fist blasted into the wall beside the bed and went right through the drywall, making a six-inch hole. Thankfully, I didn't hit a stud or a nail, or my guitar playing might never have been the same.

Mary Beth slept on.

I stormed out to the living room and paced the floor, sobbing until I ran out of steam.

When Mary Beth awakened in the morning, she found me sitting on the couch. I felt sure that when she saw the hole in the wall, she would realize how intensely frustrated I was, how upset I was, and how passionate I was, and she would be determined to talk about our issues. Or maybe she would feel sorry for me, put her arms around me, and say something like, "Oh my. Honey, is your hand okay? I'm so sorry. Let's talk about this."

Nope. That didn't happen.

When Mary Beth woke up and saw the hole in the wall, she responded emotionlessly. "Oh, that was really . . . smart," she said. "That's impressive. So you punched a hole in the wall. Now we'll probably not get our $100 deposit back from the landlord."

Her lackluster response frustrated me even more. It clearly wasn't that she didn't care; she just didn't know how else to deal with the situation or with me. And the incident made Mary Beth more fearful about our future. She wasn't afraid of me; she knew, of course, I would never hit her, or anybody else for that matter, although I had given a black eye to a few trees and steering wheels during my single days when I was trying to deal with a rage rising within me.

But we couldn't seem to talk about difficult things without an argument ensuing. She stuffed some more pain down inside her subconscious mind and went off to work, while I went off to write songs about Jesus.

Why is my wife so closed down? I pondered. *Why is she so upset about our life together? We got along so great when we were dating. Why are we on such different pages now?*

Of course, somewhere in the back of my mind, I'm sure I thought, *Yeah, sure, Mary Beth is broken, but I can tweak a few things. I can fix her. After all, that's what I was born to do—fix things.*

Was I ever wrong!

I finally realized there was more going on than what met the eye. We were in an invisible but very real spiritual battle. Satan hates marriage. He loves romance and sexual desire because he tries to twist them for his purposes. Marriage, however, is a symbolic picture of our relationship with Jesus. That's why God is so pro-marriage, and that is why the enemy works so hard to destroy marriages.

While there was much conflict, there was also much love. We were still as desperately in love as two people could be, which is what fueled the fear when we couldn't connect. The truth is we probably needed each other too much. We were codependent before codependency was cool, and as a result, we were fierce, whether we were fighting against each other or for each other.

I would come to realize over the years with the help of counseling and prayer that so much of what was going on was more than either of us could "fix," no matter how relentlessly committed I was to trying. So much of my fierce determination to do it right and make it right was really motivated by a deep fear inside and a very real enemy who was taking every opportunity to fan the flame of that fear. How thankful I am for God's faithfulness to hold us together and my wife's determination to continue to love and bear with me in my foolishness and cluelessness.

Even after Mary Beth and I married and moved to Nashville, I still saw myself as part of a duo with Herbie, but most of the music business people weren't really interested in recording the Chapman Brothers. They were interested, however, in the songs I was writing. Herbie was disappointed, but he was wonderfully distracted. Soon after moving to Nashville, Herbie and his girlfriend, Sherri, announced their engagement and were married about six months after Mary Beth and me.

While still at Anderson, when Sandi Patty was working on songs for her next album, I had gone into a rehearsal room at Anderson's music suite. I wrote the song "Give Him the Glory" and gave it to Sandi. She recorded my song on her album *Songs from the Heart*, a recording released in 1984 that skyrocketed to the top of the Christian music charts.

Sandi's star was on the rise, and getting a song on one of her albums put me on the map as a bona fide songwriter. At that point, I still didn't perceive myself as a recording and touring artist who could make a living performing music onstage. I recognized, though, that one of the best ways to get my songs heard was to sing them in public, and I had a compelling sense that God had given me some things to say that I believed were important for people to hear. So I hoped to land a deal with a music company that would at least consider developing me as an artist as well as be my publisher.

Thanks to Phil Johnson and his boss, Bob McKenzie, and partially because of my success as a songwriter, the Benson Company offered me a long-term artist development contract. Mary Beth and I did the best we could to read and decipher the fine print, but this was the only offer I had, so I signed it, locking in my career with the company for the next twelve to fifteen years, with renewal options tipped heavily in the company's favor. In retrospect, I know that was not a good move, but at the time, I thought it was the greatest deal ever—I was twenty-two years old, and I was under contract with a major record company until my midthirties. What could possibly go wrong?

Mary Beth and I had decided it would be wise for us to wait four to five years before we tried to get pregnant. Mary Beth had just turned twenty, and I was twenty-two. We agreed we had a lot to learn before we were ready to be parents.

Because I was gone so much, Mary Beth wanted a puppy to keep her company. We discussed it and decided it might be a good opportunity to see how we would do at raising something before we had a baby. I scanned the newspaper and found a newly born litter of "peek-a-lhasa-apso-poo" puppies, so we went and picked out one and named him Peso. So far we hadn't even been able to keep a plant alive—not a good sign—so we were really stepping out in faith to get a puppy. Peso had a habit of chomping on anything we left lying around, and when Mary Beth made the mistake of leaving her purse within reach, Peso found the package of her birth control pills and must have thought he'd discovered a doggy treat. He devoured the entire package!

As soon as she realized what the dog had done, Mary Beth called the vet. She was more concerned for Peso than for herself. After all, she'd missed only one pill.

I'm not exactly sure what the directions on the package say, but I can confidently tell you from experience that missing just one tiny little pill can have life-changing implications.

We were barely eight months into our new life together when we found out that Mary Beth was pregnant. Grappling with the thought that we were going to be parents was bittersweet. We were very excited and very scared! Of course, we knew this new life was a miracle, and Mary Beth had always said her greatest desire was to be a mom. That's one of the many things that had brought us together when we were first getting to know each other. But . . . now? Really, God? Are you sure about this?

He was sure.

I threw myself into high gear as a songwriter, and given the career opportunities and relationships that were already developing, combined with my plans to record an album in the near future, Mary Beth and I decided I would not go back to school in the fall of 1985. Mary Beth had taken an administrative job in a Nashville hospital that provided great benefits and a steady source of income for us, but we really didn't want her to go back to work after the baby was born. Between her job, my steady, albeit meager, royalty checks, and my $100 demos, in which I would produce, play, sing, and record song demos for other songwriters at my publishing company, we had scraped together enough money to buy our first car together. It was time to put the green Ford Pinto out to pasture.

We were so proud of our brand-new maroon Honda Civic hatchback that we purchased without air-conditioning or any other extras we couldn't afford. But Nashville summers get a lot hotter than the Ohio summers Mary Beth was used to. One morning when I was driving her to work, she quickly began to feel a wave of morning sickness coming on. With no time to pull over to stop and no receptacle in our brand-new car for her to get sick into, I did the only thing I could do—I cupped my hands to catch her breakfast. Sorry, I know that's gross . . . but it was our first ever brand-new car!

About five months into the pregnancy, I went in to the Benson Company one day to do some writing, and everyone in the large building on Great

Circle Road seemed to be speaking in hushed tones and whispers. "Did you hear? Can you believe it?"

"No, what's going on?" I asked.

"Phil Johnson and Bob McKenzie left the company this morning."

"They what?" Phil Johnson and Bob McKenzie had been running Benson when I had first moved to town.

"They quit. Both of them. They are gone."

"What? No!" I said. *Phil can't leave. He's the guy who is going to help my recording career get moving. All of my hopes and dreams of having a music career are wrapped up with him.* My songwriting was doing well, and we were getting ready to develop my recording. Now with absolutely no warning, he was gone.

Two days later, Mary Beth and I saw Phil in the company parking lot. "Phil! What in the world is going on?" I asked.

Phil gave us a confident smile and a thumbs-up. "Don't worry," he said. "There are just some changes going on, but everything's going to be okay."

"What does all this mean?" I asked. "You're the reason I signed with the company. Do I have a future here? I'm with you."

Phil touched his finger to his thumb and formed the okay sign. "Everything will be just fine," he said quietly. "Once I get settled, I'll come and get you, and we'll figure this out."

Nevertheless, the dashed development deal with the record company was a major setback for me; I felt as though the door had been slammed in my face. I was disappointed and scared. What were we going to do? I had been on track to record an album, which would hopefully lead to opportunities to provide for my family. I had left school to pursue my music career full-time, Mary Beth was five months pregnant and was freaking out. Suddenly, overnight, what little security we had was gone. While I continued to say the right words, "I know God is gonna take care of us . . ." inside I was panicking. *How are we going to survive? How in the world am I going to fix this?*

Worse yet, I wondered if I had missed God's leading.

Somewhere in the middle of my confusion, I remembered a conversation Phil and I had had before I signed the agreement with the record company. "This is great, Phil. But what happens if you ever leave the company?"

"Oh, don't worry; I'm not going anywhere," Phil had said at the time. "But just in case anything were to change, I'll put a 'key man' clause in your agreement. If Bob or I ever leave the company, you will have the option to leave too."

Nowadays, "key man" clauses are nearly nonexistent in the music business, but thanks to that one little clause, I had the option to get out of my contract. Otherwise, I would have been locked in to a songwriting and artist development deal for more than a decade with a company in which most of the key people who were interested in working with me and developing my career were gone.

I remembered something I had read by Oswald Chambers in his classic devotional book, *My Utmost for His Highest.* Chambers basically said, when you don't know what to do, trust God and do the next thing. Take the next obvious step in front of you and trust God to lead you. This is a truth I've had to return to many times as I've wrestled often with a condition my pastor and friend Scotty Smith calls "the paralysis of analysis." Partly because of my fear of doing the wrong thing or messing up, I want to consider every possible option before I make a move. A passage in Isaiah says, "And your ears shall hear a word behind you, saying, 'This is the way, walk in it,' when you turn to the right or when you turn to the left" (30:21). I noticed something after looking at that verse so many times, wanting to hear that voice tell me which way I should go before I made a move. The fact that it says you'll hear this voice directing you "when you turn to the right or the left" means that there is movement already going on, even before we hear the voice telling us, "This is the way, walk in it." That's what the faith journey is all about—taking steps, sometimes in total darkness, and trusting God to lead and direct us. God used that truth then—and many times since then—to direct and redirect my life when I didn't have a clue which way to go.

Although the Benson Company had been kind to me, I exercised the option and struck out on a new adventure.

Bill Hearn, Peter York, me, Dan Raines, and Billy Ray Hearn celebrating the signing of my record deal.

Chapter Nine

The Cool Kids and a Country Boy

My next steps felt more like running on a treadmill in the dark than an adventure. Mary Beth's salary was soon to be disrupted or possibly eliminated by the birth of our baby, and that made me nervous. Because of my Sandi Patty cut, among others, plenty of publishers were interested in signing me as a songwriter, but my prospects as a recording artist were not looking good. I went back to Opryland and worked in one of the shows there for a while and continued to record demos for other writers at night, occasionally even being hired to sing background vocals on records.

I met with Greg Nelson, Sandi Patty's producer, with whom I had developed a friendship as a songwriter, and Greg suggested I talk with Lorenz Creative Services, the company with whom he worked. One conversation with Greg was pretty transformational. He asked, "What do you want to do besides write songs for other people?"

I took a deep breath and responded, "Well, I know it may seem like a long shot, but I'd love the opportunity to record my own songs as well as write them for others. I know I'm not a great singer, but I feel like there's a special connection between me and people when I sing them my songs."

Greg listened to me and was painfully honest. "You're not necessarily a great singer," he said straightforwardly. Greg was working at the time with three of the greatest voices in Christian music—Sandi Patty, Larnelle Harris, and Steve Green—so even though his words stung, I understood what he meant. "But your songs . . ." Greg continued, "When you communicate your songs, people respond. I think God has given you a unique gift. I believe in that, and I want to help you. I think we need to get a really good recording of your voice on one of your songs." Most of my recordings were songwriter demos I had recorded myself as opposed to fully produced professional recordings.

I had been hired to sing background vocals on "All the Time," a song I had written that was being recorded by an artist named Tony Elenburg. Tony and I hit it off immediately, and we struck up a friendship. He and his wife, Cindy, would become very important to Mary Beth and me in the difficult days ahead. Greg Nelson was the executive producer, and a guy named Phil Naish was producing the record. Phil was a world-class keyboard player who was working alongside Greg on all the records he was making at the time with Sandi, Larnelle, and Steve. Phil had also been a member of the Belmont Reasons when he attended Belmont College a few years ahead of me, so we had an immediate connection. At the end of the recording session, Phil, knowing that Greg was pitching me as an artist, said, "Hey, why don't you go in the studio and sing a lead vocal on this song. It might be good to have a version of this song with you singing for Greg to use." Little did I know that would be the first of countless hours I would spend in studios with Phil Naish as my producer.

Greg took that recording, along with a few others, and began to introduce me to heads of other record labels in town, hoping one would be interested in me as an artist.

None were. Each one passed on me. They liked my songs, but my singing . . . well, let's just say they were underwhelmed.

Undaunted, Greg said, "Let me pitch you to Sparrow Records."

Sparrow? I thought. *The "cool kids" in Los Angeles? No way would they ever be interested in a country boy from Paducah like me.*

Billy Ray Hearn had founded Sparrow Records in 1976 after building the Myrrh record label into a powerhouse contemporary Christian music division at Word Records with artists such as Petra, Honeytree, and others. At Sparrow, Billy Ray had furthered the careers of Keith Green, the Second Chapter of Acts, John Michael Talbot, and many other top contemporary Christian artists. The label had just signed three new acts: BeBe and CeCe Winans, a brother-sister team, both of whom were incredible singers with class and style; Tim Miner, who had a strong, soulful voice; and Margaret Becker, a Pat Benatar–style rocker with a big voice packed inside a tiny body. I was a guy with a southern accent and an unimpressive voice, but Greg said that Sparrow was in the process of signing some new artists, so it was worth a shot.

Unfortunately, although Sparrow was interested in me as a songwriter, they too passed on me as a recording artist. Just as I expected, Billy Ray had responded, "I'm just not sure he has the voice." Rejection is tough on a man's self-confidence, regardless of his career, and singer/songwriters are not exempt. Especially when that singer/songwriter is wired to please people. I was thankful for the interest in me as a songwriter, but I couldn't let go of the belief that God was giving me songs, a passion and a gift for communicating, and a sincere, if not remarkable, voice that I was supposed to use. So as much as I hated the feeling of rejection, I continued to meet with record companies, write songs, and record demos for others.

I had been hired to sing on some country-gospel demos for James Isaac Elliott, a songwriter buddy of mine that Sparrow had recently signed. I didn't realize it at the time, but God was weaving my life together with some great people who would be a big part of my story in the days to come. Much as had happened with Tony Elenburg and Phil Naish, James and I hit it off, and we began to write some songs together. We would eventually go on to write a couple of my most important career songs, "My Redeemer Is Faithful and True" and "His Eyes," among others.

I sang the demos for James, he took them to Sparrow's offices in Nashville, and they sent them on to Sparrow's home office in Chatsworth, California.

Apparently, Billy Ray Hearn was walking down the hall in the Sparrow building in California when he heard the James Isaac Elliott demos being played in someone's office. He stuck his head in and asked, "Who are you listening to?"

"These are some new songs from one of our writers in Nashville."

"Is that him singing?"

"No, I don't think so . . ."

"Something sounds familiar . . . that voice . . ." Billy Ray said. "I'm curious. Find out who sang those." Sparrow called James Isaac Elliott, and he told them I had sung the demos. When that information was passed along to Billy Ray, he recalled, "Ah yes. That's the guy Greg Nelson was telling me about."

Billy Ray called Greg and said, "I want to revisit that Chapman guy. Has he signed anywhere?"

That same day I had gone to Word Records to meet with Neal Joseph. Neal had produced my first cut on the Imperials' *Side by Side* album and had graciously met with me many times to listen to my songs and give me his honest input. Like many others in Nashville, Neal had a great belief in me as a songwriter and had offered to sign me as a writer to Word. But now, as I discussed with him my desire to record my own songs, I was hearing that familiar speech again. "Steve, I just don't think we have any place for you on our roster as a recording artist. I'd love to have you as a songwriter . . ."

Greg Nelson knew about the meeting and had just received the call from Billy Ray. He called Word and left a message for me to call him. When I did, I could hear the excitement in his voice as he asked, "Did you sign anything?"

"No, and I don't really think there will be anything to sign. They passed . . . again."

"Great!"

"Great?"

"Yes, Billy Ray Hearn called, and he and his guys want to come to Nashville to meet with you."

"Billy Ray Hearn? The cool kids? Are you serious?" I could hardly believe it, but sure enough, a short time later, Billy Ray sent his representative, Peter York, and his wife, Michelle, to visit with me. Peter and Michelle took Mary Beth and me out to dinner, and it was immediately apparent that Peter came from a world very different from Paducah. Peter was the coolest guy I'd ever met.

Sitting at dinner, Peter sounded as though he'd just come off the set of a surfing movie. "So, bro . . . I'm really diggin' your music . . ."

I tried my best to sound cool and failed miserably as I responded, "Well, um . . . Mr. York . . . Peter, I'd love to be on Sparrow Records."

No doubt, Peter returned to California thinking, *What in the world are we going to do with this hillbilly*?

But Peter must have been convinced that I was at least worth a shot. A short time later, Sparrow Records offered me a recording/publishing deal . . . without ever having heard me in a live performance. That does not normally happen in the music business!

The year 1986 brought much promise as I entered into a copublishing deal between Sparrow Records and Lorenz Creative Services, with the plan being that Sparrow would develop me as a recording artist and I would begin making my first record in the next several months. Unable to afford a good lawyer at that point, Mary Beth and I sat in our car in the parking lot of Lorenz Creative Services on Music Row in Nashville and did our best to read through the contract one last time. We prayed, I took a deep breath, and I signed it! In my heart, I trusted these people and believed God had opened this door of opportunity and would take care of us.

The company gave me an advance of $250 a week against future royalties, which we saw as God's way of providing for us, since the money replaced Mary Beth's salary almost to the penny. Mary Beth really wanted to be a stay-at-home mom with our baby, and I thought that was a great idea too.

On February 24, 1986, we excitedly made our way to Baptist Hospital—Mary Beth was ready to deliver our baby. After seven hours of labor, Mary Beth still seemed to be in a great deal of pain even after receiving an epidural, and the doctor noticed the baby's heart rate decreasing. Suddenly, the atmosphere in the room shifted from calm to frenzied as nurses and doctors converged around Mary Beth's bed. The doctor announced that the baby was fine, but they were going to need to do an emergency C-section to deliver the baby quickly. I could see the concern in Mary Beth's eyes. I know she could see the panic in mine, even though I tried to act confident.

A little after 7:00 p.m. a beautiful little girl named Emily Elizabeth Chapman came into the world. I studied her tiny fingers and perfectly formed fingernails, amazed at how God could fit so much of His goodness and beauty into one tiny little person. Although we hadn't planned for Emily, she was certainly God's perfect plan for us.

Before Emily was born, we'd moved to a townhouse so we'd have an extra bedroom we could use as a nursery. Shortly after Emily arrived, we realized that the townhouse was going to work for only a short season. We wanted to have our children close together, and anticipating that we'd need more room, we began searching for a small house.

On a Sunday afternoon in April, a real estate agent came knocking at the front door of our townhouse to take us house hunting, so we left hurriedly. Mary Beth had been sterilizing baby bottles on the stove, and as we rushed out the front door, which we seldom used, we forgot to turn off the burner.

We went out for a few hours, looking at houses within our price range on the southeast section of Nashville. We found a few just across the county line and were excited about the possibilities. We returned home, however, to discover fire trucks and equipment in front of our complex.

Oh no! Somebody is in trouble! I thought.

Somebody was. And it was *us*! Our townhouse had caught on fire, and everything inside was burnt to a crisp, waterlogged, or saturated with smoke.

We later learned that because we had left our car at the townhouse and had ridden with the real estate agent, our neighbors had thought we might still be in the building, along with our newborn baby, maybe taking a Sunday afternoon nap. The firefighters had courageously fought through the fire, all the way to the second floor, trying to save our lives. When we were allowed back in the building, we traced the black handprints along the wall where a fireman had felt his way through the smoke, up the stairs, and into Emily's nursery, where our neighbors had told him she might be sleeping. We cried at the thought of what could have happened.

While the building wasn't burned to the ground, it was clear it would have to be gutted and rebuilt before anyone could live in it. My friend Tony Elenburg, whose album I had sung background vocals on several months earlier, and his wife, Cindy, lived nearby and invited us to stay with them. Other good friends, Geoff and Jan Moore, brought some of their clothes for us to wear, since all of ours, including the baby's, were ruined by the smell of smoke baked in so deeply that no amount of washing could remove it.

The cleanup process after the fire was backbreaking and sad. Anything that wasn't scorched had to be thoroughly washed, several times, and sometimes still thrown away because of the odor. Mary Beth's mom and dad, Poppy and Mamaw, as Emily would eventually call them, were incredible in-laws from day one and, as always, came quickly to help however they could. They spent long days helping to scrub, clean, and repair anything that was salvageable from the fire and helping Mary Beth attend to our infant daughter, Emily, not yet two months old. We also spent many hours and many rolls of quarters at the laundromat trying to get the smoke smell out of baby Emily's new toys, clothes, and stuffed animals. She was the first grandbaby, so she had quite the collection of stuffed animals.

Mary Beth, her parents, and I worked feverishly for a week, making only a small dent in the mountain of cleanup chores ahead of us, and by the Sunday after the fire, we were all exhausted. I had called my parents shortly after the fire to tell them what had happened, but I hadn't encouraged them to come help. I didn't doubt they'd come if we needed them, but I knew my dad had to work at his music store, and after Mary Beth's mom and dad showed up, I felt sure we could handle things. But as we worked through the week, occasionally, someone would mention my parents. "Where are Herb and Judy? We could sure use an extra hand." I wasn't paying attention.

My mom arrived with my grandmother on Sunday afternoon. Mary Beth and her parents welcomed them but quickly asked, "Where's Herb?" At first, Mom made excuses for him, but after a while, Mom was steaming. "I told him we should have come to help," she said. "He wouldn't listen to me."

I knew she was speaking out of anger, hurt, and stress that may have had nothing to do with the fire, so I tried to diffuse the situation. "No, no, Mom. It's okay. I understand that he's busy and has to work, and I didn't ask you guys to come." In my own cluelessness and my lack of sensitivity to what Mary Beth was experiencing, I found myself defending my dad.

We were all tired and exasperated, and emotions quickly took over. The conversation spiraled downward as our voices escalated in volume and intensity, and searing comments flew back and forth. Somewhere in the midst of the battle, I even heard mention of Mary Beth and the baby going back to Ohio with her mom and dad. I couldn't believe what was happening, and I was terrified at what felt like my family getting ripped apart.

Finally, I couldn't take it anymore. In the midst of the caustic, chaotic yelling, something rose up inside me. I stood up and stepped into the middle of the room. I raised my hands in the air like a traffic cop and shouted as loudly as I could, "Satan, you will not have my family!" I didn't know where Satan was, but it definitely felt like he was there, and I was going to make sure he could hear my declaration.

The noise and commotion stopped instantly. Whether it was shock at my uncharacteristic actions or a spiritual realization that struck my in-laws, my mom and grandma, and Mary Beth, I'm not sure. But we all calmed down and even awkwardly apologized.

Later, I confided to my wife, "Sweetheart, there is a real enemy, but it is not you and it is not me. We love each other, and we are committed to each other."

I called my dad to tell him what had happened as my mom and grandmother drove back home to Kentucky. I knew somehow that this was a defining moment in our early marriage. I wanted my wife to know that she and our baby were most important to me, even over my relationship with my parents, so I asked her to listen on the phone while I spoke to my dad. I also had a good conversation with her dad about the challenges I felt I was facing in trying to find my place as the man in her life. While he didn't have much to say, he listened and responded with kindness and encouragement, as he would do many times in the future, and I was very grateful.

Unfortunately, the fire and all that came with it brought my songwriting and discussions about recording an album to a screeching halt. We had a brand-new baby, were living out of suitcases in the basement of our friends' house, and were trying to salvage what we could and replace what we could afford. I battled that old familiar voice telling me, "You have to fix this . . . it's all up to you," and felt like I was failing miserably. Stress was high, and arguments were frequent. Desperate, I spent a lot of time on my knees asking God to give me wisdom to know how to take care of my family and praying with Mary Beth that God would strengthen us. We were both thankful for good friends who loved us well, cried and prayed with us often, and helped us laugh when we desperately needed it (and will hopefully never write a book about all they experienced in those trying days with the Chapmans).

Eventually, we purchased the house we had been looking at the day of the fire. As Mary Beth commented, "It needed a big hug," so we worked on the house with Poppy and Mamaw, and after several weeks of scrubbing, and wallpaper stripping and reapplying, and many gallons of paint, we moved in to 586 Blakemore Drive in LaVergne, Tennessee.

A couple of years earlier, just after Mary Beth and I had gotten married and while I was still working with the Benson Company, I had spent a day cowriting with Geoff Moore, another Benson writer and artist. Geoff had been hired a few years earlier to sing a demo of my song "Built to Last," which would become my first cut as a songwriter. We hit it off immediately, and since he was also newly married, we spent much of our initial writing session discussing the challenges of married life. Soon we followed it up with a double date in which our wives met and became great friends. At the time, Geoff was touring with his band the Distance and was looking to add a guitar player for his upcoming tour, which included several dates as an opening act for two major Christian rock bands, Petra and DeGarmo and Key. I mentioned that, as a developing artist, I'd be interested in taking the job for a short period of time if there might be an occasional opportunity for me to play a song of my own at some of the shows so as to familiarize people with my name and my music. Geoff thought that was a great idea and invited me to be a part of the tour, my first professional touring experience. So in the fall of 1986, at twenty-four years of age, I took my first flight in an airplane on our way to Detroit, Michigan. This was it. I was on tour!

The music was flowing again as I began to write and make plans to record some of my songs for my first album. I sensed that Sparrow was still a bit tentative about whether I was going to work as an artist. They had just signed three new artists they were very excited about and were reluctant to put up all the money to do a full record, so Greg Nelson's 19th Street Music production company, along with my copublisher, Lorenz Creative Services, agreed to split the costs to record a few songs, then evaluate whether to move forward.

Phil Naish and I went into the studio together and recorded three songs. We worked all day and late into the night for several weeks trying to make

In the studio with Sandi Patty and Greg Nelson.

these the best three songs ever recorded. They had to be great. This was my shot!

All the while, Mary Beth and I prayed. Fortunately, the record company liked what they heard, so they said, "Let's go ahead and finish the album." Mary Beth and I were flown out to Los Angeles for my first photo shoot. As two kids who had barely ever traveled a few miles from home, we were tremendously excited to be going to Los Angeles. Since we would hopefully be going on tour soon, Mary Beth had devised a plan: she would get on *The Price Is Right* and win either a motor home or enough money for us to buy one to tour in. I'm serious . . . that was her plan! She went and stood in line for hours while I had meetings at Sparrow's offices. She made it into the audience for the show, but unfortunately, she never heard, "Mary Beth Chapman . . . come on down!" No motor home for us.

We debuted my first radio single, "Weak Days," at the Gospel Music Association's 1987 conference held in April in Nashville. I handed out vinyl 45 records with the song on it to all the radio programmers I met. I was scheduled to perform at a new artist showcase during the event, and Billy Ray Hearn, founder of Sparrow Records, was to attend. This would be the first time he would hear me perform live.

The night of the showcase I was terribly nervous, thinking, *Don't screw this up!* Sure enough, Billy Ray Hearn was sitting in the crowd. Sparrow had already signed me, and I had recorded the album, but the album wasn't out yet. They still had time to dump me!

I planned to perform two songs in the showcase: "Hiding Place," a song I had written on the piano, and my first single, "Weak Days."

As a songwriter and a musician, I wanted to perform "Hiding Place" the way I had written it—using a piano. I wasn't the greatest piano player, but knowing that most people were going to use recorded backing tracks, it seemed that I could have more of an impact by performing the song by myself and letting people see that I was a musician as well as a writer. I didn't have a piano at my house, so I had practiced on a Yamaha DX7, an electronic keyboard. But when I sat down at the grand piano on the showcase stage, it had a totally different feel. I was so nervous my fingers were trembling, and I could barely get the piano keys to make a sound. I felt I was in one of those dreams where you're running as fast as you can but you're not getting anywhere. It was like trying to get sound to come out of a wooden table. And the more nervous I got, the more my voice began to tremble along with my fingers. This was not going well at all.

I fumbled through my song, and I knew it was awful. Even Mary Beth, my biggest cheerleader, later said, "Oh, that wasn't good. It didn't sound very confident." But she added, trying to give me a little hope, "I could tell you were very nervous, and I'm sure they knew that too."

Fortunately, I had a recorded sound track for the song "Weak Days," and I performed my single with the track. Although I've never enjoyed singing to a sound track as much as playing live, that song went over much better with the showcase audience.

Afterward, I talked briefly with the founder of Sparrow. "Glad you did that one song with the sound track," Billy Ray Hearn said to me. That's pretty much all he said—not exactly the gushing compliment I was hoping for.

Later, when Billy Ray saw Greg Nelson, he asked, "You didn't sell me a bill of goods on that Chapman guy, did ya?" . . . half joking but half serious.

Greg assured him I had simply been extremely nervous.

My debut performance had not evoked high levels of belief. I didn't know that at the time, but if I had, I would not have blamed anyone for wondering about my potential. Nevertheless, within the year, "Weak Days" climbed to number two on the charts, and everyone at my record label was feeling much more confident . . . and so was I.

The proud parents with our baby Emily.

Chapter Ten

Divorce Is Not an Option

My first album with Sparrow Records, titled *First Hand*, was released in May of 1987. The initial radio single, "Weak Days," a song about the importance of spending time with God on the days in between Sundays, found a ready audience and seemed to resonate with listeners. With songs like "My Redeemer Is Faithful and True" and "Hiding Place," my desire was to be the voice of a friend encouraging and challenging others from my own experience, and that seemed to be what people were connecting with most in my music. Well, that and the fact I had a really cool mullet!

I was busy writing more songs and performing more concerts—mostly just me with my guitar doing an acoustic program—at churches or in small auditoriums. The fact that my songs were doing well on the radio continued to open doors for more opportunities. "Weak Days" rose to number two on the contemporary Christian music charts, so Sparrow and I began thinking about a follow-up album. I began writing songs and preparing to go into the recording studio. It was on one of our many late-night drives from Nashville to Ohio to take Emily and Mary Beth to see Mamaw and Poppy that my thoughts began to turn into song lyrics. In fact, many of my songs were birthed on those drives. This night as I drove in the dark, I was thinking about the eyes of Jesus, how the very same physical eyes of Jesus that had looked out at the crowd of five thousand before He fed them and had filled with tears at Lazarus's grave were the same eyes that were watching me as I drove. He knew what I was going through. I began to write a song called "His Eyes," which I would go on to finish with my dear friend James Isaac Elliott.

Another good songwriter friend of mine, whom I had worked with at Opryland, Jerry Salley, and I were talking one day about a Scripture passage that was particularly encouraging to us at the time. We were both intrigued by the apostle Paul's honesty in 2 Corinthians when he talks about his weakness as something he isn't ashamed of but rather boasts about because, in his weakness, Christ's strength is made perfect in him. As two guys who were painfully aware of their weaknesses and shortcomings, we found ourselves so encouraged by Paul's words that we were inspired to write a song called "His Strength Is Perfect."

My second album, *Real Life Conversations*, came out in 1988, and good things started happening fast. My record label and I introduced the album at a gathering for Christian radio stations during GMA week in Nashville. In the audience at that event was one of my favorite singer/songwriters, Michael Card, also an artist at Sparrow. Michael had written several big songs, including "El Shaddai," recorded by Amy Grant.

When Michael heard me sing my song "His Eyes," he stood to his feet, smiling and clapping his hands, giving me a standing ovation right there in front of the other Sparrow artists and radio personnel. Michael Card was the only person in the crowded room who stood up after my performance, but seeing him applaud my song like that was tremendously encouraging. Michael was a song craftsman, and to have his support thrilled me and gave me a sense that the song was going to have a significant impact.

It did. The *Real Life Conversations* album contained several significant career songs, including "His Eyes," which became my first number one song on the radio charts. In 1989, it was voted pop/contemporary recorded song of the year by the Gospel Music Association. The album also contained "His Strength Is Perfect," a song that would increasingly have more

Me serenading the new girl in my life, baby Emily.

meaning to me over the years. That same year I won the Dove Award for best songwriter of the year. I was blown away! Even though I had a sense that God had entrusted to me a gift of connecting with people through my music, I had no idea it would evoke that sort of response.

As exciting as all of this was, along with the bigger and better opportunities for my career came more time away, more expectations and demands on my time, and more stress on Mary Beth's and my marriage. From the beginning, we were a team. Mary Beth is smart and has a great mind for finance, organization, and administration. I, on the other hand, am the creative one. She was my first booking agent, sitting on the edge of our bed with her photocopied sheets of prospective booking calls spread out on the blanket beside baby Emily and making phone calls. "Hi, this is Mary Beth calling from the office of Steven Curtis Chapman," she'd say, hoping Emily would stay quiet so it would sound professional. Mary Beth was also my first merch guy and sound man, meaning she would set up the table and sell my T-shirts and records, and during the concert, she would sit at the mixing console and start my sound tracks when it was time for me to sing. This was a great arrangement, except for when she felt I had said enough to set up a certain song, which was often. I've always been known to have a lot to say between songs, and sometimes when I stopped to take a breath, she would start the track, even though I had more to say! She would later giggle and say, "I felt like you had made your point. Besides, what are you going to do, fire me?"

Mary Beth was excited with me about the success we were having, but we realized that even though financial pressures were fewer and our hard work together was paying off, the struggles in our relationship were intensifying. In some of our hardest moments, I wondered if I needed to change my career path and take a "real job" rather than pursue a music career. One of the challenges that continued to surface was the fact that, for Mary Beth, security and safety came in the form of a predictable schedule and structure. And our life was turning out to be anything but that. I had made a commitment to my bride, and I was determined to honor it and do the right thing, even if it meant walking away from music.

At one point, in desperation, I even sat down with Mary Beth's dad and asked his advice. "Maybe I need to try to get a job at the Nissan auto factory or something," I suggested.

"Don't even think about it," he responded. "You do what you believe God wants you to do. Mary Beth is tough; she'll be okay. She just needs some time."

We were still crazy in love with each other, and there were plenty of sweet times mixed in with the bitter. We made a promise as we spooned one night in our small full-size bed never to get a queen-size bed so we would always sleep close. We held hands when we walked and still loved kissing—most of the time. But there were also those awful arguments and a lot that was broken between us, and there was nothing I could do to fix it, try as I might.

Whenever we'd argue, in my misguided attempts to be the good spiritual leader of my home, often my position was, "This is what the Bible says, and this is how we need to do these things." I was trying to do the right thing, but in doing so, I was subtly rebuking Mary Beth, implying that she was not as spiritual as she ought to be—or worse yet, not as spiritual as *me*!

The message Mary Beth heard was that she wasn't good enough, that she wasn't spiritual enough, that if she'd just read her Bible or pray more, our problems would go away.

Mary Beth often said, "I am not the person people expect me to be as your wife." She sometimes expressed a sense that she wasn't the person I needed, that she wasn't the same type of woman Ruth Graham was to Billy Graham or Gloria Gaither is to Bill Gaither—the woman behind the man. "I'm not that deep, spiritual person you need," she said. She didn't doubt that we should have gotten married in the first place. She just felt she wasn't the best counterpart for me, that she didn't fit the persona of the person married to someone out onstage proclaiming the gospel.

My mom and dad were my spiritual role models. They had struggles, but when they did, they'd get on their knees and pray. "God's Word is our counseling manual," one of them would say. "We just need to trust God."

I saw this work for them, so naturally, when Mary Beth and I married, I believed that was the best way to deal with conflicts. But then reality poked holes in my idealistic view when my parents began to experience serious problems in their marriage.

"Divorce is not an option" was a statement I had heard my parents say over and over again as I was growing up. And I think they truly believed that. Mom and Dad did far more right than they did wrong; they were deeply committed in their relationship to Jesus, they loved their boys, and they took time to care for people around them who were struggling. My dad's music store and my mom's little space at the photography shop where she worked were counseling offices more than anything, it seemed, as they prayed and encouraged people. But as so often happens, after my brother and I left home, our parents became more isolated.

At one point, when I called home, Dad said, "Well, your mother and I are not getting a divorce, but we need some space, so we're going to spend some time apart."

"What? What are you talking about, Dad?" I began asking my dad some hard questions.

When I called Mom, I heard the same thing. "We're not getting a divorce; we just need some space. Don't worry; we're going to work this out."

I shook my head in amazement. Who *are* these people?

After that, it was a series of inevitable steps to divorce court.

My parents had always been like spiritual heroes to me. I'd watched them work through all sorts of problems and arguments, often ending their disagreements on their knees, praying and asking each other and God for forgiveness and for wisdom. I knew they had counseled numerous other couples who had experienced troubles in their marriages. Now my own parents were calling it quits, and I was devastated.

Out of this painful experience, witnessing my parents dissolve their marriage, I realized that merely saying the words "Divorce is not an option" was not enough. I also realized with time that my parents were two broken people with some deep wounds of their own who despite their bad choices had done an amazing job modeling for my brother and me the love of a family and a deep faith in Jesus.

As usual, I turned to music to express my thoughts and emotions and most of all my commitment to Mary Beth. This experience had shaken us down to the foundations of our relationship, and I needed her to know that I was serious when I said I would never leave her, that I was not depending on mushy feelings but on a solid commitment I had made—to God and to her. As long as we stayed close to Him, I believed He would hold us together, even with all our differences and disagreements. On our first anniversary, I had established a tradition of giving Mary Beth three red roses, one symbolizing each of us and the center rose symbolizing Jesus. We understood that the best marriages are not two people—but three. And it is the One in the center who holds it all together. The closer we got to Him, the closer we would stay to each other. I've continued bringing home three roses over the years, always for our anniversary but occasionally just as a reminder that we are in this thing together with God.

I had promised Mary Beth I would be with her no matter what, and now more than ever I wanted her to be sure of it. So I began writing these words:

> Tomorrow morning if you wake up,
> And the sun does not appear
> I, I will be here
> If in the dark we lose sight of love,
> Hold my hand, and have no fear
> 'Cause I, I will be here
> I will be here when you feel like being quiet
> When you need to speak your mind,
> I will listen and

I will be here when the laughter turns to cryin'
Through the winning, losing, and tryin'
We'll be together 'cause I will be here.

So much of our own personal story and struggles were written in every line of that song. I never expected that in the years to come the song would be sung at thousands of weddings as a pledge of commitment between brides and grooms. As only God could, He would take a song born out of heartache and pain and use it to greatly encourage many on their own journeys—something He has done so many times in my life.

I sat down with Mary Beth and played a recording of the song for her on Mother's Day. She didn't know I had written it, and I waited until the recording was finished before I played it for her. She cried, and so did I.

The failure of Mom and Dad's marriage scared us, because we both admired my parents' marriage. If Mom and Dad's marriage could fail, so could ours. So with the wake-up call of my own parents' divorce, we began to seek wise counsel wherever we could find it—from our pastor, friends, professional counselors, and others.

My ideas of building a strong marriage were similar to those of my parents, but now my parents were divorced. And it was clear that I had a lot to learn about how to love my wife well. To be honest, we both had a lot to learn, and we acknowledged it. We were trying to figure out how to balance my creativity and my being in the studio and on the road for concerts with Mary Beth's need for structure and plans. I'd often tell her I'd be home from the studio at six o'clock, but then something marvelous would take place during the creative process that would keep me at the studio until eight o'clock or later. "I can't dictate creativity," I'd try to explain to Mary Beth. "You just have to trust that I love you and will get home as soon as I can."

"That doesn't work for me," Mary Beth would say. "I'm used to my dad coming home after work at the same time every day. That's what love is to me."

I would respond, "Sweetheart, I love you with all of my heart, and I'm asking you to please trust me. I'm really trying hard to follow God's plan for my life and our life . . . can't you see that?"

She could . . . but she couldn't.

We'd get down on our knees and pray, but when we'd get up, Mary Beth wouldn't necessarily throw her arms around me and say, "Oh, thank you, sweetheart, for being such a godly leader."

We need help, I thought. I wanted some accountability. More than that, Mary Beth and I needed a referee!

We sought out a professional counselor who began by administering a personality test to each of us. After the counselor analyzed the results, he said, "Well, guys, if I could put your test results on a graph, Steve, where you go up, Mary Beth, you go down. Where you go down, she goes up. The two lines sort of make an X. As much as you thought you were on the same track, more often than not you are at cross-purposes. You have some real challenges because of your differences." Everything in both of us wanted to scream, "Thank you so much, Captain Obvious!" We actually had to pay him for that information.

We already knew we were so different from each other, of course. Mary Beth and I had gone to several marriage conferences. But unlike most couples, it wasn't the wife saying, "Let's go!" It was the husband thinking, *If we go to this conference, we are going to get fixed!* Mary Beth was reticent, but she was willing to go with me. I really wanted to go because I was sure that if we could just get a list of things to do, we'd solve our problems.

Of course, at most of the conferences, the leader would say something like, "Okay, guys, here's how you function. You just want the facts; you're not into talking about feelings. And women, here's how you operate. You are more feelings oriented." Mary Beth and I would look at each other and say, "Nope. Not us!" So we'd quietly slip out and go see a movie or something.

Worse yet, at this point in my career, I had recorded a couple of albums and was becoming known in the Christian community, so many people looked at us as the ideal Christian couple who had their marriage all together. And I was getting ready to release the song "I Will Be Here," which would only increase that notion. The fact that we were so "not all together" added stress on top of stress, because we knew we weren't what we were supposed to be.

While many of the books we read and conferences we attended left us feeling even more frustrated and beyond help, somebody recommended the book *Intimate Allies*, by psychologist and marriage counselor Dan Allender and his friend Tremper Longman. As I read it, I realized that Mary Beth's and my differences were not accidental; they didn't take God by surprise. In fact, He made us that way so we could be each other's complement. He created us for each other. Of all the people on the planet, God created an incredible treasure and gave her to me. If I loved her well, with God's strength and wisdom, even if I stumbled and failed, I had the opportunity to help bring out the love and beauty in my wife. In the same way, even with her brokenness, Mary Beth would be the one who would call out the glory of God in me. Yet in doing that, she would also expose my selfishness, weaknesses, self-righteousness, and pride.

She pulled down my mask and let me see myself for who I really was in a way that no one else ever could. That's the beauty and danger of marriage. Prior to that, I was convinced I was a pretty good guy. I'd tried to do all the right things. I never got in trouble. I always ate my vegetables (except for sweet potatoes, which are questionable as a vegetable anyway) and washed behind my ears. I was Mr. Heath High School, for cryin' out loud. I was born to be Mr. Fix-it. So everything should work out. But when it didn't, I was mad.

Through my relationship with Mary Beth, I was realizing there was an ugly anger rooted deep within me. I seldom let it be seen, but it was there nonetheless. God began to show me more of my *self*—and it wasn't pretty. As Mary Beth was pretty good at reminding me, I wasn't perfect either.

I began to understand that even a lot of my desire to fix everything was based in my own selfishness as much as and sometimes even more than in my desire to glorify God. I wanted to be in control. I also realized that something far more mysterious and complex was going on in and through Mary Beth's and my relationship than I ever imagined. God was showing me once again, as He had several years earlier, that I was just as broken as Mary Beth and that I needed His grace and forgiveness just as much as Mary Beth or anyone else.

Although I didn't fully realize it at the time, being a part of her journey would profoundly reveal parts of me that God wanted to use for His glory and to help other people. And her being a part of my journey would facilitate what God wanted to do in and through Mary Beth.

Dan Allender's book helped me realize why Mary Beth's and my marriage was going to be so hard—that God was doing something mysteriously beautiful even in our messes, that I was the one guy chosen by God for her, that she was the one woman chosen by God for me, and that despite our differences we were together by design. It was our brokenness that would make me more aware of my desperate need for God's grace in my life.

Knowing these things didn't solve all our problems, of course, but it definitely gave me a greater sense of hope and purpose for the hard days we had been through as well as the ones ahead.

The growing Chapman family.

Chapter Eleven

More to This Life

Mary Beth had gotten pregnant again soon after we had moved into our new home, and we were excited to be parents again. But at twelve weeks along, while visiting her parents in Ohio, she called to me in a panic from the bathroom. With tears in her eyes, she told me something was wrong and we needed to get her to a doctor quickly. She felt sure she was having a miscarriage. She was. Even though it was early in the pregnancy, it was a traumatic experience that broke our hearts. The miscarriage also gave us an even greater sense of the miracle that our little girl, Emily, was.

In her heart and mind, Mary Beth had already mapped out the strategic time frame for having our children. We hoped to have our kids close together so there wouldn't be too much space between Emily and our next child. We had gotten pregnant so easily with Emily that we assumed that when we actually *tried* to get pregnant, it would be a simple matter. Not so, as the miscarriage taught us.

As soon as we could, we began trying to have another baby. I, of course, felt it was my duty to remind her that practice makes perfect. She was not amused. To Mary Beth, this was serious business.

As the ultimate planner, this time she was leaving nothing to chance. She went to the pharmacy and purchased an ovulation kit.

I was performing at a concert nine hundred miles away from home when Mary Beth's ovulation kit revealed it was the optimum time for her to get pregnant. She called me and said, "You need to come home."

I could hear the intensity in her voice. "Why? What's going on?"

"I need you to come home *now*!" She explained the ovulation window of opportunity.

"Sweetheart, I have a concert tonight."

"I need you to cancel your concert," she said matter-of-factly, "and come home."

"And what do you suggest I tell the audience? Am I supposed to walk out onstage and say, 'Sorry, folks. My wife is ovulating, and I have to go home and make a baby!'"

"Yes!" Mary Beth responded.

"As much fun as that would be, I really don't think I can do that, sweetheart."

Mary Beth's mind was already working on contingency plans. "All right, then, when you land at the airport, you need to come straight home. Dennis and Laura will come and get Emily so we won't have to worry about the baby. You are going to come straight home, and we are going to make a baby!" (Dennis Disney and his wife, Laura, were good friends who lived in our neighborhood. Dennis and I had met in a physics of sound class at Belmont a few years earlier. As I was working on my first record, I had mentioned to Dennis that I might need a manager, even though I didn't really know what a manager did. He wanted to work in music business management, so he took me on as his first client. He was a great believer in me even when I wasn't sure about myself and was an important part of my early career.)

Sure enough, Mary Beth was waiting for me when I arrived at the airport. We had only a matter of hours left on her ticking ovulation clock. Dennis and Laura took Emily to their home after I sheepishly greeted them, embarrassed that they knew precisely why they were babysitting. More modest about such matters than Mary Beth, I could barely make eye contact with our friends. That didn't bother my wife in the least. We hurried home and . . . well, how do I say this delicately . . . while it may not have been the most romantic welcome home, I certainly wasn't complaining.

Mary Beth and I knelt beside our bed that afternoon, held hands, and prayed, asking God to bless us with another child. Our prayer went something like, "Heavenly Father, we know the gift of life comes from You, and we're asking You to bless us with another baby if it's Your will. We did our part, God; now we're asking You to do the rest."

Nine months later, on October 2, 1989, our son Caleb Stevenson Chapman made his grand entrance into the world. We had no doubt about the date of Caleb's conception.

About six months after Caleb was born, we were surprised to discover we were pregnant again. We were at Chuck E. Cheese's with Herbie and his wife, Sherri, and Mary Beth's brother, Jim Chapman Jr., and his wife, Yolanda. Both Sherri and Yo were pregnant. On the way to the restaurant, we had stopped at a store to pick up a few last-minute things. Mary Beth had been feeling a little strange, so unbeknownst to me, she had purchased a pregnancy test just to rule out the untimely possibility, as we were still unsure whether to stop at two children or try to have a third child at some point in the distant future. After greeting everyone and settling Emily and baby Caleb in with the other kids, my wife went into Chuck E. Cheese's restroom . . . and came out pregnant. With tears in her eyes, she informed me we were going to have another baby—relatively soon!

Emily saw that Mary Beth was crying and ran to her. "Mommy! Why are you crying?"

Mary Beth explained to Emily that she had just found out she was going to have another baby, and her tears were happy tears.

In what came to be a classic Chapman moment, four-year-old Emily put her hands on her hips and asked, "What in the *world* are we going to do with another baby?"

"I don't know," Mary Beth whimpered. "That's why I'm crying!"

Mary Beth gave birth to our second son, Will Franklin, on February 6, 1991. We now had three children under five years of age.

My third album, *More to This Life*, launched four number one hits, including "I Will Be Here," and in 1990, I received my first ever Grammy nomination and ten nominations for Gospel Music Association's Dove Awards. I took home five Dove Awards that year. For Mary Beth and me, our heads were swimming with all the success. Yet as crazy as it sounds, I was still battling those little voices telling me, "You're just an average singer who happens to be a fairly likeable guy, but eventually, they're going to figure out you're not that good."

My next album, *For the Sake of the Call*, featured five number one singles, and I was honored with more Dove Awards and my first Grammy for best pop/contemporary gospel album.

After working in a little room writing songs for several years, suddenly, it seemed I was everywhere—doing concerts, interviews, television and radio shows, and all the while writing more songs. We were finally able to afford to build a house, something neither of us ever imagined we'd get the opportunity to do, but something Mary Beth had been hoping we could do now that we had three little ones.

Ask anyone who's ever done it and they'll tell you that few things in life will test a marriage more than building a house. Working with builders and subcontractors alone is enough to drive a novice crazy, not to mention the myriad decisions that have to be made when you design your own home. The project will either draw you together in a deeper bond of love or make you consider murder! Or both!

Although I had grown up in Paducah, we had lived far enough out on the edge of town to be out in the country, where I had two fishing ponds nearby, plenty of wide-open spaces, and a couple hundred acres of farmland next door. When Mary Beth and I began looking for property, I wanted to live out in the country rather than in the city. We found a perfect place,

Roses for my bride.

complete with a pond just like the ones I had grown up fishing in, out in the country but still within a short drive of Nashville.

We sold our house in LaVergne and lived in an apartment in the Civil War town of Franklin, about a thirty-minute drive south of Nashville, while contractors were building our house.

Around that same time, Emily began kindergarten at the elementary school across the street from our little two-bedroom apartment. On her first day of school, Mary Beth and I walked Emily out the front door, across the street, and to the school. Of course, we videotaped the whole affair.

After a few months of living in a cramped apartment, I wanted to do something special for Mary Beth to celebrate our seventh anniversary. I purchased tickets to the Broadway show *Les Miserables*, which was playing at the Tennessee Performing Arts Center in Nashville. Mary Beth would have been thrilled simply to see the show, but I wanted to really do it up right, so I decided to have a limousine pick us up at our apartment and transport us to our favorite restaurant downtown. Following dinner, I planned for us to take a romantic ride on the Nashville trolley to the show and then afterward have the limo bring us back home. But when I investigated the cost of the limo, I had sticker shock.

Most of the limos cost about $50 an hour and had a four-hour minimum. I figured our evening might entail about six hours . . . that was a lot of money just for the limo. So I kept calling around, trying to find a deal.

I found one, J. D. Limousine Service . . . and I dialed the number.

"Hello," a brusque voice answered. "This is J. D." I should have guessed that this was not a primo operation right there. But I didn't.

"Hey, J. D., it's my wife's and my anniversary, so I want to do something special for her and have a limo take us downtown to the restaurant and bring us home after the show at the theater. Every place I've called has a four-hour minimum, and they want way too much money. I just want someone to give us a ride downtown and then bring us home . . . I was thinking about spending around $50."

"Tell ya what," J. D. proffered, "I can make that work. I'm free tonight. I can fit that into my schedule. How does forty bucks each way sound?"

"Wow, that sounds good!"

J. D. was going to pick me up in a parking lot around the corner from our apartment. Then I'd show up at the door with flowers in hand and a special anniversary ring I'd bought for Mary Beth.

I told Mary Beth, "Okay, you get ready. I'll be right back, and your surprise will begin." She looked at me skeptically but nonetheless excited.

I drove to the parking lot and left my car where I was to meet the limousine. I had visions of grandeur, anticipating a shiny, black stretch limo in which I would escort my bride to dinner and the theater. *Mary Beth is going to love this!* I thought.

I should have known I was in trouble when I saw the limo. An old, dingy, dirty, white stretch limousine pulled into the parking lot. A man wearing a gray leisure suit and snakeskin cowboy boots got out of the vehicle. He clomped over to me and stretched out his hand. "Hey, Steve. I'm J. D.," he said in a molasses-thick country drawl.

Oh boy, I said to myself. *What have I gotten myself into?*

He opened the back door to the car and said, "Let's go get your bride." I reluctantly slid into the backseat and instantly realized the limo's interior unfortunately matched the exterior. I was dressed up, and I wasn't sure I wanted to sit back in the seat. I glanced around and noticed that the privacy glass separating the front seat from the rear was tipped in toward the driver's head. J. D. tried to knock the glass back into place before getting in the car. "Sorry about that," he said. "We had kind of a rough night last night."

In front of me, I saw a television—not built into the car but on a table, attached with duct tape so it wouldn't slide off. The television had a videotape slot in the front. As we went around a curve, I heard something sliding behind me. I turned around and looked in the window compartment behind the seat and saw that J. D. had stocked the car with videotapes. I picked up a tape titled *Bambi* but not the Disney version! Suddenly, I realized, *I am in a pornmobile!*

My mind was racing. I could imagine Mary Beth all dressed up, ready for our big night, and me showing up with J. D. and this limo. *How can I get out of this?* I thought. About that time, we pulled up in front of our apartment. I decided to tell J. D. I had changed my mind.

Too late. Mary Beth had seen the limo.

"Oh! You got a limousine for our anniversary!" she gushed and gave me a big kiss. "Happy anniversary!"

"No, I didn't. Um, I mean, yes, I did, but it's not what you think. I mean, it is, but it's not!"

"Oh, that's so sweet."

"Well, it's actually not sweet. It's nasty!"

Somebody told me that confession is good for the soul, so I admitted my mistake to Mary Beth. "Okay, this is terrible. I made a mistake. I got the cheapest limo I could find, and I'm paying the price now. It's the pornmobile! It has adult movies in the back window, and its dingy and dirty. I don't even want you to ride in it."

Mary Beth looked at me, then looked at the limo, with J. D. standing by the door. J. D. waved and smiled. Mary Beth looked back at me and said, "You know what? Come on. It will be fun. We'll make the best of it. You went to all the trouble; we've got the limo; let's just go and have fun. It will be a story to tell."

Mary Beth and I carefully got into the car, trying not to touch anything. I knew she had to be grossed out because she was steeped in the tradition of cleanliness is next to godliness. "I can't believe you did this," she said, laughing. "This is so funny."

I buried my head in my chest, mumbling, "I'm so sorry . . . I'm so sorry . . . I've learned my lesson. I'll never get the cheapest limo ever again."

Mary Beth was cracking up.

I was already thinking ahead. "Sweetheart, don't worry, when we get to the restaurant, I'll tell J. D. we have changed our plans and we don't need him anymore." I figured I could call Herbie or one of the guys in my band to give us a ride home. "I'll send him away."

All the way to town J. D. talked to us through the broken privacy window. "Oh, it's your anniversary. That's great! Thank you so much for allowing me to be a part of it." He really was a nice guy . . . in spite of it all.

We arrived at the well-known, classy restaurant downtown, and J. D., in his leisure suit, bounded out of the car to open the door as tourists gawked, perhaps wondering which famous Nashville celebrities were getting out of the limo—as dumpy as the vehicle was. Remaining inconspicuous was impossible!

I hurried Mary Beth into the restaurant, and I stepped back to settle up with J. D. I tried to explain to him that we had changed our plans. "J. D., my wife and I have decided that we're not going to need you to take us home."

"Naw, naw, I'm gonna pick you up. I'll get ya back home."

"It's okay, J. D. Really. We'll be fine."

"Well, all right, if you're sure," he said.

Our deal was for $40 each way, so I gave him $40 and a $20 tip. J. D. took the money without looking at it and drove away as I hurried in to rejoin my wife.

Inside the candle-lit, quiet, romantic restaurant, the maître 'd ushered us to our table, where I had arranged ahead of time to have our traditional three red roses waiting. A piano player provided soft, romantic music in the background. The mood was perfect.

"Can you believe I did that?" I asked with a laugh, still thinking about the limo.

Mary Beth giggled as we received our menus. We started perusing our options, although I already had my heart set on the filet mignon. We were basking in the atmosphere when suddenly we heard clomp, clomp, clomp!

Oh no! I recognized the sound of J. D.'s cowboy boots clomping across the hardwood floor and echoing through the quiet restaurant. It got worse.

From across the room, I heard, "Steve! Hey, Steve! J. D. here." He made his way to our table. "Hey, man, you paid me too much money."

"Oh, it's okay, J. D. I wanted to give you a little extra because we weren't using you to go home."

"No, I said $40 and you paid me $60," he said loudly enough for everyone in the restaurant to hear. He tried to hand me back some money.

"No, no, J. D., really, I wanted you to have it," I said.

J. D. finally accepted the cash and left happy, and Mary Beth and I proceeded to have an amazing dinner. Just as I had planned, we caught the Nashville trolley to the show and took our seats for the presentation of *Les Mis*.

Mary Beth, however, was worried about how we were going to get home.

"Oh, don't worry. I'll call someone at intermission," I said. At the conclusion of the first act, I went out to the lobby to make a call. Cell phones were a relatively new idea, and we didn't have one yet, so I found a pay phone with about twenty people standing in line. I waited a while, but then it was time for the next act to begin, so I went back inside the theater.

"Did you get someone?" Mary Beth asked.

"No, there were too many people in line at the phone, but I'll go back out after the next act starts, and hopefully the line will be shorter." That's what I did, but the line was still long. I didn't want to miss too much of the show, so I went back inside again, assuming I could make the call after the show.

When the show concluded, we wiped the tears from our eyes, deeply moved by the powerful music and message. But when we walked out of the auditorium, the line at the pay phone remained.

"Sweetheart, *Les Mis* is a show with strong Christian themes, so I'm guessing there are people here we know. Record label people, friends from church. Surely, we'll see somebody we know."

"Are you serious? I don't want to ask somebody for a ride home."

"If we see some friends, we'll tell them the story, and they'll think it is funny."

"Okay," Mary Beth said reluctantly.

We went out and stood on the street corner, watching people exit the theater, hoping to see someone we knew. Crowds of people flowed past us, and I didn't spot a single person I recognized.

Finally, a man and a woman approached us with quizzical expressions on their faces. The man peered intently at me and slowly said, "Are you who I think you are?"

I quickly looked him over and decided he looked safe enough. "Ya know, I kinda hope so," I said.

Beside me, I could hear Mary Beth mumbling under her breath, "You've got to be kidding."

"Well, you look like Steven Curtis Chapman," the man said.

"Why, yes, I *am* Steven Curtis Chapman!"

"I can't believe it! I love your music. My wife and I came to *Les Mis* tonight, and I'm a minister of music at a church in Dixon, Tennessee. We sing some of your songs."

The next words out of my mouth were, "Now, tell me, where exactly is Dixon? I'm not familiar with which direction it is."

Mary Beth was shaking her head. "I know where this is going," she whispered. "We're going to ride home with these people!"

I proceeded to tell the minister of music and his wife about J. D. and his limo. "So we're kinda stuck and trying to find a way home."

"Oh, we'll take you," the man said. "We'd love to take you home."

Mary Beth was sending me very loud messages with her eyes. "Are you crazy? We're going to ride home with perfect strangers?"

"He's a minister of music," I said sideways. "He's a good guy."

The kind minister of music and his wife drove more than two hours out of their way to take Mary Beth and me home after we'd canceled J. D. and his limo. It wasn't quite the perfectly executed romantic evening I'd had in mind, but we sure made some great memories that night—as well as some new friends!

HAPPY
Birthday
Emily

Chapter Twelve

It's an Honor Just to Be Nominated

In the early stages of my career, I patterned much of my approach in my concerts after Dallas Holm, intentionally keeping the night focused on the message more than the musical experience, while still doing all I could to make sure the music was great. It was important that whenever I could, I ended my concerts with a Billy Graham–style altar call, inviting people to respond to the message of God's grace and love. As the concert venues got larger and the production grew more elaborate, my managers and the record label folks encouraged me not to end the evening that way. "People are buying tickets to come to a concert," they said. "They are not attending a church service. Do you really need to sing four verses of 'Just As I Am' or 'I Surrender All'? Just give them a concert. Share your testimony and your stories, but don't feel like you have to turn the event into an evangelistic crusade."

That was (and always has been) somewhat of a challenge. If I was going to take time away from my family, I wanted to know I was doing something of eternal value and significance. This was a calling as much as a career for me. I love music, and I know it's a powerful thing, but for me, music is not the end in and of itself. It's a means to an end. I want to do my music in a way that draws people in closer to hear what God might be saying to them.

On the other hand, I understood the tenuous balance between being in the music business and having a music ministry.

I talked with Steve Green, one of the most gifted and respected artists in Christian music. Steve was a missionary kid with a heart for evangelism, so he understood my passion. I also spoke with Michael Card, who had formed a management company called Creative Trust with Dan Raines to help guide his own efforts to use the talents God had given him in the wisest way.

Wanting to be a good steward of the talents entrusted to me was not a new issue for me. From the beginning of my career, I had leaned heavily on the wisdom of godly advisors around me. This wasn't the first time I'd heard the name Dan Raines in that regard. While I was working on my second album, my producer, Phil Naish, had told me, "You should meet Dan Raines. He's going to manage my productions. He's a smart guy with great ideas and a great heart."

I talked with Dan Raines and signed a management agreement with Creative Trust in 1989. It was one of the wisest moves I've made in my entire career, as Dan would become one of my dearest friends, walking alongside me, providing great support and counsel in the years ahead.

Despite the busy-ness and challenges Mary Beth and I were experiencing, we enjoyed some of the perks of our success. One of those was the opportunity to attend the Grammy Awards, the annual gathering of artists, music industry personnel, and music aficionados celebrating excellence in every musical genre. The first time Mary Beth and I attended the Grammys the show was held on February 22, 1989, in Los Angeles at the Shrine Auditorium. My album *Real Life Conversations* was nominated for an award in the category best gospel performance, male. Dan Raines and his wife, Evelyn, went along with us, as did my producer, Phil Naish, and his wife, Becky.

I had been to Los Angeles previously, but I wasn't familiar with the city, so Dan suggested a Moroccan restaurant called Dar Maghreb in Hollywood that was one of his favorites. "I love this place," Dan said. "I try to eat there

At an event to honor one of my heroes,
Dallas Holm (middle right),
along with Twila Paris and Eddie DeGarmo.

every time I get to the city. When I used to live in Los Angeles, I ate there two or three times a week."

"Well, okay," everyone said. "We definitely want to eat there."

We arrived at the Moroccan restaurant on Sunset Boulevard in Hollywood and were seated on the floor on bean-bag-style pillows. I assumed it was simply the waiting area. Wrong. It was a genuine Middle Eastern restaurant where the customers reclined to eat. That was weird enough for me, but a few minutes later, the waiters started bringing all sorts of food but no silverware. This was definitely finger food.

Dan was loving it. "Man, isn't this great?" he said.

Phil was up for the experience too, and everyone was having fun sopping up all sorts of food with the bread. I was doing the best that a boy from Paducah could do, wondering, *Where are my meat and potatoes?*

Suddenly, the lights in the restaurant dimmed, and the sounds of exotic Middle Eastern music filled the room. Then out from behind a curtain emerged a half-naked belly dancer dressed in traditional garb, complete with a sheer skirt, scarves, veil, headdress, and tiny finger cymbals. The dancer undulated her way around the room, dancing in front of each group of customers.

I knew Phil well from working in the studio, and I had been working with Dan for a while now, so I was comfortable with him too. But I wasn't sure how Evelyn was going to respond. She was very proper and from a sophisticated family in Nashville.

Evelyn looked at Dan as though she was ready to wring his neck. "You didn't tell us about a dancer," she said tersely, pretending to be angry.

"I don't remember this part," Dan said in a panic.

"You ate here three times a week, and you didn't notice the belly dancer?" Evelyn asked, giving Dan the evil eye.

Mary Beth and Becky were good sports, laughing and giving Dan a hard time too. "Yeah, Dan," Becky teased. "Three times a week! What's the dancer's name?"

Phil, who has the best wheeze laugh I have ever heard, was cracking up.

The belly dancer worked her way from table to table, picking one person from among each group of customers upon whom to lavish her charms. When she got to our table, she stopped right behind me. That was awkward enough, considering the low angle at which we were seated. There was no good direction for a conservative, Christian boy from Paducah to look! After a while, I looked up sheepishly and quickly averted my gaze. Oh my! I didn't know what else to do, so I just kept my eyes looking straight ahead.

Apparently, the dancer regarded me as a challenge and made me her target. When I didn't respond to her efforts, she put her finger cymbals right next to my ears and snapped them together. Ching, ching, ching!

Phil burst out laughing so hard I thought he was going to throw up. Finally, the belly dancer looked at Mary Beth and Becky and mouthed the words, "He's not going to look at me, is he?" Everyone at the table thought that was hilarious, and the belly dancer gave one last ching and moved on to the next table.

It was my first Grammy Awards experience—Stevie goes to Hollyweird!

The Grammys themselves were awesome. Seeing the many superstars of music was intimidating but interesting. It was fun (and a little embarrassing) just to see the outfits people wore. Mary Beth had purchased a new evening gown made from some sparkling type of material, and before going into the theater, she stopped in the restroom. Coming out, she ran into several of the guys in the Red Hot Chili Peppers who were dressed more provocatively than the belly dancer, wearing socks—only socks—in enough strategic locations to keep them from being arrested. Mary Beth received a shock to her system and laughed as she came over to me. "Okay, I guess I'm not in Springfield, Ohio, anymore!"

I didn't win an award that night, but I smiled when my fellow artist and good friend Larnelle Harris did, and when Amy Grant won for best gospel performance, female. Bobby McFerrin was the big winner that night for his song "Don't Worry, Be Happy," so I took that as my theme. After all, as I told my friends, "It's an honor just to be nominated."

The following year my album *More to This Life* was nominated in the best pop gospel album category. Mary Beth and I attended the show again, this time in New York, but again, I didn't win. Still, as they say, it's an honor . . . well, you know.

My album *For the Sake of the Call* was released in late 1990. It, too, was nominated for a Grammy in the category best pop gospel album. Once again, Dan and Phil accompanied Mary Beth and me to the award show, this time at Radio City Music Hall in New York on February 25, 1992.

Mary Beth and I enjoyed going to the before parties and the after parties, and it was fun to mingle among some of the performers. Most of all, Mary Beth looked forward to receiving her Grammy goodie bag, a bag of treats given to nominees that included a few CDs by artists on the show, some bottled water, containers of skin care products, a few small electronic gizmos, and other items provided by advertisers.

"Do we really have to stand in line for a bag full of stuff we don't really need?" I asked.

Mary Beth looked at me as though I had dropped in from outer space. She was as excited going through the bag as a kid discovering the treats in a Christmas stocking on Christmas morning. Just then, walking down the hall happily swinging his goodie bag, came actor Danny Glover, star of movies such as *Lethal Weapon* and *The Color Purple*. Mary Beth looked at me and raised her eyebrows. "If Danny Glover is not too good or embarrassed to get his goodie bag, then Steven Curtis Chapman can get his bag too!"

"Okay," I relented. "Let's go get our dang Grammy goodie bags."

That night the gospel awards were presented during the pretelecast segment of the show, but that didn't diminish our enthusiasm. As a kid, when I was feeling really confident—which wasn't too often—I had occasionally dreamed about someday standing on the stage and receiving a Grammy

Award. I could imagine my name called out as a nominee and then walking onstage to accept the award.

It was a dream come true when the announcement was made: "For best pop/contemporary gospel album . . . the Grammy goes to . . . Steven Curtis Chapman!"

I stood to my feet and smiled, trying to act calm and collected, knowing the television cameras were on me, as I walked up to the stage to accept my very first Grammy Award. Not Mary Beth. She jumped up on the seat, wearing her fancy dress, and started cheering, "Yeaaahhhh!"

Bonnie Raitt was sitting behind us watching my wife and me. She leaned forward and tapped Mary Beth on the shoulder and said with a smile, "You're really excited. Do you know that guy? You must be his wife."

"Yes, I am," Mary Beth said. "Yes, I do! That's my husband, and I'm his wife!" And then it struck her. "And you're Bonnie Raitt!" she squealed, realizing for the first time that she was talking to one of our all-time favorite artists and a music icon.

And yes, I must admit, although it's an honor just to be nominated, it's even more of an honor to win.

Throughout much of 1991, I worked on the *For the Sake of the Call* tour, my first major tour with a band and a tour bus, the whole deal. Prior to that I had traveled to venues in a van and most of my concerts had been simply me performing with my guitar; now it was a full-blown production on a tour that was several months long. I'd always said that when I was able to put a band together on the road, I wanted my brother, Herbie, to be with me, so I asked Herbie to play bass for me on that tour. I hired friends to be in my band, not the seasoned pros my record label preferred, but we had great relationships, we had fun, and we played well together.

The following year the Grammy Awards were back in Los Angeles on February 24, 1993, the same day as our daughter's birthday. My album *The Great Adventure* was nominated for best pop/contemporary gospel album.

I was just as excited as I had been the first time when my name was called, although Mary Beth didn't stand up on her chair this time. I stepped onto the stage to accept my second Grammy Award, this one also presented during the pretelecast portion of the show.

Mary Beth and I had learned something from the previous year. The winners are asked to pose for a picture holding their awards, and these pictures are flashed on the television screens during the broadcast. "In ceremonies held earlier tonight, the following Grammys were awarded . . . for country album of the year . . . for gospel album of the year, Steven Curtis Chapman, *The Great Adventure*." The producer had instructed me, "Give us a moment and look at the camera, because we'll show this picture later in the night."

Mary Beth had an idea. "You need to write a message, 'Happy birthday, Emily!' That way when the family is at home watching, she will see it." I thought it was a great idea, but I didn't have a pen or a piece of paper on me. Mary Beth fumbled in her purse and found her lipstick, and I tore off the back cover of the program. I wrote on the cover using Mary Beth's lipstick, "Happy birthday, Emily!"

When I received the award, I took a moment to explain, "Today is my daughter Emily's seventh birthday, and I'm hoping they will use this picture on TV later tonight, and she'll see it."

Sure enough, that is exactly what happened. Sitting at home with Mamaw and Poppy, Mary Beth's mom and dad, without a word of warning, Emily suddenly saw my picture with the birthday message on television. She could hardly believe her eyes!

Mary Beth and I were seated next to a distinguished-looking, white-haired gentleman. During intermission, I walked back to where Phil Naish was seated. "Dude!" Phil said excitedly. "Do you know who you are sitting next to?"

"Ah . . . no . . ."

"That's George Martin!"

"Okay . . ." I said, obviously clueless. (I apologize to all my music friends who are shaking their heads as they read this.)

"George Martin," Phil repeated. "He produced the Beatles' albums!"

I walked back to my seat and tried not to say anything stupid to one of music's greatest producers.

That same year at the Grammys I was asked to be a presenter, and I had the honor of presenting Celine Dion with her very first Grammy Award for her performance of the song "Beauty and the Beast."

There were other things about the Grammy Awards that I observed. As I watched the adoration being lavished upon the performers and the superstars of the moment, it struck me that the show was really a misguided sort of worship service. In that room, the focus was on worshiping the gift rather than the Giver, the creativity rather than the Creator. Certainly, we wanted to honor the excellent work and the artistry involved in the music business. And I think many artists realize that the gift of music and the ability to create it are gifts from God at their core, which is why so many are inclined to thank God when receiving an award for something they created. But I also got a sense that this was a place where gods of our own making are worshiped for a season and then tossed aside when something new and more exciting comes along. And somewhere mixed in with all of it, I had to admit that a part of me very much enjoyed the admiration of people as much as anyone. My observations were both heartbreaking and heart-exposing at the same time.

My experience at the Grammys also helped me realize one more reason why I was so thankful for a wife who kept my feet firmly on the ground. Mary Beth and I enjoyed the celebration and had a great time together, but we also felt a little out of place.

After the show was over, we went backstage to where the performers' and the presenters' limousines were brought around. An attendant with a radio communicated with the attendants on the street level. We stood in a line of about twenty-five or thirty people waiting for the elevator to take us down to street level when the attendant announced that our car was ready. While waiting in line for the elevator, I heard someone say with a distinctly British accent, "Well, I think it was a great show."

"Yeah, yeah, man, you played great," a man with a rough, raspy voice agreed. I recognized both voices immediately. I partially turned my head so I could see for sure who was standing behind Mary Beth and me. I nudged my wife and whispered, "Don't look now, but Sting and the Boss, Bruce Springsteen, are standing right behind us."

Mary Beth whirled around and saw the two rock stars within inches of us. "That's Sting . . . and Springsteen," she said quietly but excitedly.

"Yes, I know," I said, trying to act cool.

She hit me in the arm. "And you told me not to bring my camera!"

"Yes, exactly. Because this would be the moment when you would totally embarrass us both by asking them to take a picture with you."

"Yes, I would! What's wrong with that?"

"Nothing, but we're supposed to be here as peers. Even though we know we're not, they don't know that. We're supposed to blend in. You don't blend in when you start taking pictures of the superstars!"

"But that's Springsteen . . . and that's Sting!"

"Yes, I know. Blend in!"

About that time the attendant with the radio noticed Sting and Springsteen standing in line with us. Perhaps their car was next in line, but I doubt it. The attendant near the elevator called out to the music icons, "Mr. Springsteen, Sting, please come ahead. Your limo is ready."

The rest of us standing in line were waiting patiently. It really wasn't fair that the attendant allowed the stars to jump the line, but they were, after all, Sting and Springsteen.

Most of the people continued talking and were not offended. All except one person—the Queen of What Is Right. As Springsteen and Sting started to walk around us, Mary Beth called out playfully, "Hey! Wait a second. We're all waiting in line here."

I wanted to be invisible at that moment. My wife had just called out Sting and Bruce Springsteen!

The famous stars laughed and waved as they proceeded to the elevator. Before entering the elevator, Sting turned around and called back to Mary Beth and me but mostly to Mary Beth, "Come along. You can join us."

Mary Beth climbed on her high horse, put her arms over her chest, and said, "Nope, we're just going to wait our turn like all the rest of the people here."

The other people in line clapped in good-natured applause.

Springsteen may have been the Boss and Sting a polite Brit, but to the people in line backstage after the Grammys, the most memorable person there was Mary Beth.

I only hoped we wouldn't bump into Sting or Springsteen at the after party!

Chapter Thirteen

Tears for Cheers

As my career continued to grow, I crashed into an obstacle I had never anticipated—my own success. Everywhere I went people started treating me a little bit like a rock star, albeit on a much smaller scale than the Boss and Sting. While I appreciated the kindness and the attention, it was a struggle for me. I wanted to play my music for as many people as I could, and I certainly wanted them to enjoy it and have a great time at my concerts. But I also wanted the ultimate purpose of my music to be to lift up Jesus and not Steven.

The problem came to a head for me in Memorial Auditorium in Chattanooga, Tennessee, the first night of sold-out concerts. We received an incredible response from the audience, who applauded and screamed. People in the front rows called out my name and wanted to touch my hands and feet while I was onstage. It was awesome . . . and it was scary!

We finished the show, and I went back to the dressing room, closed the door, and dropped to my knees. Tears filled my eyes, and I began to cry. "God, I'm sorry," I said. "Somehow this doesn't seem right, and I don't know what to do with all of this." I thought about the Scripture passage that talks about how Jesus needs to increase and I need to decrease. Here I was singing songs and hoping to point people to Jesus, the man who had made nothing of himself and had loved and served humbly (Phil. 2:7), and yet I was being cheered and celebrated . . . and it felt really good . . . yet somehow really wrong.

David Huffman, one of the young management guys on the tour and a close friend, came into the dressing room to give me a high five and tell me what a great show it was and found me in tears. "Are you okay, Steven?" he asked.

I waved him off, and he left. I learned later that he had gone out into the hallway and had run into my good friend Charley Redmond, who had been back by the audio board during the show and was coming backstage to congratulate me on a great performance. Charley saw the look on David's face, his eyes huge as though he'd seen a ghost.

"Do not go in there right now," David said.

"What's wrong?" Charley asked.

"I just came out of Steven's dressing room, and he's on the floor, crying."

"Why is he upset?"

"He doesn't know if this is right. Is it okay? He's never had people grabbing at his shoes on stage and all the rest."

Charley came in and found me. I pulled myself together and explained to my friend what I had experienced. "I liked the applause, I really did . . . but I wasn't sure that I should," I told him.

Charley listened and then said, "I know with the bright lights in your eyes all you could see and hear were the kids in the front rows. But what I saw back in the auditorium were the husbands and wives holding hands and hugging each other when you sang 'I Will Be Here.' And I saw people celebrating their faith in the Lord. I saw kids enjoying music they could relate to. Nearly thirty-eight hundred people left here tonight excited about Jesus. I know you don't want to be a rock star, but, Steve, what you did brought honor to God." I appreciated Charley's encouragement.

My pastor, Scotty Smith, came out on the road to see the show and get a feel for what was happening. Scotty understood the dilemma I felt. He had been backstage with me at the Dove Awards in 1990, when I had been nominated for ten awards and had won five of them for my album *More to This Life*. As much as I was thrilled and enjoyed the honors and the affirmation for doing a good job, I didn't know what to do with what I was feeling. As I carried around the five awards, I was fighting back tears born out of my concern and confusion. It was a weird paradox. "Scotty, I'm winning these awards, and I love it, and I want to embrace it, but I don't know how to handle it." Part of the struggle was the fact that I was singing songs inspired by and written about my relationship with Jesus.

Scotty's advice was something like, "The fact that you feel this way and are even concerned about this attention and adulation tells me everything I need to know about the condition of your heart. If you ever lose that, then I'll start to worry about you."

Fortunately . . . and unfortunately, Mary Beth was not impressed with my "fame." She was my most vocal cheerleader, but she was also my quickest critic. She didn't mind saying, "It's great that the audience loved you at the concert. I know the people were standing and cheering last night, but right now I really need you to help me wash some dishes and take out the garbage."

Mary Beth has remained unimpressed with my celebrity. Sometimes frustratingly so! (Maybe I should try changing my name to something cool like Sting.) "Can't you be just a little impressed?" I sometimes want to ask. But on the other hand, I'm very thankful she hasn't been.

The truth is she's always been my biggest fan and thinks I should win every award I'm nominated for, and even some I'm not. But her honesty has been a great gift to me.

Gradually, I came to understand that while the pleasure of the applause feels good and that I receive great satisfaction from doing a good job—and that I sense God's pleasure as I sing—I am well aware that every song I write and every note I sing come from a gift that He has entrusted to me. And when people have acknowledged that I've done something that moved them emotionally or spiritually or when I have received an award, I've tried to accept it with genuine humility and then turn the honor in God's direction.

As I wrestled with this, I felt that God gave me a beautiful picture of how I was to handle the applause and adulation when it came. In China, after someone performs onstage, appreciative members of the audience present the musician with a bouquet of flowers. I sensed my heavenly Father saying to me, "You know I gave you this gift and all the glory is Mine. And I know that you know it would be foolish to think otherwise. When people applaud you or express appreciation when you do your craft well, it's as if they are presenting you the bouquet of flowers in their desire to give it to Me. You have to receive the flowers from them—you gather them up in your arms and breathe in their fragrance and enjoy their beauty—and then bring the flowers to Me, just as I know you will. You don't have to put on any airs of false humility. In fact, I want you to take pleasure and joy in receiving the flowers; that brings Me joy. But then just bring them to Me."

God knows what a visual learner I am, and that simple yet profound mental picture has been an incredible help to me. While I'll never have it all together in this area, this idea has helped me humbly and gratefully accept the applause of people who enjoy and appreciate my music instead of letting it go to my head.

With that said, even more difficult than handling the approval of people has been dealing with the insecurity I've felt when criticized. I've heard other recording artists say, "One thousand compliments plus one criticism equals one criticism." Remember the Little Leaguer walking back to the dugout in shame after striking out or the boy who broke the pool skimmer and decided he would never do the wrong thing again? That little guy is still in there, of course, and he still desperately wants to do everything right, to make everybody happy.

Early in my career, I was honored to sing at a Billy Graham Crusade.

At the close of the evening, after the service was over and people were leaving the stadium, I went backstage to say good night to Dr. Graham and to express my appreciation to him. Dr. Graham and his son Franklin were in a room talking by themselves. I listened respectfully as Dr. Graham said,

Mary Beth Chapman

Backstage with Billy Graham.

"I don't know, Franklin, I think I could have been more clear on that last point. I probably should have found a better illustration . . ." I stood there amazed as Dr. Graham verbally replayed various elements of his message—a message that God had used to inspire and bless thousands of people and to draw nearly two thousand people to respond to Christ. Yet Billy Graham was expressing his own insecurities.

Afterward, I asked Franklin, "Is that common for your dad? I would never have imagined that sort of second-guessing being typical of your father."

Franklin smiled. "Daddy does that every time he comes off the platform."

In a way, I found that encouraging. If Billy Graham still had insecurities, there was hope for me!

With Mary Beth in Wyoming for "The Great Adventure" video shoot.

Chapter Fourteen

Breakdown

My career was continuing to gain momentum, and I was performing about 150 concerts a year, finishing up the *For the Sake of the Call* tour while writing songs for *The Great Adventure* album, when Will Franklin was born in February of 1991. We had a new baby, Caleb was still a toddler, and Emily was starting kindergarten, so there were a lot of expectations and emotions swirling around Mary Beth and me.

As much as I tried to tell myself this was just an intense time for us, something seemed to be getting worse at a time when so much good was happening. We were building our dream house on five acres in the country, complete with a fishing pond in the front, there was great excitement about my career, and many amazing opportunities were coming my way. We had three healthy and beautiful children. But Mary Beth was really struggling, and I was scared because I didn't know what to do to fix it.

I knew my career and the demands on our schedule were a constant source of tension between Mary Beth and me. Several times over the previous few years I had found myself at my wit's end and wondering if I should stop touring or maybe even quit music altogether because of the strain it was putting on our marriage and family. But at the same time, I was feeling the weight of all the expectations that came with my flourishing success. I was trying to find the right balance between my family and my career. I felt pulled in every direction.

I had heard Dr. James Dobson on the radio show *Focus on the Family* say something like, "You, as a husband, are responsible for the emotional well-being of your wife." Whether or not Dr. Dobson actually said that I'm not sure, but that's the message I heard. To me, that meant if my wife was not doing well, it was my fault. Her emotional health was my responsibility as her husband. If she was broken, I had to fix whatever had caused it. I had no idea that fixing someone—even myself—was impossible.

At the Sparrow offices, I met with what I referred to as my pastoral advisory board, which included my pastor, Scotty Smith, and my former pastor, Al Henson. I had given these men permission to speak into my life regarding my marriage and family. We were talking about an upcoming tour, but I wasn't sure my marriage could survive it. That in itself wasn't new.

For much of my career, I'd felt as if I'd lived with one hand on the microphone and one on the plug. "Okay, I'll sing you another song, but I may have to pull the plug at any moment."

I greeted the guys, and after some small talk, I began talking about the tour. But something about being with these men who genuinely cared about me, not just my work or what I could do for them, caused me to momentarily veer into an entirely different conversation. "If I were honest with you," I said quietly, "I think I could sit here and cry for a while. I feel like a failure on just about every level." Then I quickly regained my composure and got back to business. "But let's push on. Here's what I'm working on, and here are some of my song ideas for the new album and tour."

Al Henson, in his typical kind and sensitive way, stopped me and said, "Hang on, Steven. Before we get to all that business, what's going on? What do you mean you feel like a failure? What does that mean?"

"I don't know," I said. "I'm a failure as a husband. I feel like I'm failing my wife. She's in a very dark, hard place. She's overwhelmed and can't handle it, and I can't handle it. I don't know if my wife believes I love her. I don't know *how* to love her the way she needs me to love her.

"Our schedule is demanding. I'm trying to say no to some things, but it's still not enough. I'm just trying to keep all the plates spinning . . . and as a result, I don't feel like I'm doing anything very well, most importantly, taking care of my wife and my family.

"I see my wife struggling, and it breaks my heart. I've seen pastors who have regarded their ministries almost as a mistress. Or artists whose work becomes more important than their families, and they end up losing their families. I won't let that happen, I *can't* let that happen, but I know that just saying it isn't enough. I'm trying to take care of my wife. I just don't know how."

I admitted to the group that I was willing to give up my career. "I think I might have to quit," I said. "I don't know what else I'd do, but maybe I could get a job where I'd be home more. I don't think I love my career more than Mary Beth, even though she might not believe that, and I'm willing to give it all up for her." I paused and searched the eyes of the men in the room through my tears. "Guys, please help me to understand what I need to do. If you guys think I need to quit, I will. Listen to Mary Beth, listen to me; I don't want to spin it. Help us walk through this thing."

The guys in that room all knew and loved Mary Beth and cared deeply about our marriage and family. I trusted them to tell me the truth. "Steven, you keep talking about being a failure, but do you realize that you can't fail? We know you want to please God, to hear Him say, 'Well done.' Well, let us remind you of what you already know, that because of the grace of God and the fact that Jesus has already taken all the failure on Himself, it's actually impossible for you to be a failure in His eyes. That's what's so amazing about the grace of God. Just like the Bible talks about in Romans 5, you are *standing in* the grace of God right now, justified and righteous because of what Jesus has already done. You can't mess it up!"

They went on to talk about the specific struggle between Mary Beth and me. "Steven, we've watched you and Mary Beth and have counseled you both for a while on this journey, and we don't believe you quitting music is the answer. You and Mary Beth will still be broken, and you two will still have trust issues. No matter what job you have, those problems will still persist. That doesn't mean you don't need to have strong accountability and counsel in your life to keep you challenged and sensitive to loving and caring for your wife and family well. That's why we're here, but we believe you are on the journey you're supposed to be on."

It was all truth I knew in my heart, but I really needed to hear it at that moment.

The meeting continued for quite a while, and by the time I walked out the door, I felt a huge weight had been lifted off me. It was as though the breath was coming back into my lungs and my heart was beating with excitement. I left feeling incredibly encouraged, knowing that I was not alone, that despite my failures and confusion, God was not done with me. In fact, quite the opposite was true.

Because it's the way I process whatever is going on in my heart and my life, these thoughts began to take the form of a song. I started writing about a day that begins like every other day, feeling overwhelmed by all I have to do. I'm just trying to make this day better than the one before, a feeling of being trapped in this "small life" of my own making. Then as I open the Bible and read about God's grace having set me free from the prison of sin to live as a forgiven new creation in Christ, a lightning bolt flash of revelation hits me. It's as if God is saying to me, "I created you and saved you to live a life of following Me and trusting Me on a great adventure! And the great news is it's not up to you to fix everything and you can't mess this up, because I've already taken care of that on the cross. This journey is going to take us over some mountains with breathtakingly beautiful views, and there will be some very dark valleys I'll lead you through, with plenty of flatland in between. But I'll be with you and I will lead you if you'll trust me and follow me. So come on, we've got a trail to blaze . . . this is the great adventure!"

Doing my James Dean impression while shooting a music video.

Not only did I record the song as the title track for my fifth album, but I also got to make my first music video for "The Great Adventure." I wanted to try to capture the revelation and emotion I had experienced that had led me to write the song. We shot the music video in Jackson Hole, Wyoming. We constructed a small, stark room where I began singing the song, representing the small, closed-in life I experience apart from God's grace. When the chorus came, the walls fell down around me, and suddenly, I realized I had been in the middle of the wide-open spaces of the Grand Tetons the whole time, with breathtaking beauty, life, danger, and adventure all around me. It was meant to say this is life. This is what I was made for, what we all were made for as we live our lives in what Eugene Peterson refers to in the Message as the "wide open spaces of God's grace" (Rom. 5:2).

By the time I actually did the recording, we had moved into our new home. By all outward appearances, life in the Chapman home was wonderful, but I knew Mary Beth was still struggling.

There were beginning to be days when it took everything she had to get out of bed, and on a few occasions, I found her curled up in a fetal position in her closet. "I don't know what's wrong, but I can't do this," she'd cry. I'd hold her for a while and we'd pray, but I was scared, concerned, and heartbroken for my wife, and I didn't know what to do. There was just so much going on, and being the incredibly strong woman she is, she would get up and start going again, until she couldn't.

We previewed *The Great Adventure* album at the Christian Booksellers Association convention in Dallas, which at that time was a gathering of about fourteen thousand of the industry's movers and shakers, by far the biggest moment of my career up to that point. I went to Dallas for four days of rehearsal with the band prior to Mary Beth's arrival over the weekend. She planned to be with me for the promotion and album launch, including the big concert on Monday night at the convention. All totaled, I was scheduled to be in Dallas seven days. The first night I was in Dallas Mary

Beth called me from home in the wee hours of the morning and said, "I'm in so much pain; I think I'm dying."

At first, I thought Mary Beth was emotionally distraught, but no, she was talking about physical pain in her stomach and abdominal area. "Sweetheart, you can't ignore this. You might need to get to the hospital," I suggested.

"Oh no. I'll be okay," she tried to reassure me.

Thankfully, her mom was visiting and was going to stay with our children while Mary Beth was in Dallas. Around 3:00 a.m. Mary Beth crawled to her mom's bedroom and repeated her concerns. "Mom, wake up. I'm in so much pain. I think I'm dying."

Meanwhile, I was worried sick. *What should I do? Do I need to go home?* After all, I thought, *I'm responsible for the well-being of my wife.* But the record label was spending an enormous amount of money. The label had just been purchased for millions of dollars by EMI, and music mogul Jimmy Bowen was involved in the transition. I had never before played such a large arena. All the expectations were huge.

Mary Beth knew all she had to say was, "I need you here," and I would have caught the first flight or rented a car to drive home, but she had said, "I'm okay. Mom is here."

Back at home, Mary Beth called a good friend to stay with the children, and then she and her mom rushed to the emergency room. The hospital admitted her, and that morning she had emergency gall bladder surgery.

I stayed in Dallas and checked in with her mom constantly while Mary Beth was in surgery. Being the amazingly strong woman and supportive wife she has always been, Mary Beth got on a plane and flew to Dallas three days later to be with me for the launch of *The Great Adventure* album.

The concert and launch were a great success, creating enormous advance anticipation. *The Great Adventure* album was released in the fall of 1992, so we were once again gearing up for a major tour, the biggest and most involved of my career up to that time. We had a full band; all kinds of crew members; trucks filled with audio, sound, and lighting equipment; and tour buses for the band and the crew. Even with all the excitement, I felt the heavy burden to come through for everyone. In addition to the concerts, in every city I was scheduled for television or radio interviews, meet-and-greet events, and all the things that go into making a concert tour successful.

A day before the tour was to begin, I was home dealing with last-minute details. Dan Raines came to our house, and we were talking through yet more schedule changes and some additional concert dates and interviews. This was going to be big, and life was going to get even crazier.

Dan, Mary Beth, and I were standing in our driveway discussing all that was ahead of us when I began to sense the fear and frustration building in my wife.

Tears welled in her eyes, and then she lost it completely, screaming and crying. I tried to calm her, but she was inconsolable. Finally, I picked her up and carried her into the house, kicking and screaming. She was terrified, and so was I.

She had been through surgery alone, she was trying to get settled into a new house alone, I was getting ready to leave for the biggest tour of my career while she stayed home with three young children alone, and all the sadness had finally exploded into a rage.

Dan stayed with us until Mary Beth calmed down. He told us about a friend in his church, a Christian psychiatrist, and suggested we talk to him.

At that point, I was willing to talk to anyone who could help us. Both Mary Beth and I had always been open to wise counsel, but this seemed different, and we felt more desperate than ever.

We went to the doctor, and after listening to the story of our struggles and unique challenges, he helped us understand that Mary Beth was suffering from clinical depression. He began to connect the dots of what Mary Beth had been feeling and experiencing for a long time. While the diagnosis certainly didn't make everything okay, it did begin to bring some much needed clarity to our struggle. He talked about using medicine to help balance out some of what was going on physiologically.

Both Mary Beth and I expressed our concerns about her having to take pills to be able to function in a more healthy way. I still felt a heavy weight of responsibility to fix what part of this brokenness was my doing, and I was sure much of it was. Maybe we just needed to pray and read the Bible more and try harder. The doctor understood our concerns but said, "Look, we take medicine for high blood pressure or to control cholesterol. This is no different. As many counselors have told you, you do have some unique challenges in your life and need to continue to address those. But your body is not operating the way God designed it to function. There is something going on within your brain chemistry. Certain levels are out of balance, but that can be helped with medication."

My heart broke as I began to realize everything my wife had been dealing with. This clearly wasn't a matter of choosing not to be sad or frustrated, or deciding to be happier and trust God more.

We talked with our pastor, Scotty Smith, who also encouraged us to be open to the medical help. "Most Christians are reluctant even to talk about such things until they are on the other side of it," he said. "But this is a much more common situation than you know, and medicine can be a gift from God to help." We were grateful for his wise counsel.

It was (and has continued to be) very hard for me to watch my wife battle depression. Even to this day I sometimes wrestle with questions such as, *Could I have done something else that might have helped? Would my wife have struggled less had I done things differently?* Nevertheless, it was a milestone for us when we realized that God wasn't necessarily going to fix things simply because we prayed harder or *did better.* We were going to have to live with the brokenness and hold on to each other and the promises of God.[1]

In the midst of this situation, I wrote the song "Go There with You." Like the song "I Will Be Here," many people resonated with the lyrics and drew strength and encouragement from them. But like so many of my songs, it came as a result of my own struggles. It was so important for me to say to Mary Beth, "Wherever this takes you, as dark as it might get, as unfixable as it is, I want to be there for you and go there with you, wherever this journey takes us."

The truth underlying all our hurt and struggle was that we were in an intense spiritual battle. Mary Beth and I were committed to our marriage, and I had even written songs like "I Will Be Here," declaring our commitment loud and clear. We were battling a real enemy who hates that we would stand as a couple committed to God and to each other. I knew the fact that I had written about marriage invited attacks from the enemy, who was trying to take us out, as had happened to so many other well-meaning, God-honoring couples. We were aware of that and had discussed it frequently with our friends and counselors. The enemy seemed to know our vulnerabilities and weaknesses, and we were learning the importance of keeping ourselves surrounded by those who would stand with us and fight for us.

The only thing we could do was declare to each other what we knew to be true: There is an enemy, but you are not the enemy; I am not the enemy. We are in this thing together, and as long as we stay committed to Jesus and to each other, nothing can tear us apart.

And only God can fix us. That was an ongoing lesson for me. It still is and will be until we get to heaven.

Backstage at the Dove Awards with Emily.

Chapter Fifteen

His Strength Is Perfect

Despite her ongoing battle with depression, Mary Beth never lost her sense of humor or desire for a good party. As I was nearing the end of The Great Adventure tour, Mary Beth announced to me that we had been invited by our good friends, Brent and Laurie Lamb, to a pajama party. The idea of dressing up in pajamas to spend the evening with friends at a hotel ballroom in downtown Nashville sounded like torture to me. But Mary Beth reminded me that I had been gone on the road for quite a while and this was something she really wanted to do. So in a moment of weakness, I agreed and decided to make the best of it. I went shopping and purchased a pair of the most ridiculous pajamas I could find, one-piece knicker pajamas with a button-up flap in the back and little penguins printed all over them. I decided if we were gonna do this we were gonna do it right. What I didn't know was that it was a huge setup to get me to a surprise thirtieth birthday party. Mary Beth convinced me to leave the house in our pajamas without a change of clothes. (In an evil twist, she had already packed some clothes for *herself* and hidden them in the trunk of the car, but her plan was to leave me in my pajamas for the evening.)

We walked into the hotel ballroom, and immediately my mind told me we had walked into the wrong room. There were about two hundred people in the room all looking at us . . . and all dressed up in nice *normal* clothes. My immediate instinct was to turn around and run out the door,

At my surprise 30th birthday party with my mom and my grandpa and grandma Rudd.

which I did. But as my mind began to process the last few seconds that had just passed, questions began to race through my mind: *Is that my grandmother and my grandfather in the front of that group of people? Is that my best friend from high school and the president of my record label standing behind them? Did I just hear "Happy Birthday, Steven" shouted out by that large group of well-dressed people in that room?* It slowly dawned on me that I had been *had*! My wife had tricked me into a surprise birthday pajama party in which I was the only one wearing pajamas! She, of course, quickly went and changed into nice dress clothes. It turned out to be an amazing night of laughter and fun thanks to my wonderful (and somewhat wicked) wife.

The song "His Strength Is Perfect," which I recorded on my second album, came from my confrontations with the places in my life where I felt weak and inadequate. Whether it was as a husband, as a dad, as a follower of Jesus, or even as a singer/songwriter who wanted to use his gifts to the glory of God, it seemed like I was (and continue to be) constantly reminded of my weakness. I was the kid who had written the song about wanting to hear Jesus say, "Well done . . . you did well with all that I entrusted to you" when He returned. How could I do well with all this obvious weakness in my life?

Just like my very first song, so many have been written as a response to my understanding and experiencing the transforming truth of God's Word in my personal experience. I was so encouraged when I discovered that one of the greatest followers of Jesus, the apostle Paul, in his own intense struggle with weakness, came to this amazing realization: "My grace is sufficient for thee: for my strength is made perfect in weakness" (2 Cor. 12:9 KJV). In that same verse, Paul goes on to add, "Most gladly, therefore, I will rather boast about my weaknesses, so that the power of Christ may dwell in me" (2 Cor. 12:9 NASB).

According to Paul's experience and God's Word, the places of weakness and brokenness in my life are actually the very places where the power of Christ can be seen and experienced at its greatest. This was really great news.

Maybe there is a place at the table for me after all, I thought. And apparently, God continually wants to bring me back to that realization by reminding me, "I can use you if you continue to depend on Me in your brokenness."

When it came to my voice, for example, I felt I had a very fickle, fragile, inconsistent instrument. Sometimes it worked well, and at other times, it didn't. I felt audiences expected better from me, so I tried to give it to them and almost felt guilty that I was some sort of fraud when I couldn't.

Even after I won five Dove Awards in one year, a little voice still haunted me, saying, "Sooner or later, somebody is going to demand a recount!" Not that plenty of music reviewers didn't question my singing abilities. They did! But somehow my songs seemed to break through to the public and bypassed the barricades raised by the reviewers.

In the recording studio, I struggled with my voice as well. It seemed that every time I worked on an album, my voice grew weak and started to fail. Living in Tennessee has never helped either, where allergies pose a constant challenge for singers. (Ironically, any allergy doctor will tell you that Music City is a terrible place for singers to live because of all the allergens floating in the natural basin in which Nashville is located.) I went to the doctors, and they loaded me up with all sorts of medical concoctions to get me through. I joked that someday I was going to be stripped of all my awards for "juicing" because I had so much medication in me while making the albums.

Because I was performing in front of larger crowds, I felt an increasing burden to make sure that what I was saying onstage was biblically accurate. I knew what the Bible said about teachers having even greater responsibilities and accountability before God (James 3:1), and although I didn't really consider myself a teacher, I was the guy with the microphone in front of thousands of people.

My sense of inadequacy was further reinforced after one of my early album successes, when I was invited to the Last Days Artist Retreat hosted by Melody Green, wife of the late Keith Green. A great group of Christian artists such as Dallas Holm, Matthew Ward, Phil Keaggy, and about forty others gathered in Lindale, Texas, for a couple of days simply to encourage one another, hear some insightful speakers, and pray together. Although the retreat was inspiring, it raised more questions for me. I wondered, *Am I really equipped for this? These guys seem to understand so much more of the Bible than I do. Maybe I need to stop what I'm doing and go to Bible school.* I had taken a few biblically based classes at Anderson, but I'd never attended Bible school. *Maybe I should*, I thought.

Yet God seemed to be using me in that place where I was not confident in my own abilities, in my voice, or in my biblical knowledge.

I studied hard to improve my understanding of the Bible and read books such as *The Pursuit of God* by A. W. Tozer and others that attempted to grapple with deeper theological issues. So I wasn't being lazy; I was just very aware of my inadequacies.

And it seemed that any time I began to feel more confident about my singing, I'd get sick again and start struggling with my voice. I wouldn't lose my voice completely, but it would grow raspy and scratchy, and I wouldn't have the confidence that I could hit some of the high notes in my songs during my live concerts. That became a self-fulfilling prophecy.

Following the success of *The Great Adventure* album, my record label wanted to do a live recording and video in Seattle in May 1993. At that time, I was doing an energetic show, wearing a headset microphone and running all over the stage and out into the audience. I was compared by *Billboard* magazine to Garth Brooks, saying I was the guy who might take Christian music to the masses, similar to the way Garth had crossed all music genre lines with his concerts.

The record label secured the services of High Five, the top-tier production company that had produced Garth's big events, to produce the video. It was a huge deal, with multiple tractor-trailer trucks packed with equipment off-loading into the arena, a big stage, and cameras on cranes shooting from every angle, including backstage.

The record company was pouring an enormous amount of time, money, and effort into the project, and then it happened. With all the pressure of this huge production, four or five days before the concert, my voice went south on me again. By the night of the concert, I was in the worst voice I had experienced in a long time. I didn't feel terrible physically, and I could talk, but I couldn't hit the notes at the top of my range. I sounded like I was fourteen years old and going through puberty again! Of course, everyone around me, including Mary Beth, kept trying to encourage me by saying things such as, "Oh, it's not that bad," which I knew was code for, "Dude, you sound awful!"

We couldn't reschedule the concert and video shoot because it was a sold-out venue, plus the elaborate advance production equipment and personnel were all in place.

Why, of all times, could my voice not be strong? I wondered. I instantly knew the answer. Because it's me!

We did the entire concert with my voice weak and raspy. I could talk softly, but singing really was a great adventure! I never knew what sort of sound might come out of my mouth. I had to give it my best effort, though, because even if we could clean up my vocals in postproduction, this was a video production and I had to "sell" the songs during my live performance. So if I backed off the high notes because I was afraid I couldn't hit them, that wouldn't be good. On the other hand, if I went for the high notes and missed them, my face would show it, and the audience would cringe, "Ooo, he really can't sing!"

I didn't want to disappoint the crowd, but I figured I might as well admit my problem. "Guys, I'm really struggling vocally tonight," I told them, "and I hate it for you, because I want to be my very best for you, so I'm gonna do my best to give you more." Despite my weaknesses, the Seattle audience was tremendously supportive, and we had a great time together. The crowd was amazing, and the video was outstanding.

But when we listened back to my recorded vocals, I knew I had to sing some of them when I was in better voice. To replicate the sound of me

Me and my cowboys, Caleb and Will Franklin, on the lookout for bad guys.

singing while running through the crowd and all over the stage, I went outside the studio and ran up and down the street. Then I came back in, and my producer, Phil Naish, tried to match the out-of-breath sound I had live onstage that night. The live concert video won a Dove Award, the song "Go There with You" won a Dove Award for pop/contemporary song of the year, and I received a Grammy Award—my third—for best pop/contemporary gospel album in 1994. Clearly, God was showing me again that He could use His gifts through me even when I didn't feel I was at my best. As much as I didn't like it, because I really wanted to do my craft well, He kept bringing me back to the truth that His strength really is perfect in my weakness.

Being away from my family during the early years of my career was always hard on both Mary Beth and me, not to mention the kids. I love being a dad. I love being with my family more than anyone else in the world. Besides Mary Beth, I've always felt that my children are some of my very best friends, so being away from them has never been easy for me. Mary Beth was great about reminding our children, "Your daddy loves you, but he has to be gone right now. He'll be home soon." My wife handled all of the home-life details while I was away, including Emily's dance rehearsals and Caleb's and Will's soccer games. I tried hard to be home every chance possible, but inevitably, there were many events I sadly had to miss.

When six-year-old Caleb and five-year-old Will were playing their first soccer season, Mary Beth took them to every practice and to every game. I was on a big tour at the time, so other than a few practices on weekdays when I was home, I was missing the whole season, and I hated it.

After I had missed the boys' first five or six games, our tour swept into Dallas. I checked airline schedules to see if I could possibly swing home for even a few hours, attend their Saturday morning soccer game, and still get back in time for my concert that evening. I found a flight that left before dawn, so if I got up at 4:00 a.m. and raced to DFW airport, I could get into

Nashville in time for the early game on Saturday. A 2:00 p.m. flight would get me back in time to take the stage, as long as there wasn't too much traffic between the airport and downtown. I wouldn't have the luxury of doing a sound check, but we'd been on tour for a while now, and the engineers had everything fairly well set. I decided to do it.

My management team must have thought I was crazy, but they worked with me to make the trip home happen. After staying up late on Friday night following our concert, I pulled myself out of bed at 4:00 in the morning. I made it to DFW and on to Nashville in time to get to the 10:00 a.m. soccer game.

Mary Beth and I were having a great time watching the game when there was a lull in the action—as there often is during soccer games among six-year-olds—so Mary Beth said, "I'll be right back." She nodded toward the porta-potties at the end of the field.

Mary Beth had been gone only a minute or two when Caleb suddenly broke away from the pack. He started dribbling the ball with his feet, kicking the ball down the field, weaving between the defensive players. He finally took a strong kick—from a few feet in front of the net—and scored his very first soccer goal!

I was so excited that I ran out onto the field shouting, "Yeah! Way to go, Caleb!" I instinctively lifted him up onto my shoulders and paraded him back toward the sidelines. The other parents understood. It was "Little League" soccer, after all.

Just then Mary Beth returned from the restroom. "What? What happened?" she asked.

"Didn't you see? Caleb just scored his first goal!" a friend said to her.

Mary Beth's mouth dropped wide open. "He what? And I missed it? Noooo!"

Mary Beth is far more competitive about sports than I am, and she had been there for every practice and every game. I had swept in for two hours between tour dates and had witnessed Caleb's first goal.

I made it back to Dallas just in time for the show that night, still on cloud nine from seeing my boys play soccer and Caleb's momentous first goal. Over the years, I've flown home on a number of occasions, catching red-eye flights to get home for only a few hours to attend one of Emily's recitals, or a school play, or one of the boys' games. Sure, the extra efforts have come at a price, but the rewards of being there for and with my kids and Mary Beth have been more than worth it.

Consequently, I have a practically nonexistent golf game. When people ask me to play in charity tournaments, it is usually a terribly embarrassing experience for me, because I've just not played very often. In the same way, I have a motorcycle that I ride only a few times a year. It's not that I don't enjoy those things, but there are choices we all make about how we're going to spend the time we've been given. I've tried as best I know how to let my family know they are the most important thing on this earth that God has given me, besides my relationship with Him.

Yes, there are times when I have to work, when I have to be away from home when my family would prefer that I be with them, just like many dads. I will be the first to say I have done it far from perfectly, and thankfully, my wife and family have been incredibly patient and forgiving, and God has been faithful. But through the years, as I've made the effort to be at every event possible with my family, even if it involved saying no to some great opportunities, I've never regretted it. By the grace of God, I have an amazing relationship and friendship with my children to this day. I am a blessed man.

Celebrating three albums achieving Gold record status.
(With Bruce Koblish, president of GMA.)

Chapter Sixteen

A Road Called Adoption

For some time, our eleven-year-old daughter, Emily, had been lobbying Mary Beth and me for a sister. Her Christmas or birthday list one year included a new bike and a baby sister. Mary Beth and I smiled at her requests and said, "We have three wonderful children; we're good with that number."

In 1997, Mary Beth and Emily took a trip to Haiti along with Compassion International, a relief organization with which we had been associated for a number of years. Our friend Terri Coley and her daughter Carrie accompanied my wife and daughter on the trip. Everyone was profoundly affected by the pervasive, abject poverty affecting many people in Haiti, but the group was especially touched by the needs of the children in Haiti's orphanages. Emily returned home with a passion to help the children who had no parents. She began to talk to us about adopting a child who needed a family. "We have a nice home and plenty of food, and I'll even share my room and all my stuff," she told us.

Emily was so convinced God wanted our family to adopt that she began praying that Mary Beth and I would see the light. She wrote letters to us explaining why adoption made perfectly good sense to her eleven-year-old mind. She even told us in one of her letters, "If you don't seriously consider adoption, you could be living in disobedience to God's will."

Who could argue with that?

While it might seem unusual to some people that Mary Beth and I would take Emily seriously, we had raised our children to have a heart for God and compassion for people in need. We certainly didn't want to discount her concerns for children without parents, even though we had no intention of adopting a child. We had three biological children of our own to care for, and our job of raising them to adulthood was far from complete.

Still, Emily was pretty relentless, and I had to admit that her sudden interest in adoption resonated with me. We had a few friends who had opened their homes to foster and adopt children who didn't have a family, and I was convinced that adopting a child could be an amazing experience that would deepen our understanding of God's love for us like nothing else could. After all, we were all our heavenly Father's "adopted children," so adoption must have a special place in God's heart. And as a guy who had spent so many years pondering and writing songs about the love of God and how to really experience it in a tangible way, I couldn't imagine anything more tangible than adoption. Consequently, when Emily raised the issue of adoption, I didn't rule it out and even considered that God could possibly be using Emily to communicate something to us.

I tried to be careful about what I said to Mary Beth, however. Because of my past mistakes in our marriage, when I had given the impression that she wasn't spiritual enough, I knew I needed to be careful. So I simply prayed, "God, I'm open to the idea of bringing another child into our family through adoption. I'm ready and willing and could even get very excited about it. But if this is part of Your plan, You will have to convince Mary Beth." I knew if an adoption was supposed to take place, it would have to be God who made it happen.

It wasn't that Mary Beth wouldn't be open to the idea. There's not a more loving, compassionate person on earth. She has an incredible sense of righting what is wrong in the world, and her heart was deeply moved by what she saw in Haiti. At her insistence, we had already been involved in supporting organizations and families that were committed to caring for

courtesy of the Gospel Music Association

Attending the Dove Awards together.

"the least of these." But in her practical manner, she had very reasonable and logical questions and concerns about what it would look like to add another child to our already very busy and full life.

Of course, this was a different approach for me, taking my hands off the situation, consciously trying *not* to fix it, and truly trusting God to work out the details. And while this new approach was challenging for me, it also brought a great sense of freedom with it, for I knew that if it was God's plan for us to adopt a child, He would be the one to make it happen. I knew what I was *not* going to do, but I sure was interested in seeing what God would do.

Over the next several months, any time the issue of adoption came up—which it did often, thanks to Emily—I was careful with my language even around the kids. I'd say things such as, "Well, guys, we are seriously praying about it, but adoption is something we all have to believe is right for our family, especially Mom."

If we said yes to adoption, that meant we were going to have to say no to many other things, and our calendar and my schedule were already a constant source of tension for Mary Beth and me. I prayed sincerely, "God, please show us what to do, and help me know how to lead my family. I don't want to do the wrong thing or the right thing for the wrong reasons."

I realized something was very different about this prayer. The first time—and every time—I prayed about not wanting to do "the wrong thing" in this case, I sensed God's gentle but clear answer: "Do you really think you are going to do the wrong thing by adopting a child who doesn't have a family and bringing that child into your home and your life?" He seemed to emphasize the phrase "a child who doesn't have a family." I sensed Him saying, "Whatever happens, I'm going to be with you in this. That doesn't mean it will all be easy, but this is who I am; I am the Father to the fatherless, and I will provide and take care of you."

This was not like talking about a business deal, or taking a new job, or purchasing a piece of property.

"You are doing 'true religion'; you are right in the middle of what I say is My heart for you. I am obligated by My own promise to care and provide for you. I'm going to take care of you because I have already called you to do this—to care for orphans and widows. Whatever you have done unto the least of these, you have done unto Me. This is like inviting Me into your home."

Yet over a period of months, in my reluctance to do anything without certainty of success, I kept asking, "Are You sure about this, God? I don't want to do the wrong thing."

"It's not the wrong thing!" I could hear Him saying over a spiritual loudspeaker to my heart and mind.

Nevertheless, I continued to wrestle in prayer. As I mentioned earlier, I have this strange condition my friend Scotty Smith calls "the paralysis of analysis." It probably stems in some ways from the pool skimmer experience in my childhood, among other things. I'm one of those people who desperately tries not to do the wrong thing. If I'm not completely sure something is the right thing to do, I don't want to do it, or I keep asking until I have figured out the next step.

But faith doesn't work like that.

"God, I need confirmation . . ."

"No, you need to trust."

For one of the first and only times in my life, I laid out a fleece before the Lord. "Okay, God, I trust You, and I'm willing. So if You really want us to do this, please have my wife come to me, commit to us adopting a child, and say, 'I think we're supposed to do this.' I'm not going to try to talk her into it. If this really is Your plan for our family I'm going to trust that You will make it clear to my wife without me having to say anything."

Meanwhile, Emily kept up her full-court press. She wrote more letters, and in at least one she reminded Mary Beth that she had three able-bodied children to help her. Emily had eight-year-old Will Franklin and nine-year-old Caleb scrawl their signatures at the bottom of her adoption pledge as witnesses. We still have that letter. We kept it in case we ever needed to cash in on their services.

Emily bought a book about international adoption using money relatives had given her in birthday cards. She read it to Mary Beth, pointing out interesting facts she had gleaned from the book, as they rode home from school and to soccer practice and any other opportunity in which she had her mom as a captive audience. This girl was tenacious!

Although she had made no commitments, in an unguarded moment with me, Mary Beth had commented, "If and when I think about adoption, for some reason I picture a little baby girl from Asia."

Well, I thought, *that's a start.*

The kids' campaign did all the pushing; I simply stayed on the sidelines and prayed. When I was asked to sing at a benefit event for Bethany Christian Services, a Christian adoption agency, held at a hotel ballroom in downtown Nashville, I took Emily along with me. Mary Beth conveniently had to take the boys to a soccer event that night, but she did make a deal with Emily that she would read any information Emily wanted to bring home to her.

Much of the Bethany event centered around adoptions in China, which was their focus at the time, to the point of even discounting their administrative fees. A discount? That really piqued Emily's imagination, so she loaded up on materials about adopting from China. "Mom can't pass up a good deal!" she said.

Ever so slowly, like a cruise ship turning incrementally into port, Mary Beth's heart began to turn toward adoption, but she still had several obstacles blocking the way. "Okay," she said, "because we have three children already, we are over the limit China allows families to have to adopt Chinese children." Mary Beth had been reading up on adoptions.

"Well, is it worth a phone call?" I asked.

"All right, if you want to call Bethany Christian Services and ask them, fine. But it says here in the book that if you have three biological children in the home, you can't adopt from China."

The next day, while Mary Beth and I were in the car, I called Bethany Christian Services. "I have a question," I began. "We already have three children at home. That negates our ability to adopt from China, right?"

The woman from Bethany replied, "You know what? That *was* the case, but just a month ago the Chinese government raised the number to four children in the home."

"Oh, really?" I said, trying hard not to smile. I looked over at Mary Beth and said, "Well, sweetheart, apparently the Chinese government changed that law last month. Now you can have up to four biological children in the home—and still adopt."

Mary Beth's eyes widened. "Okay . . . well, I read that most children being adopted from China are two to three years old. Can you ask them if that's still the case?" Even though she had been slow to admit it, Mary Beth had already been having thoughts and even a dream about a baby girl from China. Whenever she even considered the idea, for reasons we would only know later, her mind always went to the picture of a little girl about nine months old. "Ask about the age of the children Bethany is placing." She whispered, "They probably aren't placing babies under the age of one."

I turned my attention back to the woman still on the phone. "Can you answer another question for me? What general age are the children being adopted right now?"

"Well, the babies we are seeing adopted right now are usually somewhere between eight and ten months old," she said.

"Wow . . . okay. Can you please hold on a second?"

I turned again to Mary Beth and repeated the information. "Any more questions?" I asked her.

I recognized that the cruise ship had started to move, so we decided to pray more seriously about the possibility of adopting in general and adopting from China specifically. Mary Beth and I spent a day together discussing the possibility, and strangely, everything we saw reminded us of China. At one point, just for fun, we started discussing what we might name another little girl in the highly unlikely event that we might adopt. Mary Beth mentioned that she had always loved the name Hannah, which means "gift of God's grace." Randomly, I said something like, "If we actually adopted a little girl at this point in our lives, it would kinda be like Abraham and Sarah in the Bible . . . you know, how Sarah laughed at the idea that God would really add a child to their lives when they thought it was impossible, and that's why their son was given the name Isaac, which means 'laughter.' We should find out what the Chinese word is for laughter and put that in her name . . . kind of like our Isaac."

I was half joking, although I did think it would be a pretty cool story if we actually ended up adopting. But how in the world would we ever find out the Mandarin word for laughter anyway?

Later that afternoon, I accompanied Mary Beth to a doctor's appointment. While in the waiting room, I randomly picked up a *Reader's Digest* magazine and flipped it open. There I found an article about a Chinese couple's desperate search to find a cure for their son who had an unusual heart disease. The story stated that the boy's name was Shao-Han. They called him Shao Shao. Then in parentheses it said, "Shao comes from the Mandarin word *Xiao*, which means 'laughter.'" What? There it was! The Chinese word for laughter . . . and it was used in a name! And the last part of the name Shao-Han was also part of the name Hannah, which Mary Beth had mentioned liking earlier. Her name would have to be Shao-Hannah.

"Mary Beth! You are not going to believe this!" I handed her the magazine and told her to read the article. I watched her face and waited for the reaction. And wow! Was there ever a reaction! She screamed and dropped the magazine to the floor in shock.

The ship had turned.

It was as if God was smiling and saying, "Okay, so you wanted to know the Chinese word for laughter and if it would work in a name? We checked that one off the list. What else?"

That experience, along with our phone call to Bethany, was teaching me something about the heart of God that I hadn't really considered before. He loves to surprise us. He has an incredible sense of humor, and He loves laughter. He even knows the Chinese word for laughter! I hadn't thought a lot about God having fun before, but I began to realize that if He created everything, He also created fun. Joy and delight and surprises and, yes, even fun are all His ideas, and it seemed like He was having a lot of fun taking us on this journey.

About a week later, we were driving down Hillsboro Road together as a family. As usual, the kids were badgering us about adoption. "Mom, Dad, are we gonna adopt? Can we adopt a baby from China?"

Although their persistence was a little annoying on one level, it was a beautiful thing on another. After all, they weren't begging to go to Disney World, or for a new bicycle, or for something frivolous.

"Okay, listen up," I said. "Here's what we can tell you. We are on Hillsboro Road right now. You guys may not know this, but there is a little town known as Hillsboro, and if we stayed on this road long enough, we'd arrive at that town. So we're gonna get on Adoption Road."

The kids interrupted me with wild cheers. "Yeah! All right! We're on the road!"

"Whoa, slow down," I cautioned. "We'll get on Adoption Road. Whether or not we will ever get to Adoption we're not sure about yet. We may have to make some turns. There may be some detours. We may hit a roadblock and go somewhere else. But from Mom's and my perspective, we're willing to head down the road. We'll see where God directs us. Can you guys be okay with that?"

Another cheer rose in the back of the car. "Yeah, yeah! We're on the road!"

Not only were Emily, Caleb, and Will able to comprehend my illustration, but that concept gave Mary Beth a sense of peace as well. The pressure was off. We were on a journey, but at any point, God could redirect our path.

He could recalculate the GPS at His discretion. More importantly, He could lead us as we took each step—or not. That was liberating for Mary Beth. It really was a step of faith in a way she had never previously experienced.

A short time later, she and I were doing a magazine interview by phone, with both of us on the call at the same time, Mary Beth on the house phone and me sitting outside on the porch steps. At some point in the interview, the subject of adoption came up. We mentioned that with great trepidation we were praying about adopting a child.

Sitting on the porch, listening to Mary Beth respond, I heard her say, "I've come to the realization that if I am going to live by faith, I'm going to have to take some steps in the dark. I don't like that. I like to know where I'm going. I like to see everything laid out neatly. I'm organized, and my husband drives me crazy with his creativity and spontaneity. But I realize that faith in God implies that you are taking a journey into the unknown and you are trusting that God is going to be there."

I was amazed at what I was hearing, but Mary Beth wasn't done. "I've called myself a woman of faith for years," she said, "but I think this is the first time I've trusted when I can't see. So we're going to take the next steps, trusting God and believing that this is the direction we should go."

Tears welled in my eyes. I had asked God to let me hear the words from Mary Beth's mouth. This was a confirmation in my heart and mind that we were supposed to adopt.

Jamming with my boys on the back porch.

Chapter Seventeen

Tuesday's Child

"Monday's child is fair of face; Tuesday's child is full of grace," states an old rhyme first found in A. E. Bray's *Traditions of Devonshire*. That has been my prayer and my goal any time I have had an opportunity to represent Jesus in a mainstream environment. One such opportunity came in a most unusual manner.

The same year Emily and Mary Beth took the life-changing trip to Haiti I experienced a mission trip of a different sort—I was asked to be a part of the team that announced the Grammy Award nominees to the world during a nationally televised press conference in New York. Along with four other presenters—Richard Marx, Jewel, B. B. King, and rapper Busta Rhymes—it was my honor to read the names of the nominees.

Prior to the press conference, I was sharing a dressing room with Richard Marx when I overheard someone tell Richard, "I hear Stuttering John is going to be here for the press junket today, so be on the lookout."

I knew very little about Stuttering John other than he was a character on *The Howard Stern Show* and was known for asking shocking, inane, or crude questions during interviews.

Following the presentation of the nominees, each presenter worked the press junket separately, going from interviewer to interviewer answering questions. All of the exchanges were similar, with the only differences being the logos on the microphones. Most of the questions were expected, such as, "Hey, Steven Curtis Chapman, you've won a Grammy. How does that feel?" My answers were equally typical.

For me, interviews are one of the most stressful things I do because I never know what questions are coming. But I've always believed that part of why God has given me the platform I have is so I can try in some small way to bring the light of Jesus into these places with me. The Scripture passage 1 Peter 3:15 has always been a great reminder to me whenever I'm in such situations: to always be ready to give a reason for the hope that is in me, and to do it with gentleness and respect. That's what I've tried to do.

I had done an interview with all the major networks, including CNN, E! Entertainment Television, FOX, and a host of others, when a disheveled guy who looked like he'd just walked in off the street approached me with a camera and a microphone. His camera looked like a home video camera. Mr. Disheveled stuck the microphone in front of my face. "So what's your name?"

"Steven Curtis Chapman."

"And you were nominated for a Grammy today?"

"Yeah, I was."

"What's your category?"

"Gospel music," I said. "Best pop gospel male performance."

"Oh, okay." He looked as if the wheels in his mind were turning, as though he knew he was on to something. "So what do you think about Howard Stern?"

Suddenly, it was as if fireworks began going off in my brain. My heart started racing, and my mouth got as dry as cotton. With the cameras rolling and the microphone in my face, I knew there was no good answer, and I suddenly realized, *This is Stuttering John, and I'm on* The Howard Stern Show *right now!* Although I hadn't noticed a logo on the microphone, there was no doubt in my mind.

A few weeks earlier, while channel surfing on our television at home, I had run across the Stern spectacle. The "show" featured little more than the host, Howard Stern, and his cohorts making degrading comments about the physical anatomies of various strippers—not exactly the kind of fare you would want your kids to watch, or yourself for that matter. I could hardly believe that such a thing would even be on television. I changed the channel but had seen enough to know that *The Howard Stern Show* was bad news. Before seeing that clip of his show, I hadn't known much about Stern other than the fact that he was quite successful and had been around a long time in New York as a shock jock radio broadcaster before moving to television.

So when the disheveled interviewer asked for my opinion of Howard Stern, I wanted to say something bright and clever, something that would give an account for the hope I have, something that would speak the truth in love . . . all those things I had prayed about ahead of time for moments like this. What I really wanted to do at that moment was to take the easy road and say, "I don't watch the guy and don't know enough about him to make an informed comment." But I had seen enough of his show to know I couldn't just plead the fifth. I thought to myself, *Okay, Chapman, are you ready to step up? For such a time as this, are you ready to take a stand? You have this moment to try to bring some truth and light into the darkness, so here it goes . . .*

I took a deep breath, and after a long pause—a really long pause—I said the first thoughts that came to my mind. "Well, I have kids . . ." I stopped and swallowed hard ". . . I'm a dad. Television is accessible to kids. And there's a platform that we have access to when we stand behind the microphone, and honestly, I think Howard Stern is a guy who misuses the platform he has. He obviously has gifts and abilities, and he has access to a lot of people . . . but I think he is irresponsible with his platform." So that was it? The platform speech? It wasn't bad, and I believed it was true, but I was already thinking, *I wish I could've done better . . . and please let this be over now.*

I could see Mr. Disheveled perk up at my answer. "Okay," he said. "So do you have a message for Howard Stern?"

"Yes," I said, "I do." I took another deep breath, looked into the camera, and said, "Howard, obviously you are a talented guy and you were made for a purpose. I believe that purpose was to know the God who made you. That's what I sing about; it's what I believe. God loves you, and I believe He has a great purpose for you, but I don't believe it is what you are doing now and the way you are doing it. I hope you will find it, because I know that God loves you and has a great plan for your life. I hope you will find it."

Mr. Disheveled looked at me and deadpanned, "Okay, last question. Would you marry Rosie O'Donell for a million dollars?"

This one was easy. "No, I'm happily married. Thanks," I replied with a smile.

"All right, thanks a lot; see ya later!" The interviewer hustled away. As soon as he did, I let out a huge sigh and immediately began second-guessing my answers. A strange mix of emotions came over me. I was thankful I had spoken the truth as best as I could under the circumstances, but I also felt like I had just been in a fight. My stomach was turning, and I wanted to run to a corner and cry. I hoped the producers would find my answers too boring and the interview would disappear.

Nope. About two months later, Howard Stern aired the interview. One of the host's sidekicks said to Stern, "Hey, we were at the Grammy Awards press conference the other day, and we ran across this guy. You're going to have some fun with this."

They started watching the clip. As I spoke, Stern interjected, "Who is this idiot? He sounds like Mr. Rogers."

"So what category are you nominated for?"

"Gospel music."

Howard hit the pause button. "Oh no; oh boy. We've got us a *Christian*. Now this is going to be interesting. He can't totally blast me because he's a Christian, so he's gotta be nice, but he can't let me off the hook because everything I do goes against everything he stands for."

Amazingly, they let the entire clip play in split screen while they continued to pan me and everything I said. But the viewing audience could hear my words coming through. They played that clip several times over the next months because it stirred people up and helped with ratings.

When I saw clips of the show, that familiar sick feeling returned. I wondered, *Am I embarrassed because I looked foolish? Because I wasn't as articulate as I would have hoped? Is it my pride that is feeling beaten up? Was I a fool for Christ or just a fool who should have walked away the moment I realized I was deep in hostile territory?* Thankfully, God uses even our most feeble efforts to honor Him.

Sometime later, I heard the story of a Christian woman whose husband was not a believer, and one of the things she disliked about his lifestyle was that he watched Howard Stern's show regularly. She prayed, "God, how can I reach him and not simply yell at him?" One night she decided to sit down and watch Stern's show with her husband just to be with him.

"Who came on the show but Steven Curtis Chapman? My husband got offended at Howard Stern for attacking him and the Christian beliefs that he knew were important to me." She said her husband started going to church with her as a result of that eye-opening exchange. God really does work in some mysterious ways.

It was a lesson for me. I always want to give the right answer, but I hadn't. I didn't fix anything. Nobody said, "Yes, I'm really convicted about that. I think I want to trust Jesus." But at least one husband started a fresh journey with his wife as a result of the encounter in which I felt I had failed to represent the Lord well. It was a poignant reminder of the truth: God never calls us to be successful; He calls us to be faithful.

For quite a while after the Stern affair, I carried a deep conviction to pray for Howard Stern. I've often wondered if there might be another opportunity down the road for me to meet Howard and to share the truth of the gospel with him in a kind, gentle manner. It's been years since that show first aired, and I have yet to meet Howard, but I still have hope.

A few years later, I was nominated for an American Music Award. Although I didn't expect to win, I prepared some remarks ahead of time just in case I had the opportunity to stand at a microphone and make some comments.

Whenever I'm given the opportunity to represent the message of God's love and the gospel, my hope is to be a Tuesday's child, full of grace. I want to be unafraid and bold about speaking the truth but not offensive in the way I do it.

Jimmy Kimmel was the host of the American Music Awards show the night I was nominated in the inspirational artist of the year category. In his opening monologue, Jimmy cracked, "Okay, before we get started, here are some simple rules for the night. We're gonna keep our acceptance speeches short . . . you don't need to thank your mom and dad. We know you love them. There will be no thanking God tonight. God isn't watching the show." Jimmy's comments were meant to be funny, but I had already prepared some comments just in case I won. I had prayerfully considered what I wanted to say, hoping in some way to honor God with the opportunity.

As the show commenced, I sat in my seat praying for wisdom, fully aware that my accomplishments were not mine alone. In all such moments, I realize that, on the one hand, these moments have no eternal value in themselves, yet on the other hand, there may be something valuable, meaningful, and eternally significant in these moments if I can use them to bring honor and glory to Jesus. I also may have the opportunity to honor all the other people who were involved in the process. I assume I am there for a purpose.

I was genuinely surprised when the guys from Rascal Flatts, who were presenting my category, called out my name as the winner! I ran up on the stage and was handed the award. I looked out into a sea of famous faces. Below the stage I saw the clock ticking down, letting me know how much time I had left before the music started drowning out anything else I wanted to say during my acceptance speech.

While my family tried to quiet down back at home, I stood at the microphone onstage at the Shrine Auditorium in Los Angeles and began my acceptance speech. "Wow . . . thank you very, very much! Thank you American Music Awards for recognizing artists like myself and Mercy Me and Third Day [the other nominees that night]. We represent a whole bunch of folks who make music inspired by the love and grace of God, and we're so privileged to get to do that." I went on to thank Mary Beth and the kids and everyone else just as I had planned, and then I ended by saying, "Finally . . . Jimmy, I'm sorry, but thanks be to God for His indescribable gift. God bless you."

The crowd applauded, and I left the stage. I was actually surprised how loudly they cheered when I mentioned God.

After the show, I did interviews backstage for a while, and then my publicist hustled me off to the after party. I walked in and began greeting all of the people on our EMI team. My publicist interrupted us and said, "Hey, Steven, Jimmy Kimmel is here at the party. Let's get a picture of you two together. It will look good in the trade magazines."

The publicist introduced me to Jimmy, and he was the perfect, amiable gentleman. I started to say something about why I had disobeyed his instructions, but he interrupted me. "Hey, that was great. That was a good bit," he said. "You kinda gave it back to me, and that really worked. That was a good television moment." While Jimmy may have missed the essence of my statement, I was surprised he had heard it and glad he acknowledged it.

He moved off in a different direction, and the publicist introduced me to an older couple standing nearby. "Steven, this is Jimmy Kimmel's mom and dad."

As I shook their hands, Jimmy's dad said, "You know what, son? We loved that you said what you did about thanking God. Because Jimmy knows about that. He was an altar boy in church when he was young. He knows where all of his gifts come from, so that was good that you thanked God and did what you did." I smiled and thanked them.

It felt like a Tuesday's child sort of moment.

With Chuck Colson and Mary Beth.

Chapter Eighteen

Two Trips to Prison

Despite our differences and our intense struggles, Mary Beth and I continued to fall deeper in love. Even as we were walking the journey of trying to understand Mary Beth's battle with depression, we were committed to doing it together no matter what. As we often said, "We fight hard and we love hard," and as a result, our love grew stronger over the years.

In an attempt to take some time to recover from the craziness and give us some much needed rest, I decided to try to take a sabbatical of sorts. In theory, that sounded good, but we soon found ourselves busier than ever with some incredible unexpected opportunities mixed with several heartrending tragedies. One of the new opportunities took me to prison.

When I was a kid, my church youth choir sometimes sang for the inmates at Kentucky State Penitentiary in Eddyville, a medieval castle-like structure overlooking the Cumberland River a few miles from Paducah. More than nine hundred inmates were incarcerated in the prison. One of the inmates who came to hear us sing was from our hometown, and knowing him caused us to realize that those men in prison were people just like us, and in many cases it was just one bad decision that separated their lives from ours.

That experience started my interest in what was going on in prisons, and later continued with my friendship with Chuck Colson, founder of Prison

Fellowship. Somewhere in the mid-1990s, I read Chuck Colson's book *Loving God*, in which the former Nixon "hatchet man" tells numerous stories of life-changing, spiritual transformations. The book had a profound impact on me and to this day remains one of my all-time favorites.

I was fascinated by Colson's stories of meeting people on death row whose hope in this life was gone, yet Chuck was able to minister to them and introduce them to Jesus. Chuck didn't simply put a notch on his spiritual six-shooter; he went back year after year and spent his time teaching and making disciples of these inmates who most likely would never come out of prison alive.

I was deeply moved by the stories of the life-changing power of the gospel in some of those darkest places, and I had the thought, *Someday I wish I could experience that. If I could ever go with Chuck Colson into prison and go with him to death row, one of the scariest places I could imagine, I would do it.*

I was reading the Bible one day and came to a passage in 2 Peter 2 that talks about the person who forgets that he was cleansed from his former sins. The verse reminded me never to forget where I had come from spiritually, what I had been freed from . . . that I, too, had been a prisoner in chains, invisible but nonetheless real, and that Jesus had set me free. Not too long after that, I was on an airplane when down the aisle came an inmate in shackles wearing a prison jumpsuit and being escorted onto the plane by law enforcement officers in front of him and behind him. They sat down a few rows behind me, and when I got up to use the restroom, I noticed the inmate sadly staring out the window. Following the flight, I couldn't get that scene out of my mind, and it became the inspiration for "Remember Your Chains," a song I included on the album *Heaven in the Real World*.

Prison Fellowship heard the song somehow and reached out to me about going into the prisons to sing. "I would love to do that," I said. I accompanied Chuck Colson on several occasions, including one of the most memorable

Easter Sundays of my life in Kentucky State Prison in Eddyville. Talk about traveling full circle!

Wherever we went within the prison system, Chuck and his Prison Fellowship team walked the cells, inviting inmates to a chapel service. Some of the inmates responded positively. "Okay, I'll be there!" Others reacted violently. "If I ever get out of here, I'm gonna kill you!" Many of the inmates would not look us in the eyes but stared at the floor as we talked to them. But most of the inmates were grateful we had come.

In the chapel services, I'd sing some songs, and then Chuck would tell his story. "I'm one of you; I spent time in prison. I was Nixon's hatchet man, and I was convicted of my crimes and went to prison," Chuck told the inmates. "But I found genuine forgiveness and hope in a relationship with Jesus Christ, and that changed my life." Most of the inmates were willing to listen, and many wanted to find the kind of peace with God that Chuck had found. Taking a stand for Christ in prison takes real courage because the inmates watch for any sign of hypocrisy and often react violently.

During my initial experience in prison ministry, we were scheduled to do a program in an assembly hall. We were setting up chairs with several members of the inmate worship band when suddenly the alarms went off and the entire prison went on lockdown. That meant nobody was permitted in or out; the guards ordered everyone back to their cells or locked in where they were. Rumors had spread about a potential prison riot planned to take place during our chapel service, since most of the population rarely assembled in one location like that. It was the perfect time for rival gangs to square off.

Our team was locked in the room along with the inmates. The lockdown canceled our performance, but it gave me the opportunity to talk with an inmate, a former professional musician who had become a Christian while in prison. He told me, "I play in the worship band here. I used to perform in bars and clubs, so music represented my old life. When I got onstage and played, it was all about me entertaining people, letting them know how good I am, and being somebody special. Then I came in here and found Jesus. When some of the chapel leaders found out I could play, they wanted me to be a part of the band, but for a long time I couldn't do it; I didn't want to do it."

The man said, "I was afraid of standing up in front of everyone and playing music again, afraid I would try to steal some of God's glory. The old me would do that. I had to pray for a long time before I could stand up. Thankfully, now the new me can play and give God the glory."

His words convicted me. Around that time I was doing *The Great Adventure* concerts, and thousands of people cheered me on every night as I called out, "We're here to sing about Jesus! Come on, let's saddle up our horses; it's gonna be a great adventure!"

Here was an inmate who was concerned about pride getting the better of him and about stealing God's glory when he played in front of a captive audience of fifty or so inmates in prison. Meanwhile, I was singing in front of thousands of people who said, "Yeah! You're great. Love your music, man, love you!"

It was tremendously humbling to hear this brother's heartfelt testimony. I prayed, "God, please give me the same kind of heart and humility. I want You to get the glory and not me."

In a prison in Indiana, I got the opportunity I had hoped for years earlier to go with Chuck to death row. It was an eerie feeling as we went through a series of gates that ominously slid closed behind us. We stepped through another series of doors that clanked shut behind us, and then another, and then we were in the bowels of the prison; we had arrived on death row . . . and somehow I had an incredible sense of peace. God was here, even in this place, especially in this place. The prison guard who accompanied us removed the shackles from a man, and Chuck and the inmate—a man to whom Chuck had ministered for fourteen years—embraced for the first time without chains. It was a powerfully moving experience, and we all wiped away tears as we prayed together.

Another man on death row seemed to be waiting for us with tremendous anticipation. He had his Bible open as we approached his cell. "Brothers," he said, "I heard that you were coming, so I've been praying that God will give you boldness. This is such a hard place, and the message of the gospel is so needed here."

The man didn't ask us for anything for himself. He was concerned for the other men on death row. He had tears in his eyes as he told us his story. "I destroyed my life by making some terrible choices," he said, "and the worst part is what I did to my own family. I'm here paying the price for the things I have done, but I know my sins have been forgiven. Jesus has set me free!"

I was in one of the darkest places in the real world—the death row cell block in a maximum security prison—but this man had the light of heaven in his eyes. I thought I had come to minister to him, but as it turned out, he was praying for us, encouraging us, and ministering to me. The song "Free" on my *Signs of Life* album was a direct result of my work with Prison Fellowship and particularly inspired by my visit with this brother on death row that day.

I think one of the reasons I was so affected was because I was in a place where, apart from the grace of God and the gospel of Jesus Christ, everything was broken beyond fixing, and yet I was experiencing God in one of the most profound ways I ever had. It was a powerful lesson I would find myself learning over and over again in the years ahead.

One night in 1997, my booking agent, John Huie, called and invited Mary Beth and me to view a prescreening of the movie *The Apostle*, starring Robert Duvall, Farrah Fawcett, Billy Bob Thornton, and June Carter Cash. I had recorded a song called "Lord of the Dance" that had a "swampy" feel to it on my *Signs of Life* album, and the song had piqued the imaginations of the movie's sound track producers. Although they wanted mostly old gospel songs, they wondered if I had anything original that might work in their movie.

Actor Robert Duvall had personally financed the production and had written and directed the thought-provoking, though deeply troubling, movie about a confused, convoluted, fire-and-brimstone-style preacher, Euless "Sonny" Dewey, whose marriage is falling apart because his wife is having an affair with a man in the church. Sonny takes off on a run from the law after an altercation with his wife's lover in which he slugs him with a baseball bat at a church softball game. He disappears for a while and eventually resurfaces out in the country as a new man with a renewed call to preach. He gets himself another church gig as Apostle E. F. but is soon caught and imprisoned. The movie ends with Apostle E. F. out on a chain gang. He's still a mess, but he is still preaching.

After I viewed the rough cut of the movie, Duvall's character reminded me of Peter, the rambunctious disciple of Jesus, so I wrote the song "I Will Not Go Quietly," and Robert Duvall decided to use it in the movie. Since it was the only original song on the sound track, the producers wanted to do a music video for the song.

I offered some ideas for the video concept, and the producers said, "We love it; let's do it." In the video story line, I go into a prison, similar to what I had done with Prison Fellowship, and there I meet and minister to Sonny, the Robert Duvall character.

We went to the old, abandoned Tennessee state prison and shot the video, a mini-movie *with Robert Duvall*! He and I are sitting in a cell, and I'm singing to him, while various video clips cut away, showing portions of the movie. The whole day was one big pinch-me moment.

Duvall is a fascinating fellow and is genuinely interested in learning about the people around him. He looks deeply into people, and it is easy to understand why he is so successful. He was especially intrigued by Emily. "That girl has a light in her eyes," Duvall said. "She's going to do something to change the world."

The movie premiered at a private showing in New York. Mary Beth and I received an invitation that read, "Ed Harris, Christopher Walken,

Matt Damon, and Val Kilmer invite you to the private screening of *The Apostle*."

Mary Beth said, "We're definitely going to this event!"

We found the address in New York, an unmarked, nondescript building, similar to where an album listening party for a new album might be held in Nashville. The small theater seated about a hundred people, many of whom were famous movie stars or other high-profile people. Everyone was dressed casually, but it was obvious that Mary Beth and I were the outsiders, so we took a seat about ten rows up in the theater, trying to be inconspicuous. "Just sit down and try to blend in," she reminded me.

Actor Val Kilmer came in and sat down right behind Mary Beth and me. It was one of the few times in our lives when Mary Beth was starstruck. I knew she would love to meet him but would be too intimidated, so I figured, *Aw, what the heck. Why not?*

I turned around and said, "Val Kilmer, my name is Steven Curtis Chapman, and I'm a musician; I have a song that's part of the sound track. Of all the people here, you are the one person my wife would really love to meet." Meanwhile, Mary Beth was smacking me on the leg and whispering under her breath, "I can't believe you're doing this."

"What? You're usually the one doing this sort of thing," I whispered back.

Val reached up and shook Mary Beth's hand. "Well, it is very nice to meet you," he said with a big smile.

Mary Beth was thrilled. "Thank you," she whispered to me. "That was really cool." We sat back in our seats and tried not to look as out of place as we felt.

Just then Robert Duvall and Matt Damon walked in at the front of the theater, and everyone milled around the man of the hour. Duvall looked across the room and spotted us in the theater seats. His countenance brightened, and he called out, "Steven Curtis! Hey, buddy. Come on, get over here!" So much for being inconspicuous!

"Come on," I said to Mary Beth. "Come with me." We walked down to the front of the theater, and Duvall welcomed us and introduced us to his friends. "Good to see you, buddy. How's that Emily? Matt Damon, do you know this guy?"

Duvall was the quintessential kind-hearted connector. "Matt, this is Steven Curtis Chapman. You young guys are good people. You need to work together." I had no idea what that would be, but I was sure open to the possibilities. (Actually, I'm still waiting for my role as a sidekick to Jason Bourne!)

After the screening of the movie, we attended a reception where we found ourselves chatting with everyone from June Carter Cash, who played Duvall's mother in the film, to Michael Stipe from R.E.M. and Sheryl Crow. It was crazy!

Duvall came to Nashville to do some media for the movie and the album, and we were together at a Music Row studio, along with Emmylou Harris, when the news broke on television of a shooting at Heath High School, the school I had graduated from in Paducah, Kentucky. On the Monday after Thanksgiving, the first day of December, a freshman had senselessly opened fire on a group of his fellow students who had gathered in the school lobby for a daily prayer time before classes began. Three girls were dead, and five other students were injured, one of whom was paralyzed from the chest down.

When my brother Herbie and I attended Heath, he and his friends had been instrumental in founding a student-led organization known as Christian Youth Fellowship, or CYF Club. Mrs. Owsley, a devout Christian, was our faculty sponsor. When Herbie graduated I became president of the group. Besides meeting for spiritual encouragement and prayer, for one of our service projects we sponsored a child through Compassion International.

The club had evolved over the years and because of rulings related to separation of church and state, it no longer met on school property, but a group of students met on their own each day to pray before classes. That day, about thirty-five or forty kids had gathered around 7:45 a.m. when the shooter opened fire. My dad had given guitar lessons to two of the students, as well as the young man who had done the shooting.

The local newspaper, the *Paducah Sun*, printed a large one-word headline across the top of the paper: WHY? It was the question everyone was asking.

In a school that once had a Bible club and where students still voluntarily gathered to pray each morning—as they did the morning after the shooting—forgiveness, rather than revenge, took center stage. Students gathered in the library to make signs that were posted throughout the school. A large handwritten sign near the school trophy case summed up the attitudes of many: "When people genuinely turn to God, no matter what kind of mess they've gotten into, He responds with love and forgiveness."

As an alumnus of Heath, I was asked to sing at the combined funeral for the three students, and some of the relatives specifically requested that I sing Michael W. Smith's song "Friends." How could I refuse?

On the way to Paducah, I called Michael and asked him to pray I could get through it. Michael knew what it was like to have his song used in the best of times and in the worst situations. This was one of the worst, so my friend prayed for me.

More than two thousand people, including almost the entire high school student body, assembled at Bible Baptist Church for the funeral service. This was one of the first tragic school shootings in America. Several major news outlets and television networks covered the service. I looked into the brokenhearted faces at the service and prayed, *How do I present the hope of the gospel without trying to slap on a Bible Band-Aid?* I didn't want to say the wrong thing. I wanted to speak the truth, but I also wanted to be sensitive to the families and friends so consumed by grief.

I sang "Friends" as well as a song I had written earlier called "Not Home Yet." It was one of the most difficult things I had ever done, but I was amazed to see the hope of heaven and the power of God's promises put on display for the watching world.

Barely a month later, Mary Beth and I joined our church small group, consisting of four other couples with kids, at the home of our friends Terri and Dan Coley to watch the University of Tennessee in the college national championship football game. At halftime, Mary Beth wasn't feeling well, so we left early. So did Lori Mullican and her two little girls, eight-year-old Erin and five-year-old Alex.

We had just gotten in bed when we received a phone call informing us that Lori and the girls had been in a terrible auto accident—a seventeen-year-old driver had slammed full speed into the side of their car—and they were in bad shape at Vanderbilt Medical Center. Mary Beth stayed with our kids as I threw on my clothes and raced to the hospital to be with Lori's husband and my close friend, Ray.

Lori had suffered a broken neck, multiple cuts and bruises, and severe abrasions, but she was alive. Their youngest daughter, Alex, had suffered life-threatening injuries but had survived. Their daughter Erin had not.

There in the hospital, trying to make sense of it all, I couldn't begin to imagine the pain of losing a precious little girl. All I could say to Ray that seemed appropriate was what I had sung in Paducah a few weeks earlier: "We are not home yet." As we grieved together over the next several days and wrestled with all the why questions, I was deeply affected watching the Mullican family hold tightly to their hope in God's Word and His promises, that Erin was with Jesus and they would be with her again.

For the first time in my life, the words of 1 Thessalonians 4:13, which tell about how we grieve differently than those who don't have the hope of God's promises and His grace, became very tangible and real to me. In the darkest and saddest time imaginable for this family, they had a hope and a peace that comforted and sustained them. Moved by what I witnessed, I wrote the song "With Hope" to sing at the funeral for Erin. Ray and Lori also asked me to sing "Not Home Yet." It was an unforgettable service for me, marked by great pain but also great hope.

As we grieved with friends who had lost a daughter, I could not have imagined that ten years later the roles would be reversed, and Lori and Ray would be consoling Mary Beth and me.

Concert in the jungle with my boys

Chapter Nineteen

God Follower

Other than *Big Red*, which I read as a boy, I spent the early part of my life reading books only when required to do so. So as a young man, when I finally discovered a love for reading and the power of books, I had a lot of catching up to do.

Many of my teachers in the faith have instructed me by way of their writings. C. S. Lewis, Oswald Chambers, A. W. Tozer, and Watchman Nee are a few of the men who have mentored me with their written words as well as more contemporary writers such as Philip Yancey, the late Chuck Colson, John Piper, and my dear friend Max Lucado, to name just a few. I've found great wisdom and insight into questions I've wrestled with by observing what others have experienced and how they have processed their own journeys. I've especially been inspired by reading about men and women who have followed Jesus. Many of the songs I have written through the years have come from those insights. I've come to believe that one of the reasons God gave me the gift of writing songs and the platform of music to speak from is so I can pass on the wisdom I've learned through a song, to be a teacher of sorts, sharing what I've learned from others ahead of me on the journey.

One of the questions I found myself pondering several years ago was, "What does it really mean to call myself a Christian?" I was known as a Christian singer who wrote Christian songs, so what did that imply? I began to look at the word *disciple*, trying to get a better understanding of what it means to be a "follower of Jesus."

Somewhere in the process, I found the book *The Cost of Discipleship* by Dietrich Bonhoeffer. I have to admit I crawled through that one. Trust me, it's a long way from *Big Red*! It's a powerful and challenging account written by a Lutheran pastor who refused to compromise his faith in the face of Hitler's murderous oppression. As I read that book, it was as though God took me by the hand and said, "All right, come on; I'm taking you somewhere you've never been before." And He really did. As I read, I found a passage that talked about the fact that the disciples didn't follow Christ for the sake of a great cause or a dream. They followed him simply because Jesus called them by name and said, "Come, follow me." Something in Him drew them, and they couldn't help but follow once He called. The disciples recognized that He was more than merely a good man or a great teacher. Much more. And although it didn't make sense to some people, they were willing to abandon it all—everything they had once held dear—for no other reason than the fact that Jesus had called them. It was this same compulsion that influenced Dietrich Bonhoeffer, even to the point of costing him his life.

I was excited and inspired as I felt God taking me to a deeper understanding of what it meant to call myself a Christian, a follower of Jesus Christ. He had called me by name and had invited me to follow Him, wherever that might lead, and there was nothing I wanted more. That revelation inspired me to write the song "For the Sake of the Call" as well as other songs that formed the album by the same name.

Understanding that truth, however, did not imply that responding to the call and embarking on the journey would be easy, predictable, or safe. Quite the contrary. The places where I have experienced God in the most powerful, tangible ways have always seemed to be the most broken and even unfixable places of life, the places I would naturally want to run away from, being the fixer that I am. Yet it's in those most broken places that Jesus invites us to follow Him and experience God's grace and power in ways that can be known only there, whether in Changsha, China; or in a death row cell block in Indiana; or in my home in Nashville, Tennessee; or even in the jungles of Ecuador, as I was about to find out.

Somewhere in the mid-1990s, somebody gave me a copy of the fascinating account *Through Gates of Splendor*, one of the most significant missionary stories ever written. I was familiar with the story told by the late Elisabeth Elliot and the famous quote written by her husband, Jim, "He is no fool who gives what he cannot keep to gain what he cannot lose," but I didn't know the details.[1]

In 1956, after studying at Wheaton College, five intelligent young men—all married, four of them fathers—Nate Saint, Jim Elliot, Ed McCully, Pete Fleming, and Roger Youderian, desperately wanted to share their faith with one of the most dangerous and savage tribes on earth: the Auca Indians, a mysterious, Stone Age tribe known today as the Waodani. Hidden deep in the jungles of Ecuador, the Waodani were on the verge of extinction and had never heard the message of God's love through Jesus Christ.

The American missionaries repeatedly flew a yellow airplane over the beach, dropping various trinkets from the plane, hoping to capture the attention of the Waodani and pique their interest. They worked for months to build relationships with the Waodani, and their overtures of friendship seemed successful.

Then came the day when the missionaries missed their daily shortwave radio contact, the first time that had ever happened. On January 10, 1956, the US Air Force dispatched a rescue team to search for them, and several days later, the missionaries' bodies were found floating in the river. Their airplane had been destroyed, and they had been speared multiple times and brutally hacked to death with machetes. All five men were confirmed dead.

Two years later, Elisabeth Elliot, Jim Elliot's widow, and Rachel Saint, Nate's sister, felt compelled to go to Ecuador to continue the work and to live in the same place where the missionaries had been slaughtered. One by one, the tribal people responded to the Good News, and many of the

Waodani became Christians, "God followers," as Elisabeth and Rachel taught them. Five of the six men who had viciously murdered Elisabeth Elliot's husband and Rachel Saint's brother became God followers.

Today the Waodani are changed people. And the men who murdered the missionaries not only became believers but also became leaders in the local Christian church established by Elisabeth and Rachel. They have learned to "walk God's trail."

The story profoundly impacted me, and I thought, even prayed, "God, I'd love to go to Ecuador to see the work the five missionaries established and to stand on the beach and in the river where everything happened."

A few years later, I was contacted about being involved in a faith-based movie. I tried to convince the producers that someone needed to make a movie about the lives of the missionaries in Ecuador and the Waodani. They told me someone was already working on that, so I began to do some research and ran across some articles by Steve Saint. I wondered if he was Nate's son, who had been five years old when his dad was killed in Ecuador. Sure enough, he was. I contacted Steve through email, and he said he was in the United States for a while. Not only that, but he had with him a man named Mincaye. "My children now call this man Grandfather," Steve told me. "He is one of the six men who attacked and killed my dad and his friends, but he has become a dear man to our family. I'd love for you to meet him."

Okay, that's not the sort of invitation I received every day.

I had met brutal murderers with Chuck Colson, but most of them had been behind bars. This would be the first time I'd willingly encounter a killer outside of prison. Nevertheless, I heard myself saying, "That would be beyond my wildest dreams!"

I had written a song called "No Greater Love" inspired by the story of the missionaries in Ecuador to be included on my *Declaration* album. Steve mentioned that he might be making a trip to Nashville and bringing Mincaye with him, and I immediately had a crazy idea. What if I could get one of the very men who had taken the lives of those missionaries, but was now a living testimony of the power of God's grace and forgiveness, to be a part of the recording of that song?

I called Steve and asked him if there was any chance Mincaye could sing and if the tribe had any songs that might be appropriate for him to sing at the end of a song I had written about their story. I knew that Mincaye spoke only his native language, with Steve translating for him, and I had no idea if music as we know it was even a part of their culture.

It turns out Steve already knew something of me. When his daughter died at the age of twenty from a cerebral hemorrhage, he was crushed, wondering how a father survives the loss of his daughter. His other children gave him a CD "by a guy named Steven Curtis Chapman" with the song "My Redeemer Is Faithful and True."

Now Steve and Mincaye were sitting in my little home studio at my house in Franklin, Tennessee. I could hardly believe I was sitting across from the son of missionary Nate Saint, and I had an even harder time believing that this small, gentle man with joy and kindness in his eyes had speared the father of the man who sat right beside him . . . this was too amazing!

After visiting for a while, I asked Mincaye if he would sing for me. Steve translated my question, and Mincaye smiled and nodded. I asked Steve if he could translate the words into English for me. Here is the song Mincaye sang:

> God, creating from nothing has made all things around us.
> While our hearts are beating and we are alive, let's all believe.
> Believe without being afraid.
> I also to God's place am going.
> We believers are going to God's place.
> Let's all believe that.
> How can it be that we will go?
> If we are clean in our hearts, then let's be out of here.
> We, the believing ones, shall go up to God's place.
> All of us believers who are still living, we will be saying to ourselves,
> "We want to go up to God's place."

I used Mincaye's song at the end of my song "No Greater Love" to create a sort of duet between us. If someone had told me when I was reading *Through Gates of Splendor* that I would have the opportunity to record a duet about our shared belief in God and His love for us with one of the men who had killed Jim Elliot and his friends in the jungles of Ecuador, I would not have believed them. I also would have had a hard time believing that someday I would get to stand in the very place where those men gave their lives, but before Mincaye left my house that day, he invited me to visit him at his house—in the jungles of Ecuador. It was an invitation I couldn't pass up.

I took two trips to Ecuador with Steve Saint. The first was sort of an exploratory venture and an opportunity to spend more time with Mincaye in his "neighborhood."

On this trip, we also filmed footage that was used along with original photos and home movies of the missionaries, their families, and members of the Waodani tribe to create a powerful music video for my song "God Is God." During the evenings, before attempting to get some sleep in our string hammocks stretched between poles inside a thatched longhouse, we would sit and listen to the stories told by the Waodani and translated by Steve Saint. Mincaye spoke freely and passionately about his life as a God follower. He also introduced me to the three other men still living who had participated in the murders of the missionaries. They were all God followers now too. Mincaye told me how Jesus had washed his heart clean so that he could "walk God's trail," as he had been doing now for many years.

As Mincaye told me his powerful story through Steve's translation, I had another idea. I wanted to take Steve and Mincaye with me on tour so he could tell his story to my audiences.

The second time I went to Ecuador I got to take my sons, Caleb and Will Franklin, with me. When we reached the river where the men had been killed, Mincaye was waiting for us along with other members of the tribe. Not much was spoken there, as we could still feel a sense of the weight of what had taken place there fifty years earlier.

David Dobson

My boys and me in Ecuador.

One evening after a "delicious" meal of monkey soup, we were sitting in the hut where we ate our meals and slept. A documentary film, *Beyond the Gates of Splendor,* was being shot on location where the events had taken place. The film crew brought in a generator, and they played some of the music they planned to use in the film. One piece of music was titled "Every Tribe Every Nation," since that was the motivating battle cry of the five martyred missionaries.

A man named Kimo, one of the converted murderers, and Mincaye were close by. Suddenly, I heard a commotion and several of the Waodani talking excitedly with someone outside the hut.

"What's going on?" I asked.

Through the translators, Kimo said, "That was the sound we heard when we killed the men."

Steve Saint had been reluctant to press the Waodani for details about his father's death. He let them volunteer information, but he didn't try to pry it out of them. After all the years, he was surprised at this new detail.

"What?" Steve asked. "You heard music?"

"That's the sound we heard," Kimo repeated.

Kimo had never before heard music as we know it, and he had especially not heard it coming out of loudspeakers. Yet he was insistent that the sounds were similar. "We heard that sound in the trees and in the sky," Kimo said.

Whether it was the sound of angels or something else, we will never know, but I couldn't help wondering if Kimo's revelation answered the often-asked question, Where was God when this horrible thing happened, when His messengers were attacked, when the spears were plunged into their flesh, when their bodies were dumped into the river? Was the sound in the trees and the sky an indication that God's presence had been there even as the spears were run through the missionaries? I felt I knew the answer.

For my *Live Out Loud* tour in 2002, I had the opportunity to see my dream come true as Steve Saint and Mincaye joined me each night onstage to tell their amazing story. We also developed an eighteen-minute video that we ran behind the band and me while we performed songs related to the powerful story.

When Steve introduced Mincaye, almost every night on the tour the audience emitted a hushed gasp as they came face-to-face with the man who had murdered Steve's father. Then, inevitably, the crowd broke into applause as they witnessed the amazing love and forgiveness that could come only from God. With Steve translating, Mincaye told how the Man-maker had changed his heart, how he had been changed from a man who "lived very very badly," and how God had washed his heart clean.

At one point in the program, I returned to the stage and sang "My Redeemer Is Faithful and True," and Mincaye, who couldn't speak a word of English, sang a portion of it along with me in his native tongue in a sort of chant. To some people, it may have sounded like a mess, but to me, it was as close to the language of heaven as I had ever experienced. The audience caught the profound message, many responding in tears. I have to admit that this moment hit me afresh every night of the tour as I declared the words, "My Redeemer is faithful and true."

A few years later, I would be the one calling Steve Saint and asking the same question he had asked: "How does a dad live through the loss of his daughter?" Steve would wrap his heart around mine and remind me, "My Redeemer is faithful and true."

Chapter Twenty

The Tattoo

Few things in Mary Beth's and my marriage symbolize the differences, disagreements, and dysfunction of our relationship more than a tiny tattoo. That tattoo once again tested the mettle of our marriage.

For a number of years, Mary Beth had wanted to get a tattoo. Her dad has a tattoo on his arm that he got when he was nineteen years old, along with a bunch of his buddies. "That was a dumb thing to do," Jim Chapman told us, but Mary Beth, who was a daddy's girl growing up, saw a tattoo as a connection with her dad.

Nowadays, tattoos are commonplace. But in the late 1990s, a soldier or a member of a biker gang might sport a tattoo, but "getting inked" was still largely regarded as a countercultural statement or an antiestablishment symbol, and those aspects of getting a tattoo especially appealed to Mary Beth. She embraced the idea of a tattoo as an expression of her individuality, a sign of being her own person rather than going with the flow.

"I think it would be fun to have a tattoo," she said one day. "It goes a bit against the grain, kinda like me."

I could tell by the way she said it that this was not a random thought. "Oh no, don't do that. You don't want to do that," I said hopefully, shaking my head from side to side. "You'll never be able to take it off. Those things don't wash away, ya know." I could tell I was losing ground quickly in this discussion. I really wasn't anti-tattoo; I was just anti-tattoo on my wife!

"Oh, don't worry," Mary Beth replied. "I don't want to get a skull and crossbones or anything, just something cute, maybe on my ankle."

Over time, she continued to talk about the tattoo, and I continued to stonewall the idea. I wanted to acknowledge my wife's individuality without caving completely. "Well, it's your body, and you can make your own choices, but I am your husband, and it seems that if you know that your husband doesn't really want you to get a tattoo . . ."

After much more discussion, she reluctantly agreed to table the idea—for the moment. "Okay, I'm not going to get a tattoo . . . right now," she said. "I probably won't do it, because my fuddy-duddy husband doesn't want me to have a tattoo. But I might someday." Mary Beth resigned herself to forgoing a tattoo for one simple reason: I didn't want her to get one. But she wasn't happy about it.

When I mentioned this issue to some of our counselor friends, the consensus was, "Your wife is a unique individual. What does it mean for you to celebrate her uniqueness and embrace that?"

"Well, I realize I need to accept and appreciate my wife's qualities that make her so different from me," I said. I wanted to celebrate my wife and embrace her differences. But a tattoo?

I knew the tattoo wasn't a moral issue, as much as I wanted to make it one. My aversion to my wife having a tattoo was merely my personal preference, and I was hoping Mary Beth wouldn't want to get a tattoo simply because I didn't want her to do it.

I knew, however, that Mary Beth was a fighter, and if I opposed the idea, that would automatically make it more attractive to her, so I took a different approach. The next time the subject came up I said, "Okay, sweetheart. If you *really* want to get a tattoo, knowing how I feel about it, you go ahead." I was hoping my reverse psychology might lessen the appeal in Mary Beth's mind.

That was wishful thinking. My wife was way too smart to fall for that!

Mary Beth was quick to remind me of the bumper sticker slogan, "Well-behaved women never make history."

Oh boy. I knew what that meant.

During the summer, I was on the *Speechless* tour along with my best buddy and fellow songwriter Geoff Moore. Meanwhile, the Moore kids and the Chapman kids were all going to Kamp Kanakuk, an outstanding Christian summer camp located in Branson, Missouri, run by my good friend Joe White. Since Geoff and I were on tour, Jan and Mary Beth decided to make a vacation out of it, so they went along with the kids to Branson and stayed in a cabin. Geoff and I planned to meet them there at the end of the week following our concert in Hollywood, Florida, near Fort Lauderdale.

We were getting ready to head back to Nashville when I received a cell phone call from Mary Beth. The phone reception was terrible, crackling, drifting in and out, so I listened intently, trying to make out what she was saying.

Through the distortion, I heard Mary Beth say, "Hey, sweetie. Jan and I drove by Billie's Tattoo Parlor in Branson . . . and . . . well, we might have stopped . . . just to check it out. . . ." Then right in the middle of her sentence the phone cut out.

I redialed the number and reconnected with Mary Beth.

"So then what happened?" I asked, trying to remain nonchalant. "You went into a tattoo parlor in Branson?" I launched into my Mr. Conservative Protector mode. "You know tattoos can get infected . . . you can get hepatitis C from dirty needles. Are you aware of that?"

"Well, yeah, Jan and I went in . . . and we got to talking to this guy. You know Jan would never want a tattoo, but she was willing to go in with me, to be my eyes and ears, just to check it out, to make sure everything was okay and that this place was reputable if I was going to do it . . . and so . . ."

The phone cut out again.

"No!" I yelled. My mind was really racing now. I could feel my chest tightening and my heart thumping wildly. Immediately my mind conjured up worst-case scenarios, going back and forth, posing questions and answering them.

Did she really do this?

What are people going to think? Why did I tell her to go ahead? Because I have to learn to embrace my wife with all of her differences. Who told me that was a good idea?

I hit redial and waited for Mary Beth to answer.

Back on the call, she picked up the story. "The tattoo guy was rough, but he grew up going to church, and I was telling him about our lives. You're gonna think I'm just making this up. But this was an incredible opportunity to talk to this guy about the Lord . . ."

Right! I thought. *And this is all an excuse to soften the blow. It's the old "God used me to minister to this guy" routine . . .*

"I know this isn't the way I normally talk, but I think the Lord used me there . . . and so . . ." Mary Beth paused and then quietly said, "I got a tattoo."

"Did you say you got a tattoo?"

"Yes . . . I did," she said slowly. "And I can tell you are not happy. I got some filigree sort of vines and two little hearts to represent you and me. It's really tiny and cute. But I can tell you are not happy," Mary Beth said. "I know I have disappointed you. I did what I wanted to do, and I've made you unhappy, so now . . . I guess I should just hang up."

Okay, I thought. *The next words I say will define the next six months of my life.* "Sweetheart, I told you that if you really wanted to get a tattoo, go ahead and get one. And you did. I'm not a good liar, so I can't say I'm excited for you, because you know I've been struggling with this, but I guess I'll get used to it."

"Okay, I know you're not happy," she repeated, "and there's nothing I can do about it now."

And she hung up.

I sat there for a moment holding the silent phone. *Oh*, I thought. *That didn't go well.* I felt terrible. *What am I gonna do?*

I hollered out to Geoff, "You gotta get in this bus right now! The wheels are coming off. Mary Beth has a tattoo . . . and I'm not sure about your wife, but we gotta get to Branson!"

When Geoff and I got back to Nashville, we pulled our stuff off the tour bus, jumped in our car, and drove all the way to Branson. Along the way, I prayed, "God, I know this seems really silly, but You gotta help me." I needed wisdom about how I could respond in a way that would best embrace my wife. "How do I love my wife right now?" I prayed. "I want to embrace her differences, and I know, to You, the tattoo is not a big deal, so please help me to embrace this. I don't have to like it." Even though it was just a tattoo, it represented a lot more than that to me.

We arrived in Branson that afternoon, and Mary Beth was waiting for me in our cabin. She opened the door and greeted me with that "Am I in trouble?" look in her eyes. I knew I needed to respond carefully, because if I came across as disappointed or angry that she had gotten the tattoo, she would most likely be sad, and that could easily go from sad to mad. As I glanced around the room, I noticed she had purchased some candles, perhaps with hopes of a romantic reunion.

"Well, let me see your tattoo," I said after I had gotten settled inside the cabin.

Mary Beth pointed to her ankle. "See, here are the two hearts," she said.

The tattoo was actually much smaller than I had feared. There, on the outside of her ankle, were two little hearts outlined in red and blue, with the vine winding around them in green. "Yep. There it is . . . that's a tattoo all right . . ." I said in my best trying-to-be-positive voice.

Mary Beth knew me too well. She looked up and saw my eyes, and she knew instantly that I disliked the whole idea of the tattoo. It could have been a priceless piece of art on her body and I still wouldn't have liked it.

Her countenance dropped. She walked into the other room, flopped down on the bed, and started to cry.

I felt awful. I prayed silently, "God, what is the right thing to do?" I thought I knew. I had to celebrate my wife. I followed her into the room and tried to comfort her.

"I know you're disappointed," she said. "I still think it's cool, but I know you don't."

"It's okay," I said. "I don't have to like it as long as you like it. I love you. And it's part of you, so I'll learn to love it."

The same part of my wife that motivated her to get a tattoo long before tattoos were cool for Christians was the strong-willed part of her that could fight to hold our marriage together despite the odds. It was that same part of her personality that one day would say, "I know we're in a communist country where people say we can't do this, but maybe we can build a care center for children with medical needs who don't have a family," or say, back in our home country, "Maybe we can find a way to financially assist some other families who want to adopt." It's all part of what made me fall in love with that denim-jacket-wearing girl in the first place.

This wasn't a new part of her personality; I had seen her risky, rambunctious side before. When we were on a family vacation at the beach, I wanted to go fishing. Mary Beth chose to bungee jump. She found a place to jump off an enormously high platform with her body attached only to a big rubber band. "Come on, Steven," she said. "Come with me."

"No way. I'll pay for you to go, but I'll just stand on the sidelines and watch."

"Oh, come on, scaredy-cat."

"I'm not jumping off that thing. That's crazy!"

The kids chimed in with Mary Beth. "Dad-dy . . . Bun-gee . . . Dad-dy . . . Bun-gee," they started to chant.

For an entire year, I heard that chant over and over as they harassed me. "Mom's braver than Dad!"

The following summer vacation I drove straight to the bungee jump spot and climbed up onto that platform.

"How do you want to go down?" the attendant asked as he began wrapping the safety straps around me. "Head first or feet first?"

"I don't care!" I said. "Whichever way is fastest. Just get this over with so I can get my wife and kids off my back."

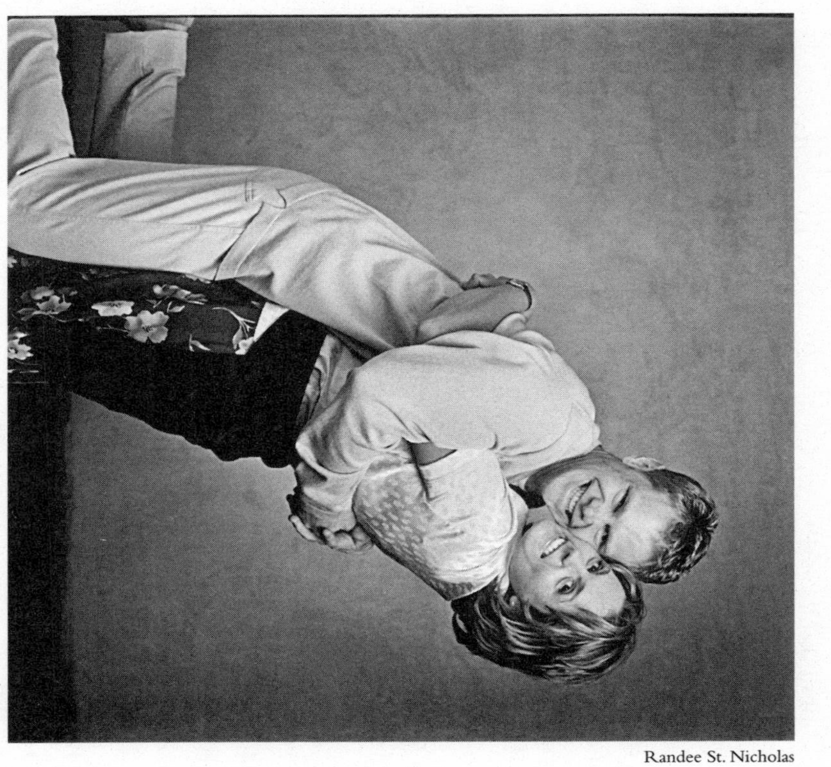

Randee St. Nicholas

I learned that celebrating Mary Beth's differences didn't mean I always had to whoop and holler and say, "Yeah!" Sometimes it was, "No, I don't see it that way." At other times, I learned to pick my battles; is this really worth fussing over? And many times, my response was more like, "Oh, okay." And sometimes, I even ended up being influenced by her and doing the unthinkable myself.

At the end of the *Live Out Loud* tour, on which Mincaye and Steve Saint amazed audiences with their story night after night, Steve said to the band members and me, "Mincaye and I want to spend a few minutes thanking you for how you have loved and served us on this tour." The day before the last concert of the tour, Mincaye, the former missionary killer, came in bare-chested with a towel wrapped around his waist and carrying a basin of water and towels. The now eighty-year-old man who had killed missionaries with his bare hands, who had hacked men of God to death with a machete, who was now a God follower, changed and redeemed by the blood of Jesus, knelt down and began washing our feet.

Steve read Scripture and translated Mincaye's comments as he went from man to man and tenderly washed each person's feet. "Thank you for loving me," he said. "Thank you for serving Jesus. I want to serve you the way Jesus has served me." We were all crying and blubbering; it was one of the most deeply moving spiritual experiences I'd ever had.

The next day the tour was in New Orleans, and several of the band members and I were still overwhelmed by Mincaye's expression of humility and love. I said, "I don't ever want to forget this moment. Mincaye, the man who killed Jim Elliot, washed my feet!" The other guys agreed.

"I have to do something to commemorate this," I said. "What is the last thing that I would do? I know. I'm gonna get a tattoo!"

I drew out a sketch of a G and an F for "God Follower" with dots similar to those the Waodani paint on themselves in the jungle and on those they accept as part of them.

I called Mary Beth and said, "I'm in New Orleans. Guess what I'm going to do."

I found a reputable tattoo parlor and had the drawing tattooed on my ankle.

When Mary Beth saw my tattoo, her first response was, "That's cool, but it's so tiny."

"Yes, it's tiny, but it's there," I said.

"Yeah, it's there, Mr. Straight and Narrow."

A few years later, she didn't have any difficulty convincing me to get another tattoo.

"Gotcha day" as Shaoey becomes a part of our family.

Chapter Twenty-one

With Hope

Shortly after Apartheid ended in South Africa, I had a chance to do a concert tour there with my band. At the time, the television news kept reporting stories of violence erupting in some of the major cities, and Mary Beth and the wives of other band members weren't sure it was a good idea for us to go. But with a strong conviction that it was a desperate time to share the "message of the peace that only God can give," we prayerfully went ahead, and the tour turned out to be a powerful experience and a great success on every level.

I had always dreamed of taking my family back there someday. The day finally came in 1999 when Mary Beth, Emily, Caleb, Will Franklin, and I boarded our flight to make the long journey to South Africa with plans to do concerts not only in Cape Town and Johannesburg but also in Zimbabwe, where we would also travel on a real safari into the wild African bush as well as take a trip to Victoria Falls. This was truly going to be a "great adventure" as a family, and since we were going to do God's work in Africa, my children were, of course, going to be perfect angels on the seventeen-hour flight. We were no more than an hour into the flight when my seat buddy, Caleb, who was in full bloom in his "spaz phase" of life, spilled his second Sprite onto his tray table, which then ran off the tray table and onto our pants. This was becoming a bonding experience for us as father and son in more ways than I had planned. I was ready to strangle him. I was feeling anything but calm and peaceful . . . and godly. I reached into my bag and pulled out my Bible, knowing that I'd better try to read some Scriptures that might snap me back to reality and keep me from losing it with my son. I could imagine the headlines: "Christian Recording Artist Duct Tapes His Child in Bathroom on International Flight." I opened my Bible to Psalm 46:10 and began to read: "Be still, and know that I am God." I was deeply convicted by that verse. It was meaningful not only for this moment but also for so many of the restless and frustrating moments in life when things don't go the way I think they should. I took out a pen and paper and began to write these words:

> Be still and know that He is God
> Be still and know that He is holy
> Be still O restless soul of mine
> Bow before the Prince of Peace
> Let the noise and clamor cease
> Be still . . .

I finished the song on the flight and went on to sing it for the people of South Africa, feeling in a way that it was a gift especially for their encouragement. It would also become an important song for me on the adventure ahead.

I included that song on an album called *Speechless*, which I was working on at the time. I also recorded "With Hope" for the album, the song I had written for my friends who had lost their daughter. I did something unusual on this album and used my touring band instead of recording studio musicians. A nineteen-year-old guy named Adam Anders (who would go on to produce all the music for the television show *Glee* as well as many other television shows and movie sound tracks) was playing bass for me at the time. He was a wiz at "programming" music, using computers to create sounds in addition to the live instruments, something I hadn't really done much of before on my albums. Adam, along with my brilliant producer and dear friend Brown Bannister, helped me create an album that had great success, especially on the radio. We had an unprecedented seven songs go to number one from that album.

While I was on the *Speechless* tour, Mary Beth was busy gathering all the necessary documents and filling out the many forms required for our journey on the road to adoption. By May 1999, we were ready. We submitted our information to Bethany Christian Services, who formally communicated our desire to adopt to the Chinese government. In January 2000, we received notification that we had been accepted as adoptive parents as well as information about the baby girl awaiting our final acceptance. We signed the forms and returned them immediately.

Mary Beth and I were so excited we could hardly stand it as we watched a photograph of our new daughter download on our computer screen. These were the days of dial-up internet speed, so we watched line by line as the picture was slowly transmitted. It almost felt like a "baby delivery" as her picture was slowly revealed to us. She was a pudgy newborn baby wrapped in blankets, and her name was Chang Yan Yan—which means "doubly adorable." And she was! Of course, we knew what her name was going to be from our earlier experience with the article in *Reader's Digest*. Her name would be Shaohannah—a combination of Shao, which we had discovered means laughter, and Hannah, the biblical reminder of God's gift. For a middle name, we added Hope. Shaohannah Hope Chapman.

We soon made plans to travel to China to receive the newest member of the Chapman family. In March 2000, we took all three kids with us—Emily, who had just turned fourteen; Caleb, our ten-year-old; and Will Franklin, who was nine. This was definitely a family affair. My road manager, David Trask, Uncle Dave, as the kids called him, went along to help and to handle the video camera. We flew from Nashville to Beijing, where we met our adoption guide, the woman who would help facilitate the process for us.

Amazingly, as we walked out of the airport, I felt instantly connected to this place so completely foreign to me. I knew my daughter was here, and somehow that made this place a part of my story. While all the details were being finalized, we managed to squeeze in some sightseeing, taking in everything from Tiananmen Square and the Forbidden City to the Great Wall of China. Then it was on to Changsha, the capital of the Hunan Province, where we were to meet our daughter at a hotel.

As we drove to the airport in Beijing to catch our flight to Changsha, a light fog grew heavier the closer we got to the airport. By the time we arrived at the gate to board our plane, the fog had completely grounded all flights. We were anxious enough already, and now we had to wait longer.

The kids and I were very excited, and Mary Beth was too, although I could tell she was scared. From the beginning of our adoption journey more than a year earlier, she had wrestled with questions and fear. This truly had been a journey of faith for her. Her heart knew this was the right thing for us to do, but her mind was filled with questions. "What if I can't love this baby as much as my other children? That won't be fair to her. What will it feel like to hold her in my arms, to wipe her runny nose, to change her stinky diapers; will I feel any different with her? What if she doesn't like me? What if she thinks I'm like the evil stepmother in *Cinderella*?" She was even worried that somehow the baby wouldn't be the same baby as the one we'd seen in the pictures we had received. Now, when we least needed delays, the fog provided her with time to start inventing all kinds of ways to freak out. Despite her strong faith and her willing heart, she sincerely worried whether she could handle all of this.

Finally, the fog lifted, and we were on our way. We arrived in Changsha and checked into our hotel. We had no sooner set foot in our room when the telephone rang. Someone at the front desk told us that the people from the orphanage were downstairs and wanted to bring our new daughter up to our room right away. This was it . . . the moment we had waited for . . . and we were so excited! Well, four out of five of us were excited. One of us was terrified.

I looked at Mary Beth; she looked at me. This is crazy! How in the world did this happen? How did we get here?

We all turned and looked at Emily, who was smiling from ear to ear!

With no time to emotionally prepare, Mary Beth had a frantic look on her face. She started pulling baby items out of a suitcase, trying to find the baby formula, bottles, diapers, and everything else we'd need to care for an infant. All of her well-planned scenarios were suddenly cast to the wind. There was a baby in an elevator on the way up to our floor. We were about to become parents for the fourth time. She sat the kids down on the bed and tried to give them a thirty-second speech, something like, "I don't know what's going to happen to your mom in the next few minutes. Just know that whatever happens I love you guys so much." They looked at each other and at me as if to say, "What is Mom trying to tell us?" I looked back just as confused with an expression that said, "I have no earthly idea."

David Trask was in the hallway ready to punch the record button on the video camera the moment the elevator door opened. Mary Beth asked the kids to stay seated on the bed for a few minutes so we wouldn't all overwhelm the baby when she got there. Just then we heard the elevator ding and the doors slide open. David pressed the button on the recorder and got the entire scene on video.

I was out in the hall with David now, and I saw a Chinese woman carrying a baby in my direction. The child was wrapped up like a mummy with only her beautiful face showing. The outer layer of blankets was a pink, polka-dot, flannel blanket that Mary Beth had made for the baby and had sent on ahead.

I sensed more than saw Mary Beth come up behind me. She came around me like a tailback skirting around the wall of linemen on a football field. She seemed drawn to our baby like a magnet.

It was then and there that I saw the miracle. I haven't seen a lot of miracles in my life, but I know I've seen at least one. Right before my very eyes, I watched my wife transform from a reticent, fretting, fearful, worried-about-being-the evil-stepmother woman into a radiant woman and mother of our infant daughter, Shaohannah. Mary Beth opened her arms and received our seven-month-old child from the Chinese woman carrying her. Tears streamed down my wife's face as she clutched the child to her breast and said over and over, "This is my baby. This is *my* baby!"

I stepped back in the hallway and for one of the few times in my life was momentarily speechless, standing in awe of divine love poured through Mary Beth. This was more than an adoption—this was a transformation of my wife's heart, mind, and spirit. David caught the entire experience on video, a witness to the work of God.

I felt something similar the moment Mary Beth placed the baby in my arms. Looking into Shaohannah's face for the first time—a child with whom I had no physical connection—I was suddenly overwhelmed, thinking, *This is my daughter. I'd give my life for her.* I hadn't expected that sort of reaction within me, and I couldn't explain it, but I knew that this, too, was a taste of heaven in the real world.

"Hey! What about us?" we heard from inside the hotel room. Emily, Caleb, and Will Franklin were obediently sitting where Mary Beth had instructed them to remain. It was time to share the joy. I moved Shaohannah back to Mary Beth's arms.

"Come on out!" I called to them, still mesmerized by the sight of Mary Beth holding Shaohannah so snugly. The kids gathered around, each one trying to get closer to Shaohannah than the other, their eyes bright.

Throughout our entire adoption process, Mary Beth had made it very clear that this was to be a one-and-done kind of deal. "I can do this only one time," she had emphatically announced. On the way to China, she had been reluctant, reticent, and worried about adoption. On the plane home, my wife was already talking about adopting another child! "Shaohannah needs a sister," she said. This was one more part of the miraculous transformation that had happened within her.

Now I was the one with my hands up, laughing and saying, "Whoa! Whoa! I'm not ready for that yet."

When we arrived back in Nashville, a crowd of more than two hundred friends, family, and other well-wishers were at the airport to welcome Shaohannah Hope Chapman to her new home in Tennessee. This was before 9/11, so the welcoming party was waiting for us right at the gate, cheering and waving welcome home signs. Although we were tired from the long flight, we were thrilled by the enthusiastic reception. The celebration was contagious, and before we left the airport, at least five other families expressed a desire to adopt a child. One of those families was Mary Beth's brother, Jim, and his wife, Yolanda. They had barely met Shaohannah when Jim said to Mary Beth, "Okay, what do we need to do to bring one of these little girls home as part of our family?"

That was music to Mary Beth's ears. One of the most emotionally difficult aspects of visiting the orphanage where Shaohannah had lived the first part of her life was seeing the many beautiful little girls just waiting for someone to love them. Because of the cultural mind-set of family structure, little boys have historically been preferred in China, while unwanted baby girls have a much bleaker future.

A number of couples with whom we talked said they wanted to adopt a child who needed a family but simply could not afford the initial outlay of money involved, which can be as much as $40,000 for international adoptions when travel and other costs are included.

"Are you serious? You're telling me you will take one of those little ones whose eyes I just looked into and be their family if you just have some financial help? Call me next week," Mary Beth said to several people wanting more information about how the adoption process worked. "We'll help you!" Not only had her heart been filled with a love for our little girl she didn't know she was capable of but it was also like a fire had been ignited in her heart to help as many little ones find a home as she could.

Never one to allow a minor obstacle to get in her way, Mary Beth began writing checks. I later teased her that we had a line of people forming out in front of our house. While I was exaggerating, the truth is we soon discovered there were a number of families praying that God would provide the necessary funds to adopt. We had to find a way to help those families and those children. I was determined to find an organization that gave assistance to families wanting to adopt and to use my platform of music to direct people to them.

I contacted Bethany Christian Services. "We're meeting more and more people who would like to adopt but need some financial assistance to do it. We want to help them all, but the need is pretty big. Is there a fund available folks can apply to for assistance?"

The people at Bethany told me they once had had an assistance fund, but it had been depleted. They acknowledged that the need was real, though, and that many Christian families were willing and ready to adopt if the financial means could be secured.

Early in my career, I began to see the value of using my stage to bring attention to Christian ministries that were doing important work. I realized that by sharing the spotlight with organizations such as Prison Fellowship, World Vision, Compassion International, and Wycliffe Bible Translators, I could help others become aware of a need as well as ways to be a part of the solution. I thought there had to be an organization that was helping families adopt who couldn't afford it otherwise.

I had even written a new song, "When Love Takes You In," about the miracle we had experienced as a family in adopting Shaohannah and was singing it at my concerts. All we needed to do was find the organization that we could partner with to help spread the word.

When we couldn't find an organization doing that kind of work, Mary Beth and I began to pray about possibly starting something to meet the need. We knew many of the issues potential adoptive parents were dealing with, and we had already been engaging in conversations with couples about the financial needs. Still, it seemed like a daunting task given the fact that we didn't know anything about starting a nonprofit organization.

Since adopting Shaoey, the nickname we soon embraced for Shaohannah, Mary Beth and I had become vocal advocates of adoption. We

Getting a kiss from princess Shaoey at home in Tennessee.

found it impossible *not* to be vocal. Not only had we become personally aware of the need, but I had also spent many years writing songs out of a desire to understand more about God's love for us and then to share that love with others through music. In all my years as a Christian, nothing had come as close to showing me the love of God in a tangible and visible way as our experience of adoption. Mary Beth and I jumped at any opportunity we were given to tell our story or be a voice for children who needed families.

Inspiration was at an all-time high for me, and in addition to "When Love Takes You In," I had written several new songs and was beginning to work in the studio on a new album. Ironically, for one of the first times I could remember in my career, I was feeling confident in my voice. It had been serving me well on tour and had been consistently strong night after night. I was almost starting to feel like a real singer.

But it was springtime in Nashville, allergy season was in full bloom, and I had been singing for hours on end in the studio. Soon my voice began to feel strained. One morning as I was trying to warm up my voice for another day of singing, I started to get a little nervous about the strange limitation I suddenly found in my vocal range. As I tried to sing a scale upward, I came to a point where I felt like my voice was paralyzed. It just wouldn't go up to the note my brain was telling it to reach and where it would normally go with ease on any other day.

I started to panic, thinking of singers who had to have surgery because of vocal nodes and the months of recovery and rehab that sidelined them. This was definitely not a good time for anything like that, as I had just come off my biggest selling album and tour to date, and there was high anticipation about future projects and plans for a busy season ahead.

I quickly went to see some of the best voice doctors in the world at Vanderbilt Voice Center in Nashville. "The good news," they said, "is there's no sign of any nodes or polyps that might require surgery. The bad news is we can't figure out what the problem is."

I returned several times to see other doctors and try various tests, including one that required needles to be injected through my throat and directly into the vocal cord muscles. Mary Beth held my hand and I tried to be brave, but I was scared to death. Just before one last visit to hear the results of the tests, I took a walk around the campus of Vanderbilt University near the doctors' office and cried and prayed. "God, I don't know what's going on . . . I don't know what to do besides sing the songs You've given me. I really don't have any other skills to speak of, and I'm not even sure what other job I would pursue if I can't sing anymore. And on top of it all, I have these new songs about adoption and other stories that I want so much to tell. But I don't know if I'm gonna be able to."

I found a bench and knelt down. "God, this gift is something You gave me, and if it's come to an end and it's time for me to do something else, I'm gonna have to trust You . . . I need You to help me trust You."

I was diagnosed with a paralyzed vocal cord, a rare condition caused by nerve damage that apparently happened as the result of a viral infection. The doctors were hopeful I would make a complete or mostly complete recovery, but there was no guarantee and no sure way to know how long it would take to heal. Needless to say, it was a scary time, as I had to begin making plans for a major album release and tour without knowing if or when I would sing again.

One night I was tucking Caleb into bed and saw tears in his eyes. "What's going on, buddy?" I asked.

"Dad, what if you can't sing again. What are you gonna do?"

"Well, we're going to have to trust God with that one. I'm kinda scared too, but I know God knows what's going on, so we're going to trust that He'll either heal my voice or show me what I'm supposed to do next."

Mary Beth and I received an invitation shortly after my diagnosis to travel to Washington, DC, to receive an award from the Congressional Coalition on Adoption Institute. The organization wanted to recognize us as National Angels in Adoption along with Dave Thomas, founder of

Wendy's restaurants, and Rosie O'Donnell, who had been speaking out about adoption. It was going to be a big deal, with many government leaders in attendance, a lot of media coverage, and great opportunities to talk about adoption advocacy and discuss ways to care for children who had been orphaned. We were even scheduled to meet with President George W. Bush the afternoon before the award presentation to talk about these issues that had become so important to us.

The organizers asked me to sing as part of the presentation.

I was so frustrated. I really wanted to sing "When Love Takes You In" at the adoption gala because I felt the song not only perfectly expressed the message and story of our adoption of Shaoey but also helped paint the picture of the miracle that adoption truly is. Yet there was no way I would be able to sing it. "God, I don't understand," I prayed again. "You gave me this song, and I feel it captures the story that so many need to hear. Now I'm not sure if I will ever be able to sing it again."

Since I had completed the recording of the song before I lost my voice, when we received the invitation to go to Washington for the award ceremony, I got an idea. I could make a music video of "When Love Takes You In" and have it shown at the ceremony. That way the message of the song could be communicated even if I couldn't use my voice.

I had just filmed a music video for the song "Live Out Loud" with Brandon Dickerson, a brilliant video director in San Francisco. We had done some of the filming in Bodega Bay, where Alfred Hitchcock shot much of his movie *The Birds*, and had even re-created a few scenes in the video for fun. All of this had been done in faith that I was going to be able to eventually sing again, and the record company had spared no expense in making the video for "Live Out Loud" to promote my upcoming *Declaration* album. There was no money left in my promotional budget to make another music video, so Mary Beth and I talked and prayed about it and decided to spend the money necessary to create a video for the song we hoped could be a powerful tool to tell the story of adoption and inspire those who saw it.

We traveled back to San Francisco to shoot the video. We rolled a grand piano out on the beach for me to play, accompanied by a few musicians. Around this scene we cut in clips of Shaoey and a few other children who had been adopted, including two of the children our friends the Coleys had adopted. The idea was for the video to tell the story of children in various places all over the world alone and waiting for a family. Then as the video concludes, hands reach in and take the hands of the children, whose eyes light up as they begin to realize they have a place to belong.

In doing the video, I worked with a sound track and didn't have to hit the notes precisely if I couldn't—I was basically acting and lip-syncing—but I wanted the video to look realistic, so I attempted to sing along with the music as it played on the speakers. I knew I would have to do some good acting, because when I tried to sing this song, I often ended up in tears of frustration. There is a high note in the song that I simply could not reach due to my impaired vocal cord, but as I was singing along to the sound track, where nobody could hear me, with the surf crashing on the shore in front of me, suddenly I heard my voice not just hitting the high note but hitting it clearly and well! It was the first step in the healing process. The doctors had told me, "When your voice comes back, it will be like plugging in the lights. It will be rough, and you will need to build up the muscle around it. But your brain will send a message to your nerves, and your voice will gradually come back. You will know if or when your voice is healed."

I knew. I called to the video director with tears in my eyes and asked him to give me a moment. Then I called out to Mary Beth and my friends the Coleys, who were there praying as we filmed, to tell them what had just happened. I was gonna sing again!

In time, I would come to realize that it was no mere coincidence that the very moment my voice began to return was during the making of a music video I never would have made had I not suffered a paralyzed vocal cord. I was supposed to create this video . . . and God would ultimately use it to influence and inspire countless families to experience the miracle of adoption.

Over and over I've met couples who have told me they saw the video on television or in a concert and decided to explore adoption as a result. One dad told me, "We saw that video, and with tears in our eyes, we drove home and asked, 'Should we consider adoption? Yes, we should.' And here is our child." He hugged a little girl and beamed with joy. It was another powerful illustration to me that when I am at my weakest, God is strong and is able to use my brokenness to get His message into people's hearts and minds. In fact, the video for "When Love Takes You In" was even shown in a meeting with government officials in China and was instrumental in encouraging them to open the doors even wider for more children to be adopted.

Mary Beth and I traveled to Washington to receive the award, and the organizers planned to show the video rather than have me sing. We spent several days at the J. W. Marriott hotel, a few blocks from the White House; we did some media interviews on the steps of the Capitol and met with some friends for dinner on Monday evening, September 10, the night before the big gala.

The following morning I had a 6:00 a.m. interview with CNN, so I got up early. Jim Houser of Creative Trust accompanied me to the interview while Mary Beth and Shaoey stayed asleep in the hotel. The interview was relatively brief, but I told the story of how Mary Beth and I had adopted Shaoey, and the producer asked to use part of the "When Love Takes You In" video. When I returned to the hotel, I excitedly told Mary Beth, "They used a clip of the video, so Shaoey is going to be on CNN! How cool is that?"

We turned on the television and watched intently, waiting for the network to loop the adoption interview again. After a while, we decided to go get some breakfast. The televisions in the breakfast room were all tuned in to newscasts of a scene in New York, where a plane had crashed into a building in Manhattan a short time earlier.

"What happened?" I asked someone.

"It looks like a plane hit the World Trade Center," a man answered. Just then on the screens in front of us, another airplane smashed into the

World Trade Center. Soon we began to hear sirens and could see smoke in the distance rising from the Pentagon. Fighter jets streaked back and forth over the city.

Our meeting with the president was canceled, as was the gala adoption event we were in town to attend. Quick-thinking Jim Houser ran twelve blocks to a rental car location he'd discovered in the vicinity of our hotel and rented a car to get us home.

We made our way back to Nashville and entered into a period of grieving along with the rest of the nation. Although our time in Washington had been drastically different than we had expected, we were grateful we had forged a new relationship with Kerry Hasenbalg of the Congressional Coalition on Adoption Institute; her husband, Scott; and many others passionate about adoption and orphan care. It seemed our hearts were melded together in our desire to awaken other Christians and get them involved in caring for orphans, specifically in financially assisting families who wanted to adopt but needed help.

I watched as the fire in my wife's eyes continued to grow to help as many children as possible come to know the love of a family, and I knew this was something God was doing in her heart. We had continued giving financial help to families on their adoption journeys and had met with some nonprofit organizations to discuss ways we could formalize a response to the great need we had become aware of. After praying and talking for several months with new friends in Washington, we turned our dream into an organization called Shaohannah's Hope, and Scott Hasenbalg became our first executive director.

Our mission was to reduce the financial barriers to adoption, but it was about much more than just writing checks to help families adopt. We wanted to mobilize churches to get involved as Christians realized and took seriously the message of James 1:27, that true religion as God defines it is so much more than attending church services, hearing sermons, or singing songs; it's about caring for the widows and the orphans.

We also wanted to help care for children who might not be eligible for adoption because of a medical condition or who were so physically vulnerable that their lives might not be viable for long. Even if a child's chances of survival were minimal, we were convinced that every child is fearfully and wonderfully knit together by God Himself and is precious to Him, so we wanted to do our part to provide medical care and treatment as well as a loving environment for as long as those children were with us. As we have learned, they have so much to teach us about the kingdom that is coming if we have eyes to see and ears to hear.

The dream that was originally birthed in Mary Beth's heart was simple: "Imagine if we could help one hundred families adopt who couldn't afford it otherwise. Wouldn't that be awesome?"

Mary Beth's dream came true. Eventually, we changed the name to Show Hope, and to date, Show Hope's adoption aid program has helped restore the hope of a family to more than five thousand children from over fifty countries, including the United States. And it's been yet another powerful reminder to me that even though on this side of heaven there is what seems to be an "unfixable" reality of children who are orphaned, if we're willing to let our hearts go there, to the "least of these," where Jesus said we would find Him, we will catch a life-changing glimpse of heaven right here in the real world.

Mary Beth with Stevey Joy just after coming home from China.

Chapter Twenty-two

Never Say Never

If someone would have asked me in the fall of 2002, "Do you think you will ever adopt any more children?" I would have told them I've learned never to say never but I felt confident our family was complete. Our lives were busy and very full. Emily was sixteen years old, and the boys were nearing their teen years as well. Shaoey was walking and talking and keeping us all excited with every new thing she experienced in life.

Musically, *Speechless*, the album I had been working on in the midst of our adoption of Shaoey, became my best-received project ever, producing seven number one songs and winning a Grammy Award. I followed that album with *Declaration*, which included the songs "No Greater Love" and "When Love Takes You In" and led to the *Live Out Loud* tour, where I first shared with audiences the joys we had experienced through adoption. While I was excited to encourage others to consider adoption, as far as I was concerned, Mary Beth and I had four children and that was plenty. I knew that a big part of my future as an artist was going to include using my voice—literally—to tell the story of and bring awareness to children who needed a family.

It was a typical Sunday morning at Christ Community Church, our home church in Franklin, Tennessee, when I took my seat along with my family and watched as our dear friends Dan and Terri Coley walked onstage with their eight children to introduce their newest member, Daniel, to their church family. They had just returned from China with Daniel, making him the fourth child to become a part of their family through adoption. I knew them well, and I knew their adoption journey had taken them to some difficult and painful places. Yet here they were with joy in their eyes, opening their hearts and their arms again to say, "You belong" to another little one who needed a family.

As I looked at them, a beautiful tapestry of different skin tones and stories of rescue and redemption, a wave of deep emotion flooded over me. I've never audibly heard the voice of God, but as clearly as I've ever heard Him whisper to my heart, I heard Him that morning. And what I heard was very different from what I would've expected. Rather than having a sense of God's conviction and even disappointment if I didn't obey, I had a strange sense that He was inviting me into something wonderful. The best way I know to describe it is like this: imagine a father putting his arm around his son and saying, "I've got an idea . . . you wanna do something crazy? I want to take you on an epic adventure. It won't necessarily be easy; it might even be hard and scary at times, but we'll do this together and you'll get to know more about me, and our relationship will grow in ways it never could otherwise." What son would pass up that kind of invitation from his dad?

Tears streamed down my cheeks, and my wife noticed me frantically scribbling something in the front of my Bible. She probably thought, *He must be getting another song idea.* She'd seen me have similar experiences before—or so she thought. Instead, I was writing down these words: "Today I commit to respond to God's revelation and give Mary Beth my full support to begin paperwork for another adoption." I went on to write more about the "invitation" I felt I had received from God. And as I understood it, this was about more than just giving a baby a home; God had shown me that somewhere in the world (probably China) there was a baby who would soon be in need of a family who would introduce him or her to the Savior.

After church that morning, on our way to lunch, I called a family meeting in the car as I drove. At this point, everyone in the family except me had already expressed a desire to adopt another child. I was the holdout. I had been wrestling with all the questions, details, and concerns of adopting another child and until that morning had come to the conclusion that we wouldn't adopt again. "I want Mom to read to you what I wrote," I said. Mary Beth read the notes I had written in my Bible, discovering for herself at the same time she informed our kids that I was ready to adopt another baby.

The car suddenly filled with cheers from the backseat, where Emily, Caleb, and Will couldn't contain their excitement. Strapped in her car seat, Shaoey was startled by all the noise from her brothers and sister and started crying—maybe because she somehow knew her reign as "queen of the world" was coming to an end. I looked over at Mary Beth and saw tears filling her eyes. She had wanted to adopt again from the time we had come home with Shaoey, and over the years since then, she had been instrumental in many of our friends adopting. So it was not a matter of convincing her; it was more a matter of keeping up with her!

It took her very little time to get the wheels turning, and before long, we were heading back to China to adopt another little girl. We even "helped" the Holy Spirit convince our dear friends Jan and Geoff Moore to adopt another baby at the same time, and they did—in the midst of a rapidly spreading SARS epidemic spawned by a highly contagious, lethal virus.

As I've often been prone to do, even after having such a powerful experience of God speaking to me about adopting another child, I found myself wrestling with the questions and the fear again. *Was I really doing the right thing in leading my family down this road again?*

I was reading the Bible one day when a particular verse struck me: "For what is our hope, our joy, or the crown in which we will glory in the presence of our Lord Jesus when he comes? Is it not you? Indeed, you are our glory and joy" (1 Thess. 2:19–20 NIV). The apostle Paul was basically saying, "I can't take anything from my earthly experience to heaven with me except for the spiritual children I've had a part in helping to get there."

Those words went straight to my heart. *What a picture!* I thought. *Imagine us getting to present our children to God as our joy and our crown in His presence. That's all we can bring with us, but what a treasure to bring to Him!*

Mary Beth and I decided to name our new baby Stevey, since we knew Steven means "crowned one." Also, because of my experience in church and the way we had come to the decision to adopt again, it felt particularly appropriate to name this little one after her daddy, something we had discussed doing before but that had never seemed right until now. After reading that passage of Scripture, I knew her middle name should be Joy. It was as though God was saying, "I've already given you hope with Shaohannah Hope; now I want to give you joy with Stevey Joy." Two baby girls, my hope and joy.

We received our referral packet from Bethany Christian Services, including a photograph of Stevey Joy, in March 2003. She was beautiful but oh so tiny. She was sickly and had weighed only 3.7 pounds when she had been brought to the orphanage. The information from Bethany revealed that Stevey Joy had been found outside a police station in a cardboard box, wrapped in a man's suit jacket. We could hardly wait to get to her and bring her home.

A few days after we received our referral picture and information about Stevey Joy, I was doing my rounds of radio interviews at GMA week (Gospel Music Association). Of course, the first thing I wanted to talk about was our new daughter on the way, the profound experience I'd had in coming to realize we were to adopt again, and what I felt God had shown me about how His instructions to care for the least of the least was really an incredible invitation to experience a deeper relationship with Him.

One of my live-on-air interviews was with two of my favorite radio people in the business, Jon and Sherry Rivers. Jon was one of the most recognizable voices and influential personalities in Christian radio, and at the time, he and his wife, Sherry, were hosts of the morning show on K-LOVE. Jon is a big guy, about six feet five inches tall, with long hair and a cowboy hat, and a voice to match his persona, so he can be an imposing character. Sherry is fun and sweet and always wants to talk about the family. We have a long history, and they know I can be a talker when we get into interviews, especially when I start talking about my family. (Many people thought it was funny when I released an album called *Speechless* because I'm known to be anything but.)

During my interview with Jon and Sherry, I could feel Jon roll his eyes and give me that "here we go again" look as I pulled out my picture of Stevey Joy and began telling the story of how we came to be in the process of adopting another little one from China. Sherry, on the other hand, was hanging on every word.

But then something amazing happened. As I talked about our journey, I noticed Jon beginning to lean in closer. I saw his eyes glisten with tears, and right in the middle of the interview, he said, "I think we need to stop and pray right now." As we prayed for our little girl and children everywhere who needed a family, Jon began to weep openly. It was a powerful moment being shared with millions of listeners around the world on K-LOVE. We finished our interview, and Jon said he wanted to talk to me. He revealed to me that at the moment he closed his eyes to pray, he saw the face of a little Chinese girl and heard a voice (he was emphatic that he *heard* the voice) saying, "Go get her." He had no intention of considering adoption and was doing his best to politely listen to me talk about it when God spoke directly to him and said, "Go get her." The next day Jon and Sherry began the adoption journey that would eventually lead them to become mom and dad to beautiful Lexi Rivers. And they began to use their massive radio platform to tell their story and inspire and encourage millions of others to consider adoption or become involved in caring for orphans in some way.

This tiny little person named Stevey Joy wasn't even home from China yet and she was already changing the world.

We were still several weeks away from having all of our travel plans in place when we began hearing troubling news about the growing concerns over SARS in China and the fact that the government was closing adoptions in various provinces until the SARS epidemic could be brought under control. At that moment, Changsha, where the orphanage was located, remained open, but it seemed certain that China would soon close the entire country to foreign travelers. Mary Beth called Jan Moore, and through a series of "impossible to get done" circumstances, the two moms made plans to head to China the following day, hoping to beat the SARS epidemic to our babies.

It was crazy! I made an attempt to talk some sense into my wife. "Sweetheart, there are still things that aren't in place for you to go get Stevey Joy. I know you're worried about her and want to get her home, and so do I, but you may get there and be turned away or even get stuck in China for a while waiting to get all the final paperwork needed."

But Mary Beth's mind was made up. "We have a daughter in China right now, and I have to go get her or at least do everything I can to try." I could see through the tears in her eyes and hear through the sound in her voice that there was no way I was talking this mom out of going to get her baby . . . and I was thankful . . . what an amazing mother . . . what a wild and wonderful woman I'm married to!

She and Jan made it to China, and, as expected, things got crazy . . . so crazy in fact that I ended up flying to China to hand deliver power of attorney documents that Jan and Mary Beth needed. All along the way, God gave us favor that opened doors other people said were closed. At several points along the way, our journey was referred to as "mission impossible." Thankfully, our God is a God of the impossible, and within a few days, Jan was headed home with a beautiful seven-month-old girl named Ashley Rose in her arms and I sat next to Mary Beth on the airplane, flying home from China with a tiny, fragile Stevey Joy asleep on my chest. She was sick and restless, so we knew this was going to be a very long flight, and I was determined not to move as long as she stayed asleep. She slept for most of the thirteen-hour flight from China to Los Angeles, and when she finally awoke, I quickly handed her to Mary Beth and made a mad dash to the bathroom!

With my namesake, Stevey Joy.

Kissing Maria good-bye in China just after I met her. This is the picture that helped convince me we were to adopt Maria.

Chapter Twenty-three

Maria

I found you in the most unlikely way

But really it was you who found me

I found myself in the gifts that you gave

You gave me so much and I wish you could stay

But I'll wait for the day

I'll watch as the cold winter melts into spring

And I'll be remembering you

I'll smell the flowers and hear the birds sing

And I'll be remembering you.

"Remembering You"
by Steven Curtis Chapman

"Well, hello there, Maria. Can I hold you for a minute?"

I lifted the cute little Chinese baby into my arms and rested her on my hip. I was a long way from my home in Tennessee and was missing my two little girls—especially their hugs—so I was happy to hold this little one for a few minutes.

It was a beautiful spring Sunday, one week before Easter, when I walked out of a church service in Beijing, China, and was greeted by a family and a little girl who would change my life forever. Tim and Amy Hedden had moved to China from the United States to work with an organization that helped care for children with special needs who had been orphaned. The Heddens and their four children had opened their home to two baby girls, Natalie and Maria, and were providing foster care for them while they prayed, hoped, and waited for a family to give the girls a permanent home. In the process, they had fallen in love with both girls and had started the adoption process for Natalie.

Tim held one-year-old Natalie, a little girl with stunning brown eyes and a cleft lip. Amy had handed me the other little one, Maria, a perfectly pudgy bundle with drool on her chin and almond-shaped eyes that were barely visible when she smiled.

As I spoke to Tim and Amy, Maria curiously played with the jade bracelet on my wrist, the one I had bought on my first trip to China and had worn ever since as a reminder to pray for the children there who were still waiting for families.

Amy gave me the *Reader's Digest* version of Maria's story. She had been found cold and blue, lying along a riverbank nearly a year ago, when she was thought to be only forty-eight hours old. She was taken to a state-run orphanage and from there placed in a foster home that had been set up by some Christians from the United States. Apparently, Maria had been born with a hole in her heart, a condition known as atrial septal defect.

Foster parents from Australia living in China gave her a home and the name Rowena, but then they were transferred back to Australia. They wanted to adopt her but were unable to because the two countries did not have an adoption agreement. That's when she was placed in the home of the Heddens, who gave her the name Maria. "We always liked the name Maria," Amy told me. "It just seemed to fit her."

I was struck by the name. For starters, you don't meet many Marias in China. And when I heard her name, I immediately remembered a song I had written several years earlier inspired by something my wife had said. Our daughter Emily was in kindergarten and had befriended a little girl named Maria, who seemed to have a hard story, from what Emily told us. As a result, our tenderhearted Emily often came home talking about Maria and how much she wanted to help her. When we considered moving Emily to another school, Mary Beth looked at me with tears in her eyes and asked, "But if Emily leaves, who's gonna love Maria?" I wrote this song and recorded it on my *Great Adventure* album.

> Who's gonna love Maria
> Who's gonna touch her
> With the tenderness she longs for
> Like the desert longs for rain
> She's got a hunger deep inside
> With every tear she cries
> She wonders if there's
> Someone out there, somewhere
> Who's gonna love Maria
> Maria, if you can hear me
> Please know that you're not forgotten
> Somebody's trying to get to you
> Who's gonna love Maria.

Now, thirteen years later, as I looked down at this little girl I was holding, that question came back to me in full force: "Who's gonna love Maria?" It seemed I had written the song for this moment. There was something about this little girl that grabbed hold of my heart and wasn't going to let go easily.

When I went to hand Maria back to Amy Hedden, I was overwhelmed emotionally. It almost felt like I was handing over my own daughter! I had held numerous Chinese children who needed a family on our trips to bring home our own adopted daughters and on trips with others. Never had I experienced such a profound emotional connection to a child I had just met. Even as I got in the car that was waiting for me and we began to drive away, I kept watching out the back window trying to catch one last glimpse of this little girl . . . and my eyes filled with tears. *What in the world was going on?*

I called Mary Beth, who was home in Tennessee. Since China is thirteen hours ahead of Nashville, it was Sunday afternoon for me and late Saturday night for Mary Beth. I could hardly contain my excitement. "Mary Beth, I just met this amazing little girl named Maria."

"Don't even think about it!" my wife quickly stopped me, half joking but also half serious. "If we are going to consider another adoption, she better know how to play guitar, because she's going on the road with you!"

"I know . . . I know," I said. "We can't adopt her, but just let me tell you about her." I went on to tell Mary Beth about the day in China, and she filled me in on events involving our kids at home, thousands of miles away from me. I missed my wife and kids, and being in China caused me to especially miss Shaoey and Stevey Joy, our two daughters we had adopted from China several years earlier. We prayed together on the phone, and before we hung up, I mentioned one last time, "Would you keep praying with me about this little Maria? I feel like we're supposed to help her find a home. There's something really special about her."

"Yes, I will," Mary Beth replied. "Be safe and call me tomorrow. I love you."

"I love you too, sweetheart . . . good night."

The next evening I did a concert that turned into a pretty amazing worship service at the Hard Rock Café in Beijing, China—of all places. Even the missionaries who had come to the concert that night (they don't actually call themselves missionaries because of the legal implications) were stunned that we were worshiping openly and freely in such a public place. The Hedden family was there too, and they had brought Maria with them, so my heart continued to grow even more attached to her.

All week long as I traveled the country with Luis Palau, Maria stayed in my mind. I even called the Heddens to ask more questions and get more information about her. They could tell I was smitten. At the time,

China had rules against multiple adoptions at the same time, and since the Heddens were already adopting Natalie, they were not permitted to adopt Maria. Nevertheless, I wondered if there was something I could do to help the Heddens navigate the adoption process. Maybe that was the answer to why I couldn't get Maria out of my mind. Amy and Tim obviously loved her and were willing to give her a home. Still, I wondered if there was something more I was to do regarding Maria. I began to think of families close to us who might be willing and able to adopt her. All the while, I couldn't shake thoughts of *us* possibly adopting her, even though I knew it made no sense whatsoever.

In addition to our already full house and full schedules, Mary Beth and I were busy with our nonprofit charitable organization Show Hope, which we had founded to help other families adopt. We had no intention of adopting another little one ourselves . . . but Maria needed a home . . . and we had one . . . and she had my heart!

I got to see Maria again when I spent the Saturday following Good Friday at her foster home, where I sang some songs for the kids and the people who were caring for them. My best bud Geoff Moore was there singing with me, along with my friend Chris Chesbro. We were playing and singing one of my favorite worship songs, "Open the Eyes of My Heart," when I noticed that a little boy had crawled into my open guitar case and was fascinated with the soft, furry lining inside. As we sang the words of that song as a prayer, asking God to open our eyes so we could see Him, I suddenly had a strong sense that God was answering me.

"I hear you saying you want to see Me," He seemed to say. "Well, here I am, sitting in your guitar case and all around you. Remember that I told you, 'Whatever you do for one of the least of these you're doing for Me'? I'm here, in these children . . . in this place . . . in this moment . . . and what you're doing for them, you're doing for Me."

I was stunned by the simple yet profound reality God showed me that day. This was holy ground. Here in this place that existed only because there were little ones whose earthly bodies and stories were broken, I was given a taste of heaven. Most of these stories wouldn't be fixable this side of heaven, but real people were compelled by the love of God to do what they could to show His love to children who needed it the most.

As I carried Maria around that Saturday afternoon listening to the children laugh while they hunted for Easter eggs, I felt like God had pulled back the veil between this world and the next for just a moment. Everything around me seemed to echo, "Taste and see, the Lord is good."

It wouldn't be the last time God would use this little girl to give me a glimpse into heaven.

It was back in 2000 on our flight home from China after adopting Shaoey that Mary Beth and I began to talk about new dreams that had been born in our hearts. Mary Beth wanted to help more orphaned children find a family, and she had a desire to go back to China and somehow help the children who were medically fragile and weren't able to be adopted. I, on the other hand, felt compelled to go back to China with my music as a way to say thank you. I believed my music and, more importantly, the message in it would be the best gifts I could offer in return for the priceless gift we had received in the adoption of our daughter. I didn't have any idea how that would be possible, but I trusted that if it was supposed to happen, God would make a way, as He had clearly done many times before.

Nearly four years later, the week of Easter 2004, I traveled to China with world-renowned evangelist Luis Palau, who was scheduled to speak in several churches and public meetings. I was going to get to realize my dream of taking my music and its message to China.

On Easter Sunday, Dr. Palau and I were involved in the resurrection Sunday service at the same church where we had been a week earlier and where I had first met Maria. The Hedden family was there also, and I saw them in the hallway carrying Maria, who was all decked out in her pink Easter dress. It was her first Easter, and Amy Hedden mentioned that she wanted me to see Maria in her Easter best in case it was the first of many we'd have together. They were not making this easy on me at all!

We enjoyed a powerful service together, celebrating the truth that Jesus is alive, that He has conquered death, and that therefore we have nothing to fear. No matter what happens in this world, because Jesus is alive, we know that heaven is our future home . . . and that changes everything about how we live in this world.

After the service, we took some pictures in the church parking lot before saying good-bye and heading to the airport. My good friend Tim Tan captured an especially poignant photograph of Maria and me face-to-face nose-to-nose as I was kissing her good-bye. I wanted to adopt her on the spot, but at that moment, I had no idea I'd ever see her again.

Back home, Mary Beth knew me better than I knew myself just then. She recognized that Maria had made an indelible impression on my heart, so unbeknownst to me, my wife was already beginning to fill out the adoption paperwork.

During the long flight home, however, I had more than twenty hours to rethink everything. I stared out the window and wept and prayed. I didn't know what to do with all that I was feeling. Slowly, reality and common sense began to win out. We already had five children, including Shaoey and Stevey Joy, adopted from China, and with Emily moving into her senior year of high school, and with the increasing activity of Show Hope, and with my schedule busier than ever, we had no business thinking about adopting another child. Besides, Maria was already more than a year old, almost the same age as Stevey Joy. If we were to adopt Maria, it would be almost like having twins, double the pleasure but also double the responsibilities. By the time I arrived back home, my careful, conservative side had kicked in and I was convinced we were supposed to help someone else adopt Maria.

When I walked into the house, resolved to tell Mary Beth my decision, she pointed at the paperwork on the kitchen counter waiting for my signature. When we were adopting Stevey Joy, on a whim Mary Beth had decided to get duplicates of all the necessary documents for another adoption . . . just in case. In her mind, Maria was already a part of the Chapman family!

I went back to work the following week and was in the recording studio when I took a break to check calls and emails. That's when I found the picture. Amy Hedden had emailed me the photo of me kissing Maria in the church parking lot in China. The moment I saw that picture I knew Maria belonged in our family. This wasn't a picture of a man kissing a little girl who was an orphan; it was a photo of a daddy—me—kissing his *daughter*!

I called Mary Beth immediately. "I know what we're supposed to do about Maria," I nearly shouted. "Let's go get her!"

Mary Beth was way ahead of me. She had all the paperwork and documents ready on our side of the process. When we arrived in China, however, we discovered there were some problems with Maria's adoption paperwork on the Chinese government's side, including her medical records indicating the heart problem. From what we understood, there was apparently no paperwork indicating that Maria had been diagnosed with a hole in her heart, or ASD.

The Chinese adoption officials asked us to come back *in a few months* to complete the adoption process after they had time to resolve her case.

"God, what is going on here?" I prayed. "What are we supposed to do? We've come all this way, and now we are being told we can't take Maria home?" Mary Beth burst into tears.

Maybe her tears touched somebody's heart, or maybe it was God's hand. For some reason, our case was reconsidered, and the Chinese adoption officials instructed us to wait, first in a room next door and then at our hotel. Hours became days as we prayed like crazy and waited. One moment it looked as though everything was moving forward, and then the next minute it seemed as if the adoption might never happen. Meanwhile, Mary Beth and I paced the floor of our hotel room and prayed some more. Again, I asked myself, *Did you really hear from God about this or were you mistaken?* I heard that old familiar voice whispering again, "Come on Steven, you've got to fix this!" But I couldn't do anything except pray.

After several more days, we received good news: despite the confusion, Maria's adoption paperwork was completed, and we were able to adopt her! We renamed her Maria Sue Chunxi Chapman, keeping the Chunxi from her given name in China and adding the Sue in honor of Amy Hedden's middle name. We said a tearful good-bye to the Hedden family, who had come to love Maria deeply. We then headed home to Tennessee with our newest Chapman.

Caleb and Will were excited to have a new sister. Ironically, Emily had been slower to warm up to the idea of adopting again, especially during her senior year of high school. Maybe she realized that some of the stress would fall on her, since I would soon be starting another tour, Mary Beth would once again have three children at home under the age of five, and the boys were not yet old enough to drive. She was also able to admit that with this being her last year at home, she was reluctant to have to share our attention with a new arrival. Regardless, once she knew I was resolved in my decision, she gave her full support. Then the moment she met Maria face-to-face our original adoption advocate fell in love with her too.

Maria was a little older than our other girls were when we adopted them, so she was already well formed by the time she became a part of our family. She was silly and witty and so much fun, but she could also be very stubborn. Talk about a strong will . . . Maria definitely had one.

Maria and Stevey Joy were almost the same age, and it was fun to notice their similarities and their differences as they grew. Stevey Joy was neat and orderly; Maria was messy, giggly, and blubbery and always seemed to have something sticky on her fingers or her face. Although they dressed alike, it was easy to tell which clothes belonged to whom. Maria's shirt inevitably had a stain or two on it. Keeping socks and shoes on her feet was next to impossible; in fact, keeping clothes on her was a real accomplishment. She much preferred being naked. There was never a dull moment around the Chapman home.

With my three little girls on a trip back to China.

Chapter Twenty-four

Cinderella

It was one of *those* nights.

Every parent has experienced those occasions when the kids are unusually hyper . . . at least I hope so, and if they haven't, I don't wanna know about it!

That was me one night with Stevey Joy and Maria.

Because I'd spent a lot of nights away from home over the years, Mary Beth and I had gotten into a routine: any night I was home during tour season, it was a given that I was on duty to get our younger children bathed and ready for bed. My assistance gave my wife a break and gave me opportunities to spend special time with our kids. I have great memories of those moments through the years, reading bedtime stories, making up my own goofy songs and stories (Loony Larry the Coconut Hunter was always one of Emily's favorites), and hearing their prayers, sometimes trying not to laugh out loud at the things they would pray about.

One night in March 2006, when Stevey Joy and Maria were three years old, I was on bath and bed duty. Ordinarily, on those occasions, I'd get the kids ready for bed and then Mary Beth would come in to kiss them good night or they'd go in and jump on Mom and say good night.

For some reason, we got a late start that night, and it was past the girls' bedtime by the time we even got started on bath time. "We gotta hurry tonight, girls," I said. "It's late. Go quick. Get in the tub."

Complicating matters further, I was getting ready for a meeting with the folks at my record label in which I planned to present some new song ideas for my upcoming album. I was still working on the songs, refining the concepts, and the performer in me wanted to make a strong impression with the new music. So it was even more important that I get the girls in bed so I could get back to work.

I hustled the girls into the bathroom and into the tub. They were splashing and being rowdy and having fun. I stepped out of the bathroom momentarily, and when I returned, I discovered the girls had hopped out of the tub. They were gone! The mystery of their disappearance was easy to solve, however, as I noticed tiny puddles of water headed in the direction of their bedroom.

The wet footprints led directly to a large box filled with Disney princess costumes. Maria and Stevey Joy loved dressing up in their princess outfits, and I'd seen them enough that I even knew which dresses went with which matching shoes and tiaras.

When I walked in the bedroom, the girls had already put on their princess costumes over their damp bodies.

"What! What's going on? What are you girls doing?"

"We're going to the ball, Daddy," one of them squealed. "We're going to the royal ball!"

"No, you're not going to the ball. You're going to bed," I said, already helping Maria out of her Cinderella costume. "Get back in the bathtub. I haven't even washed your hair yet."

I hurried them back to the bathroom and hoisted them into the tub again. I quickly shampooed their hair and rinsed, then helped them wash and dry their bodies. "Okay, now go get your pajamas on. I'm coming to tuck you into bed as soon as I clean up the bathroom."

The girls scampered to their bedroom. By the time I got there—which was only a matter of a minute or two—they were already decked out in their Snow White and Cinderella costumes again. "Get your pajamas on!"

I said in a much more *fatherly* tone. "Then get in bed, right now. Come on, this is taking way too long."

Stevey Joy and Maria slept in the same room on adjacent bunk beds with desks below them. On most nights, they ended up in the same bed, laughing and giggling until they fell asleep.

On many nights, after their baths, they'd climb up the ladder to their beds and I'd read them a Bible story or I'd make up a story about two little princesses. Then we'd pray and kiss and say good night.

But we were later than usual getting to bed that night, and I was frustrated because I still had so much work to do. I knew Mary Beth was not happy that the girls were getting to bed so late, so I was not planning on any stories.

"Read a book to us, Daddy. Tell us a story."

"No, we're not reading a book tonight; no stories tonight. We're going to sleep."

"Oh, please, Daddy, please! Just one story."

"Okay, here's the story. Two little girls went to sleep. The end!"

Even prayer time that night was going to be streamlined. The girls knew that if they prayed long prayers, they could stay up a little longer. At three years of age, they'd already learned that I was not going to interrupt their prayers, so they had a habit of praying for all of our relatives they could think of, their friends, their preschool teachers, their pets, and any other people they may have heard about around the world. Ordinarily, I didn't mind. I'd smile at their honest, heartfelt, and sometimes hilarious prayers, even if they were just stalling.

Not tonight.

"Pray fast," I instructed. "Immediate family only. Don't pray for anyone outside of this house. Mom, Dad, Shaoey, and your brothers. That's it. Okay, you can pray for your sister Emily at college. Period."

I tucked the girls in and said a terse, "I love you; I mean it; good night."

I turned out the lights and closed the door behind me, grumbling to myself. *Why can't they just listen to me?* I wondered. *They should obey the first time I say something. They need to listen to me better.* I felt frustrated and irritated at the delays, huffing and puffing like a mean old man . . . as I prepared to go write some deeply spiritual songs about the love of God and such. I didn't like myself much just then.

I could still hear the girls giggling softly in their bedroom as I walked down the stairs to my office. They'd calm down eventually now that the lights were out.

As I settled in to work, I started thinking about Emily, who was now in college at Baylor University in Texas. Although we stayed in touch by phone and email, Mary Beth and I missed seeing our daughter on a daily basis. It seemed like only yesterday I was washing Emily's hair as she splashed in the tub as a two-year-old. She used to love playing dress-up as well, and she and I had attended our share of father-daughter dances at her school. I have a great picture of Emily and me sitting on my Harley Davidson motorcycle on our way to a middle school sock hop!

Now she was all grown up, had twirled right out of our lives and had gone off to college. I guessed that one day soon she'd probably be getting married.

As I thought about how quickly the time with Emily had passed, I was even more disappointed with myself for getting upset with Maria and Stevey Joy. *I should know better,* I thought. Maria and Stevey Joy and even Shaoey, who was now in first grade, always wanted me to dance with them. Someday I'm going to blink my eyes and the little girls will be gone; they're not going to be interested in dancing with their daddy anymore . . . they may even move away and we won't be able to dance together anymore.

You're going to get only so many of these opportunities, I thought. *Is this really how you want to spend these moments that God has given you with your daughters?*

I prayed and asked God to change me, to work on my heart, and to slow me down so I wouldn't miss the special moments like these.

I thought of Emily, and of Stevey Joy and Maria and their princess costumes, and of the story of Cinderella. What if the prince had known

Ready for the sock hop with Emily.

that at midnight Cinderella would run out the door and the dance would be over? How much more would he have savored every moment he had with her in his arms?

I picked up my guitar and began putting some of those thoughts to music. I got in a creative flow and wrote the entire song "Cinderella" that night. That was unusual for me. Usually, when writing a song, I start with a chorus or maybe an idea for a verse, but the song takes a long journey before it is ever finished. That's just the way I'm accustomed to working, hashing and rehashing a song over and over. Most of my songs I've written and rewritten as many as ten to fifteen times.

That night, in working on "Cinderella," I wrote three scenarios into the song. First, the little girl is spinning and swaying without a care in the world while her daddy carries the weight of the world on his shoulders—very much the way I was feeling that very night. There is a ball at the castle, and she wants to practice dancing with Daddy. In the second section, she is older and getting ready for a dance with a guy at the prom. In the third section, a young man has given her a ring, and she is all grown up and soon will be gone. I had already experienced the first two scenarios with Emily, and I knew it was only a matter of time before I experienced the third.

In the chorus, I included a line that seemed obvious to me: "'Cause I know something the prince never knew." What I know that the prince didn't is that the clock is in fact about to strike midnight and my Cinderellas will be gone. I know how quickly that all happens.

So I wrote, "Oh, I will dance with Cinderella; I don't want to miss even one song."

The prince didn't know that his time with her was limited, that she was going to run out the door. *But I do.* The dance will be over much too soon. The key idea of the song was this: I want to savor every moment God gives me with my kids and encourage others to do the same. Don't miss an opportunity.

The ideas came together rather quickly, and I wrote the song "Cinderella," thinking, *I will rewrite this. I can make it better.* To me, it was sort of a first draft.

The next morning Mary Beth and I met with my manager, Dan Raines, about some business plans. "I want to play something I wrote last night," I said to them. "I think it is gonna be something special. It feels important. I'm sure I will rework it, but here is what I have right now."

I played and sang the song, with the three scenarios and the chorus, and when I looked up from my guitar, Mary Beth was crying and so was Dan.

"Don't touch that song!" Mary Beth said. "Don't mess with it; don't tweak it. Leave it alone. It's perfect." Dan concurred.

"You need to record it just like that."

"Ya think? Really?"

"Yes!" they both nearly shouted simultaneously.

I appreciated their encouragement, but I wasn't sure. I still wrestled with whether it was a song I should put on the new album. I've always felt that I'm a storyteller, a singer/songwriter, but I'm also a bit of a teacher. Although I've often felt ill-equipped in that regard, I've been privileged to sit under some great teachers. Much of my success as a songwriter I attribute to the great ideas they have imparted to me in sermons, books, or in person. "Cinderella" didn't necessarily seem to present a great deal of theology.

Later, I played the song for our pastor, Scotty Smith. I usually ran most of my songs past Scotty so he could check the theology before I put them on an album, so I wanted to get his impressions. "I'm not sure this is a song for the album," I said. "I don't have any Scripture background for it, like I do for most of my other songs. It's just expressing something I feel strongly about." I played the song for Scotty.

"Are you kidding me?" Scotty responded. "That *is* theology! That absolutely should be on the album. That's what it means for a dad to love his kids to the glory of God."

When I played the song for the record label folks, they agreed the song should go on my new album. So I went to work shaping the theme for the rest of the material. Over the years, on some albums, I started with the theme first and wrote the songs around the central theme, similar to what I did for my album *For the Sake of the Call*, which focused on the idea of discipleship and what it really means to be a follower of Jesus.

On other albums, I worked from the opposite direction, writing a group of songs and then looking at them and asking, "What are the themes that are emerging out of my own life experiences right now?"

For the album *This Moment*, on which I included "Cinderella," many of the songs were asking the question, "What does it mean to be fully present in this moment? With my wife? With my kids? In my relationships with friends? Out of that I wrote the song "Miracle of the Moment."

I imagined, what would it be like if we had a time machine and could go back and fix the past, or relive special moments, or redo times we had messed up or missed the opportunities. Obviously, a big part of me has wrestled with these ideas my whole life. I'm always trying to fix what is broken in the world around me. So the idea of needing to leave those past and future moments in God's hands and realize the importance of the moment I'm in is a big theme in my life. I need to keep being reminded that I can't change the past and I don't know the future. I can spend so much of my time mulling over the past or worrying about the future that it's easy for me to miss this moment and what is happening in my life right now. I need to learn how to appreciate the "Miracle of the Moment." Little did I know how much I would soon come to realize the importance of embracing the moments I had, especially with my little girl Maria.

While writing that album, I also wanted to connect with some of the writers who were creating corporate worship songs as well as individual expressions of faith. I wasn't planning to write a "worship" album, but there was an element of worship that I wanted to incorporate into these songs, so I arranged a trip to England to meet great worship leader and songwriter

Matt Redman, whose songs "The Heart of Worship," "Blessed Be Your Name," and others were being sung by congregations all over the world.

I had met Matt, but we'd never really spent much time together, so it was a step of faith for both of us to attempt to write songs together. During my time in the United Kingdom, I also worked with Martin Smith, formerly of the group Delirious?, and Stuart Townend, who wrote "In Christ Alone" with Keith Getty. I played "Cinderella" for them and was almost apologetic about it. "This isn't the kind of music you write. This might seem too casual to you. It's just a song about a dad and his little girl. You guys write the deep, spiritual songs, the great hymns of our day."

But the guys were incredibly supportive, encouraging me to use the gift of storytelling in song that God had given me. While in the UK, I wasn't sure I'd written the songs I had hoped to write, but we forged great friendships that would prove invaluable to me in the years ahead.

Matt introduced me to a young guy named Jonas Myrin, a Swedish songwriter and former worship leader at Hillsong Church in London. Matt said, "You guys need to connect and try to write some songs."

The afternoon before I was to meet with Jonas, I was walking down the street in London thinking about how God had moved there in such powerful ways in the past. John Wesley, William Wilberforce, William Booth, George Mueller, Martyn Lloyd-Jones, and so many other great Christians had once had a profound influence in this city. Yet I quickly realized I was not in Franklin, Tennessee, where I could walk into a coffee shop almost anywhere in town and find somebody with an open Bible or a group of people talking about Jesus. In contrast, nowadays, many regard England in general and London specifically as post-Christian. Much of the culture is devoid of Christian influences. I wondered, *Where is the hope for London?* I felt a sense of aloneness come over me.

I continued to walk and began to look into the eyes of the people passing me on the sidewalk and to pray for them. As I did, a phrase my pastor borrowed from Abraham Kuyper and used frequently popped into my mind:

"There's not one square inch in all of creation over which God does not declare, 'Mine.'"[1] I had the sense that God was answering my prayer with this profound thought.

I realized I could not put my foot anywhere on earth that was not God's domain, not Las Vegas, or Hollywood, or London. *This is my Father's world,* I thought. *This is my Dad's town!* "It's all Yours, God," I said aloud. "This street I'm walking down right now . . . every street in London is Yours. And so are all these people walking on these streets." My steps quickened as I started to feel a sense of hope and strength well up inside me, replacing the loneliness and sadness I had been carrying a few minutes earlier.

When I met with Jonas Myrin later that evening around an old piano in a tiny church chapel, I told him about my thoughts and the verse I had begun writing about London and some of the other places I'd been. "Yeah, yeah." Jonas instantly caught what I was trying to express. "Now what about this chorus? It's all Yours, God!"

> It's all Yours, God, Yours, God
> Everything is Yours
> From the stars in the sky
> To the depths of the ocean floor
> And it's all Yours, God, Yours, God
> Everything is Yours
> You're the Maker and Keeper
> Father and Ruler of everything
> It's all Yours.

We wrote the song "Yours" as a declaration of the truth. "All my dreams are Yours, all my plans are Yours, all my gifts are Yours. My life is Yours, my heart is Yours. Everything I am and everything I have belong to You, God." It was a prayer of declaration that would be severely tested on the road ahead.

We were excited about the song we felt God had given us. We high-fived, prayed a prayer of thanksgiving, and said our good-byes.

The song was one of my favorites on the *This Moment* album because it felt like the collective testimony of so many believers. When the album came out, with the first single "Miracle of the Moment," I began performing the songs in concert, and "Yours" seemed to instantly resonate with audiences. And then I began performing the song "Cinderella."

Everywhere I sang the song dads came up to me with red eyes. "Oh, thanks a lot, Chapman," they joked. "You got me with that song. I finally got over 'Butterfly Kisses,' and you come along with 'Cinderella!' Thanks a bunch." I laughed with them, but we all knew that God was reminding us of what a treasure our children are and the importance of making the most of the time we have with them. As I said, I had no idea at the time just how meaningful and significant that song and that album would become in my own life.

Maria and me having a goofy face contest.

Chapter Twenty-five

Does God Really Have a Big, Big House?

Of our six children, I think Maria had the loudest personality. She lived with passion. I've sometimes said I think she was cramming an earthly lifetime into five years, so she did everything big. She made no effort to conceal her true feelings. If she was happy, the world knew it, and if she was unhappy about something, she let the world know that with equal intensity. Her passion was on full display whether she was glad or mad. She loved to sing and dance, and her enthusiasm was contagious. And Maria loved her family. She especially loved us all being together. On those occasions when our entire family would be gathered around the kitchen table, Maria would say a phrase she became known for: "I love it when my whole family is together!"

With Stevey Joy only five months older than Maria, they were almost like twins. They shared a bedroom and dressed alike and did just about everything together. Getting both girls ready for preschool was always an adventure. Synchronized preschool prep—it should be an Olympic sport.

Whenever I was home, I would drive the girls to school on the mornings they attended. It wasn't a long ride, just a few miles each way, but I loved learning about my daughters during those rides. Early on, the idea of preschool was entirely unacceptable to Maria. Stevey Joy has always been the compliant and eager-to-please daughter, so she took to preschool like a duck to water. Maria, on the other hand, took to it more like a duck to a shotgun. Many times her teacher, Miss Megan, would have to pry her fingers, arms, and legs from around me to get her into the classroom. Of course, being the softy that I am, I was convinced that we should discontinue this practice altogether. But Mary Beth and all the teachers at the school maintained that Maria cried for only about the length of time it took me to get back out to my car, and she would then proceed to have a wonderful day.

She was always happy when I picked her up, but the dropping off was traumatic—for Maria and for me! I walked down the hallway away from her classroom on several occasions with tears streaming down *my* cheeks, listening to her scream as I walked away, wondering if we were doing the wrong thing by taking her to preschool, and praying that God would give her a peaceful and good day. I still remember vividly the day when she stood in Miss Megan's doorway and waved at me with a smile on her face and said, "Good-bye, Daddy, I love you, gooberhead" as I left. It was a major breakthrough and a serious answer to prayer for me. That day I also cried and prayed as I walked to my car, but this time they were tears of joy and prayers of thanksgiving. "Thank you, Father, for getting us through that valley."

One morning Mary Beth went into the girls' bedroom and found Maria sitting on the floor struggling to put on her socks and shoes. "Maria, would you like Mommy to help you?" Mary Beth asked.

Without even saying good morning, Maria looked up at Mary Beth and asked, "Mom, is it true that God has a big, big house?"

"Yes," Mary Beth replied with a smile. "God does have a big, big house."

"Does it really have lots and lots of room?" Maria asked.

"Yes, it does," Mary Beth responded.

"And is there lots and lots of food there?" Maria was our eater. Everything from Chinese food (of course!) to ice cream was her favorite. Anything that didn't move on our kitchen table was likely to end up in her mouth, and the evidence of whatever she had eaten recently was usually on her face and shirt. For a tiny four-year-old, she could put away the food! So when she heard that there was lots of food in God's big house, that was good news to her indeed.

Mary Beth recognized that Maria's questions were following a line of thought identical to the chorus of a song recorded by the group Audio Adrenaline that Maria and her preschool class were learning at school. "Yes, Maria!" Mary Beth said with a laugh. "There is lots and lots of food there—the best food ever! And you'll never run out." Mary Beth jumped ahead of Maria and mentioned another thought from the song. "God also has a big, big yard where you can play football!"

Maria looked up at Mary Beth. "Mom! How did you know?" she asked wide-eyed.

"Are you learning a song at school about God's big, big house?" Mary Beth asked.

"Yep . . . and, Mom, I wanna go there. I wanna go to God's big, big house. How do you get there? Can I go there?"

Mary Beth intuitively realized that this might be a pivotal moment in the spiritual life of our daughter, that even at four years of age, Maria was asking questions about God and heaven. My wife later said that she "wanted to make sure she didn't mess anything up, so she decided she'd better call on Steven Curtis Chapman" to help answer Maria's questions.

By this time, I had arrived back home from taking Shaoey to school, and I heard Mary Beth calling out for me. "Steven! Steven, can you come here? Maria is asking some really good questions, and I think you oughta help me answer them!"

I walked into the kitchen where they now were, and Mary Beth explained a little about the conversation they'd been having. I picked up Maria and sat her on the kitchen countertop so we could be eye to eye. This was important stuff, and I wanted her to know I was taking it, and her, seriously.

"That's so great that you want to go to God's big house, sweetheart," I said. "So do I, and so does Mom. We all want to go and be there with God someday . . . that's how He made us . . . to want to be with Him." I did my best to explain in four-year-old terms how Jesus paid the price for us to live in God's big house forever, that if we ask Him, He will come and live in our hearts so that when we leave this earth, He will take us to His big house to live with Him. The whole time I had a little legalistic voice in my head saying, "She's probably too young to understand this," but here was my little girl on her very own saying she wanted to see and even live in God's big house, so I decided in that moment to go with it. And I'm so very thankful I did.

"Would you like to talk to God about this?" I asked her.

"Yes," she said. That led to a precious time of praying with Maria. We let her talk to God in her own words, and she prayed a beautiful prayer, asking Jesus to let her live forever with Him in God's big house. She asked Jesus to come into her heart and to give her eternal life. "Jesus, please come and live in my heart, and someday can I come and live with You?"

More than at any other time in my life, I understood what Jesus meant when He said that if we want to inherit the kingdom of God, we must have childlike faith. Maria personified it! Her trust in God was so sweet, so simple, yet so real. She believed what Jesus said, and she decided, "I want to go there!"

Sitting on the sofa and quietly observing all this, Stevey Joy jumped up and said, "If Maria is going to God's big, big house, I wanna go too!"

So we repeated the process, putting Stevey Joy up on the kitchen countertop along with Maria, and she too prayed a simple yet profound prayer, inviting Jesus into her heart. Mary Beth and I couldn't hold back the tears . . . and we didn't try. Nothing in this life could bring us more joy than knowing that our children were on their way to heaven!

I still had to get them to preschool that morning, but the celebration continued once we arrived. I walked Stevey Joy to her class first, and she told her teacher what had happened that morning. Her teacher gave her a big hug. Then we walked next door to Maria's class.

Maria and Stevey Joy in their dance recital costumes.

"Tell Miss Megan what you did today," I said.

"What did you do?" Megan asked.

"I invited Jesus into my heart so now I can go to God's big, big house."

Megan and Maria wrapped their arms around each other.

Again that morning I walked down the hallway of Harpeth Hills Preschool wiping tears from my eyes, thankful that Maria's early preschool protests hadn't won out, thankful for Miss Megan and my buddies in Audio Adrenaline and the song "Big House," thankful that God put the desire in my little girl's heart to want to be with Him, and so thankful that He made a way for all of us to be where we ultimately were meant to be—with Him.

It was the morning of February 20, 2008. We never imagined that Maria would be going to God's big, big house so soon.

Visiting Maria at preschool for "donuts with Dad" day.

Chapter Twenty-six

The Ladybug That Lost Its Dots

In China, little red ladybugs are frequently identified with adoption. There are several explanations, but for whatever reason, from the beginning of our adoption journey, ladybugs have always been associated with Chinese adoptions and therefore with our three girls.

Maria was our special little ladybug, and she loved wearing all sorts of ladybug outfits. She even had a ladybug umbrella, a ladybug raincoat, ladybug boots, and the list goes on. It turns out that not all ladybugs are as calm and docile as they seem, because of all of our six kids, Maria was definitely our most feisty and strong-willed young'un.

Melissa Northup, our wonderful, compassionate babysitter who helped Mary Beth with the children, was often at her wit's end trying to make Maria behave. We realized we had to devise some sort of disciplinary measure especially for Maria. She could test any babysitter but especially Melissa because she was so sweet and tender. She had a hard time even speaking firmly to the girls, so we needed to put a program in place that would enable Melissa to invoke the dreaded "I'm going to have to tell your parents when they get home" method of discipline.

We created three little ladybugs that hung on the refrigerator, one for each of our young girls, Shaoey, Stevey Joy, and Maria. On each ladybug were three black dots stuck on with Velcro. Whenever one of the girls got in trouble or disobeyed Melissa, she took one dot off the ladybug.

If one of the girls—translated Maria—lost all three of her dots, she would be disciplined by Mary Beth or me when we got home—usually me.

Discipline with Dad sometimes involved a time-out, and I would go and sit with her, but more often the discipline involved a long talk about what she had done wrong and why it was unacceptable behavior. (According to my kids, my lectures are the stuff of legends. I know I can get a little long-winded, but I'm certain that their tales of my three- to four-hour discourses are entirely fictitious and greatly exaggerated!)

Of course, Shaoey and Stevey Joy rarely lost a dot. Maria's poor ladybug, however, often found itself dotless by the end of the day when Melissa was watching them.

On more occasions than I could count, Mary Beth and I would come home to find that all three of Maria's dots were gone. Melissa would be almost crying. "I didn't want to do it, but I had to . . ." Melissa loved Maria very much, as we all did.

"No, that's okay," I would say. "We've got to stay the course with our little passionate one. She's gonna change the world with that energy of hers. We've just gotta keep trying to steer it in the right direction."

For all the challenging moments with Maria, she brought far more joy and laughter to our home than anything with her silly ways. "I love you, ya gooberhead" was one of her favorite ways to say good night. She could always get a laugh out of us by quoting Mater from Disney's *Cars* movie: "Hi, my name's Mater, as in Tuhmater, 'cept without the tuh." She could sing every word of "Best of Both Worlds" by Hannah Montana and "I Love You a Bushel and a Peck," taught to her by her mom. When she was happy, all seemed right with the world.

Tuesday, May 20, 2008, was an exciting day for our family. That was the day our oldest daughter, Emily, now twenty-three, found her wedding dress. Over the weekend a few days earlier, Emily had gotten engaged to Tanner Richards, a good, godly young man who not only impressed Emily with his gentlemanly character but also made it through the gauntlet of her brothers' approval as well as her parents'. Since she had been a little girl, I had prayed that if it was God's plan for Emily to be married someday, He would bring the right man into her life at the right time. I was sure that Tanner was an answer to that prayer.

The couple was planning an October wedding outdoors on our property, so even though Emily had been engaged for less than a week, plans were already way behind as far as Mary Beth was concerned. That's why we were all ecstatic when Emily found the perfect wedding gown. She had made the trip to the dress boutique along with Mary Beth and her future mother-in-law and sister-in-law as well as her best friend, and they all gave her glowing votes of approval about the dress. But Emily wanted one more vote before she was convinced—mine. She called me and asked me to come see her in the potential wedding dress.

I was the guy who had written "Cinderella." There was no way I was going to miss this moment. It took me more than half an hour to drive across town to where the boutique was located, but I would have driven any distance to see my daughter in her wedding dress.

When I arrived, the women made me close my eyes and sit on a couch while Emily hid in the dressing room and the girls fluffed and arranged her gown. She came out and stepped up on a small platform, and the women instructed me to open my eyes on the count of three.

I opened my eyes, and for a fraction of a second, I saw my little six-year-old Emily standing in front of me. *How did this happen that she is now standing there in a wedding dress?* I thought to myself. *Where did the time go?* The smile on her face was worth more than the price of ten wedding dresses, and I instinctively rose off the couch to embrace my beautiful, beaming daughter. "Yes!" I said. "It's perfect." It was a Cinderella moment for sure.

Then, of course, she began to explain to me how excited she was that the shop had offered to let her purchase the floor sample for a discounted price. We argued with her for a few minutes and told her we wanted to buy

With Emily after she picked out her wedding dress . . .
a Cinderella moment for sure.

her a new one, but she was adamant that getting a good deal would make the dress mean even more to her. Like mother like daughter.

Mary Beth and I had dinner with some friends after the dress fitting and then returned home later that evening with Emily's new wedding dress to discover that Maria's dots were all gone from her ladybug—again. She and Stevey Joy were so excited to see their sister's wedding dress when we walked in the door that I decided to delay our "discussion" until the next morning and let the night be a celebration. Little girl squeals of delight echoed through the house as Mary Beth unzipped the bag containing the dress. She pulled out the gown, and the girls oohed and ahhed. Maria couldn't simply look at the dress. She wanted to wrap the lace around herself. (Of course, we had to make sure her face and hands were washed clean of any post-dinner stickiness.) This was even better than a princess costume! Not only that, but Emily and Tanner had asked Maria and Stevey Joy to be flower girls in their wedding, so Maria was especially excited about the dress and all things related to Emily and Tanner's coming day.

The next morning Maria and I made another trip to the bathroom where we would often go to have our talks about why her ladybug had lost all of its dots while we were away. Maria had just turned five a week earlier, and we'd had a great birthday celebration. She and Stevey Joy had also just graduated a few days earlier from preschool, and I had had the video camera rolling as she walked down the aisle in her tiny white cap and gown to receive her diploma. And a few weeks before that, we'd had one of our best spring breaks ever in Florida, where I had created some of my famous family videos featuring Maria and Stevey Joy. Maria was getting funnier and sillier the older she got, and she loved making us laugh. I made a home video of an impromptu song called "Dishwashin' Daddy," which I sang with my guitar while Maria washed the dishes (fortunately, she was clothed this time). We were in a really good place with Maria, and even though her stubborn streak was still alive and well, we seemed to be making great headway, with her sweetness and silliness winning out more often.

Nothing in me wanted to have this corrective conversation and discipline my little girl, who was being her goofy little self the morning of May 21. But I knew that part of why we were in a better place with her was because we were working hard at being consistent and following through with what we had told her. I knew what the right "dad thing" to do was, as much as I didn't want to do it. "Maria, you know how much your daddy loves you, don't you?" I asked her.

"Yes."

"Well, because I love you so much, when you disobey Melissa so many times that you lose all your dots on your ladybug, you know I have to discipline you, right?"

She nodded.

After a few minutes of further discussion, as we always did, before we left the bathroom we prayed together, and like many times before, I cried as I hugged her and told her again how much I loved her. I think that because shame and the fear of it were such powerful forces in my young life, I've always tried my best to make sure my children don't feel shame from me, even when I have to correct and discipline them. I'm sure I've blown it plenty of times, but that's been my desire. Like most parents who love their children fiercely and feel the weighty responsibility of trying to "train them up in the way they should go," I've wrestled a lot with knowing the best way to discipline them in each situation. One of my most frequent prayers as a dad has been to ask God for wisdom to know how to love the children He has entrusted to me in the way He would have me do it.

I wish I could do that moment over, even though I don't know I would do it any differently. I was trying to love her the best way I knew how. And I'm thankful that it ended in a very tender moment, with a prayer, a few tears, and a sweet hug from my little ladybug before she buzzed out the door to go play with her sisters.

Chapter Twenty-seven

The Accident

Certain days are indelibly impressed on our hearts and minds, sometimes on a national basis, such as the day our country was attacked at Pearl Harbor or the day terrorists attacked America on 9/11. If you survive the experience, you almost don't want to remember, yet you can never forget. For our family, Wednesday, May 21, 2008, is such a day—a day when the enemy launched a vicious, full-scale attack against us.

The morning dawned a beautiful, sunny, warm spring day in Tennessee. It was another whirlwind of activity around the Chapman home, although I had to make only one trip to the school each way that day, since Stevey Joy and Maria had graduated from preschool at the end of the previous week. They were excited to stay home and have a play day.

Caleb, our eighteen-year-old, was set to graduate from high school in a few days, and we were planning a big party for him that weekend. Emily was at Show Hope, where she had been working for the past few months since she had graduated from Baylor University, and our seventeen-year-old son, Will Franklin, had driven over to his school to audition for a play. Caleb was practicing his guitar in our music room. Mary Beth and I were in the dining room working on wedding lists and a zillion other details, now that we knew we would be hosting a wedding in a few months. I had set up a keyboard on the dining room table and was already working on some musical ideas for an instrumental called "Sisters" for the bride's attendants' and flower girls' entrance and a song called "Emily's Smile," which I wanted to be played as I walked Emily down the aisle and presented her to her groom.

Shaoey came home from school around three o'clock and immediately joined Stevey Joy and Maria playing in the backyard, about thirty yards behind our driveway. Our babysitter, Melissa, had been with the younger girls earlier in the day, but now that Shaoey was home from school and both Mary Beth and I were at home, Mary Beth suggested that Melissa take off early and enjoy the beautiful blue-sky weather. Melissa gladly took her up on the offer.

The younger girls were running in and out of the house, and I noticed Maria was carrying a Cinderella Barbie doll and was trying to tug a pair of doll-sized white gloves over Barbie's rubber hands and arms. Maria was having trouble getting the gloves on the doll, so Mary Beth offered to help her. But even my wife had difficulty getting the gloves on the doll's hands and Maria was too hyped-up to be patient, so she bolted out of the dining room, leaving Cinderella Barbie to Mary Beth.

At some point, the girls got dressed up in various outfits from their closet, pretending to get ready to go to a Jonas Brothers concert; then they ran out to play on the playground.

About that time, my cell phone rang, and I saw that it was my manager and close friend Jim Houser calling from Creative Trust. I picked up the phone and answered, but the cell phone reception was not good inside our home, so I stepped outside onto our wraparound porch to talk with Jim.

Jim told me he had been trying to get in touch with me all day. That wasn't unusual; Jim handled the logistics of my concert schedule and career, so he and I talked three or four times a week, and when he needed me, he called repeatedly until he got me. But because of the poor cell phone reception inside our house, I hadn't noticed Jim's calls. When he finally got ahold of me at 4:55 p.m., he had some good news about a potential tour with my friend Michael W. Smith. Over the years, Michael and I had performed at various venues together, but we had never done a full-blown tour. Now both Michael and I had agreed to do the tour, and Jim was working out the details with Michael's manager, Chaz Corzine, and we were close to having everything nailed down.

As I was standing on the front porch talking with Jim, I saw Will pull onto our property, slowly turn his old hand-me-down Land Cruiser through our gate, and drive up our gravel driveway, which winds past the house to the garage in the back. I noticed specifically that Will was driving slowly and was not talking on a cell phone. Although I didn't think much about it at the time, I was so grateful later that God had allowed me to notice those details and have absolute assurance that Will wasn't distracted.

The girls in the backyard saw Will pull onto our property too. Maria had been trying to get on the monkey bars on the playground but couldn't reach them, and she had asked Shaoey to help her. "Here comes Will," Shaoey said to Maria. "He'll help you get on the monkey bars." Being the world-class big brother that he is, Will always dropped whatever he was doing to play with the girls. As he rounded the corner, headed toward the garage, Maria yelled out to him, "Will!" And then our rambunctious little girl started running toward the Land Cruiser.

Shaoey screamed at her little sister, "Maria! Stop!"

But she didn't. Instead, Maria kept running toward the SUV.

Still on the phone, I suddenly heard screams out back, not the normal little girl squeals of delight that their big brother was home or that he was tossing them in the air and catching them, or even screams of mock fear in response to being chased around the backyard by one of their brothers. These screams sounded different than any I'd ever heard before.

"I hear something going on," I told Jim. "Hold on a second . . ." I headed around the porch toward the garage to find out what was happening.

Mary Beth had heard the horrifying noise too, and about that same time she came out of the house and saw Shaoey running toward her from the driveway. "Mom!" Shaoey screamed. "Will hit Maria with the car!"

Mary Beth ran out to the driveway, where Will had picked up Maria and was carrying his sister in his arms next to his heart. He cried desperately,

"Maria, wake up!" He saw Mary Beth. "I hit her with the car!" he cried. A large circle of blood was visible on the driveway. Both Will and Maria had blood all over them as well.

As Mary Beth took Maria from Will, she cried, "Call 911! And get your dad." Will tried to make the call, but he was already in shock and couldn't get his phone to work. Mary Beth ran across the driveway and laid Maria down in the grass. She immediately tried to clear the blood from Maria's nose and mouth and attempted to blow air into her mouth, trying to breathe for her. Maria did not respond.

Just then I rounded the corner, still on the phone with Jim, and the sight staggered me. "Oh, my God!" I cried loudly. I never use that phrase under ordinary circumstances. But I did that day. I dropped the cell phone with Jim still on the call. Jim could hear the screaming and the confusion but had no idea what had happened. He knew me well enough to know that something awful must have occurred.

On another line from his office, he called my road manager, David Trask, who lived a short distance away from us.

"David, I don't know what's going on," Jim said, "but something terrible just happened at the Chapmans' house. Can you head over there?"

"I'm on my way," David said, already out the door of his home.

I raced to Mary Beth and lifted our little girl out of the grass and carried her over to a rug on the floor right outside our back door in the garage. "Will hit her with the car," my wife cried. I got down on the ground and took over the rescue breathing on our daughter. Mary Beth ran inside the house and called 911. She stood at the doorway giving me CPR instructions as the dispatch operator gave them to her. I applied compressions, praying loudly in between, "Breathe, Stevey! Breathe, Stevey Joy!"

"Steven, it's Maria!" Mary Beth called out.

"What!" I looked more closely at my daughter covered in blood. It was only then that I realized Maria had changed into a maroon and pink ballerina tutu, an outfit typically worn by Stevey Joy. It was not Stevey but

Maria. I struggled to piece together what was happening. Nothing about any of this was making sense . . . it all just seemed like a very bad dream.

A paramedic who lived nearby heard the 911 dispatch on his scanner and pulled into our driveway. Mary Beth ran to him and tugged him toward the garage, screaming, "You've gotta save my little girl!"

The paramedic rounded the corner and took over for me working on Maria on the ground. I stepped back, dropped to my knees, and began to pray at the top of my lungs. "God, You can't let this happen . . . You can't ask this of us . . . we can't do this . . . You've got to heal my little girl right now . . . please, God. You can do this . . . I know You can! God, *please* . . ."

More paramedics soon arrived, and in the midst of the chaos, they moved Maria further into the garage and worked desperately trying to save her life. A few minutes later, I heard the loud grinding sound of the Vanderbilt Medical Center LifeFlight helicopter off in the distance, but I didn't see it hovering over the trees and eventually landing in a field down the road about a quarter of a mile from our home.

In my mind, I knew Maria wasn't breathing when they put our baby in the ambulance to transport her to the helicopter and on to the hospital, but I refused to give up on her.

My brother, Herbie, had been working at our barn, and when he heard the commotion, he had come running. He found eight-year-old Shaoey and then searched for Stevey Joy. Standing nearby Shaoey at the time of the accident, Stevey Joy too had watched in horror as it happened. Herbie found Stevey Joy in the house, upstairs, curled tightly in a fetal position under her bed, in the bedroom she shared with Maria. She was terrified. Outside, Shaoey continued sobbing uncontrollably.

Meanwhile, in shock, Will bolted toward the pond in front of our home. Shaoey chased after him, crying and yelling for him to come back. Caleb, who had come running out of the house at the sound of all the commotion, saw Will running and raced after him, tackling him in the grass near the pond and holding him down as Will struggled to get away.

"I can't stay here!" Will pleaded with his older brother.

Caleb continued holding him. "Where would you go? We love you, Will."

Caleb grabbed at Will's T-shirt, covered in their sister's blood. "We've got to get this off you," Caleb cried. Will tried to argue, saying he had to wear the shirt because of what he had done. Caleb ripped at Will's shirt, tearing it off his body. He wadded up the shirt and pitched it into the pond.

David Trask, having received the phone call from Jim Houser, was the first person to reach our house. Herbie met him and through his tears briefly explained that Will had hit Maria with the SUV. David called Jim to tell him the news.

David had worked with me for years as my road manager, but he was much more than that; he was like a family member to us. And the scene he came upon that day was far too familiar to him. Years ago, as a seventeen-year-old, David had hit a child with a car when the child had run out in the street in front of David's car and he couldn't stop. That child had not survived. David had often told me about the long-term effects of that accident and how devastating that experience had been in his life.

David saw Caleb holding Will tightly, so he ran to the boys and wrapped his arms around Will, who was sobbing uncontrollably. David took over for Caleb, holding Will in place on the ground and gently stroking his hair at the same time. He understood what Will was feeling. "Maria is in God's hands," David told Will.

Meanwhile, my prayer was, "Breathe life into Maria. Breathe life into Maria, right now, God." I prayed over and over, "Breathe life into Maria, oh, God . . . please!"

Our friend and nearby neighbor Lori Mullican arrived shortly after David. Nearly ten years earlier, Lori and her husband, Ray, had lost their daughter Erin when Lori and their daughters, Erin, eight, and Alex, five, had been hit by a seventeen-year-old driver. Lori and Alex had survived the crash; Erin had not. I know it was not coincidental that David and Lori—two people who understood the trauma we were experiencing from opposite perspectives, David, the person who had struck a child, and Lori, the parent who had lost a child—were the first friends to arrive at our house.

Another neighbor, Rick Wood, had been taking a walk, and when he saw the situation, he ran up our driveway to assist us. "Come on. Let me drive you to the hospital," Rick said and hopped into our van. I was in no condition to drive, so I got in the front passenger seat. Mary Beth and Lori were in the backseat, desperately making phone calls urging our friends to pray.

As we started driving down our driveway, I saw our sons, Will Franklin and Caleb, and David Trask by the pond on our property. When I saw David holding Will, I knew I had to reassure my son somehow. There were no words that could express all I was feeling, but I felt sure that Will's emotions were roaring condemnation and guilt within him. I knew he might want to give up on hope, and on life itself, if Maria did not survive. So even though we were rushing to the hospital, I had Rick stop long enough for me to roll down the window so I could call out to Will. My heart was breaking for him even as I knew his was being shattered. "Will Franklin, I love you!" I yelled at the top of my lungs. "Your father loves you!"

I wanted him to hear something from me at that moment, something that confirmed no matter how horrible the situation he was still my son, something that might help him survive the crushing weight of guilt and shame I knew he must be feeling.

A few minutes earlier, as we were hurrying to get into the van to follow the ambulance, a young police officer had pulled in and stopped me at the back of the house, near where the accident had happened.

"I need to talk to you and get a report," he said. "What happened?"

In the midst of the chaos, I somehow understood that the young police officer was simply doing his job, but unwittingly, he was being terribly insensitive to the situation. "I just need the facts," he said. "I need to know what happened."

In staccato phrases, I hurriedly tried to give him a brief summary of what I knew. "Well, my son was coming home . . . I was standing on the porch . . . I saw him . . . he didn't see his little sister . . . he came around the corner . . . she was in the playground . . . she was running toward him . . . he was in a car that was up high and didn't see her . . . that's what my little girl told me."

"Well, I'm going to need to talk to your son," the officer said.

I understood that, but I also understood that my young son was on the verge of slipping or had already slipped into a state of shock or worse.

"No," I said. "You will not talk to my son right now. He will talk to you later, but not right now."

"I need to get my report," the officer reiterated. "I need to talk to your son."

I got square up in the policeman's face and yelled at him, "You *will not* speak to my son right now! You can get your report later, but he is dealing with the trauma that his little sister might be dead!" I was frantic to get into the van to chase after the helicopter transporting Maria to the hospital, but I didn't want this guy going after Will once I was gone.

When the officer finally relented, we pulled out of the gravel driveway and onto the main road, past the open area on a neighbor's property where the helicopter had landed. The paramedics were loading Maria onto the chopper as we passed by, and I was tempted to stop and wait until they took off, but that would serve no purpose. We had to get to the hospital as fast as possible, and we were headed right into Nashville's rush-hour traffic. I saw the helicopter take off through the trees moments after we passed by.

The ride to the hospital seemed like it would never end. Mary Beth was in the backseat, and between praying and screaming and crying, she continued calling friends, urging them to pray. I sat in the front praying out loud over and over, "Breathe life into Maria, God. Please, breathe life into her."

As I was praying, I was simultaneously and rhythmically pounding on the inside of the car door. "Please, God. Breathe life into Maria." I felt almost as though I was breathing for Maria. I kept striking the car so hard that Lori reached over from the backseat and grabbed my arm. "Just keep praying, Steven," she said, trying to calm me down.

As we raced to the hospital, I made up my mind that I wouldn't leave there without Maria . . . regardless of what the doctors told us . . . and I feared the worst . . . but I was prepared to pray and beg and plead and remind God of all the times He had done it before . . . and I wouldn't stop until Maria was breathing again. *I don't care what people think*, I thought. *I'm gonna bar the doors if I have to and keep praying until God brings our little girl back to us. I've heard all the stories. I know God can do it. He has done things like this before, so I'm gonna pray until He does it. They are gonna have to cuff me and drag me out of there, because I'm not giving up on God or Maria. I'm not leaving until we leave there together, as a whole family.*

David Trask followed behind us with Caleb and Will. Caleb contacted Emily, who had just gotten off work, and told her to go straight to the hospital. She met Tanner and headed downtown, aware that Maria had been hit by a car but little else.

When we finally arrived at the hospital, we rushed to the emergency room, but it felt as though we were moving in slow motion, in a blur of sights and sounds that didn't connect. Geoff and Jan Moore and several of our close friends were already there, as were Mary Beth's brother, Jim, and his wife, Yolanda.

A hospital staff member ushered Mary Beth and me away from the hustle and bustle of the emergency room. I barely remember passing a few friends on the way and receiving a few quick hugs as we were led into a little room. Then it was just Mary Beth and me and a couple of doctors.

"We tried everything," one of the doctors quietly said to Mary Beth and me. "We pulled out everything in our bag, we emptied the bag, and I'm so sorry, she didn't . . . she didn't make it."

Mary Beth stiffened and screamed, her tears unrestrained. "No! No!" she cried again and again.

I heard the doctor's words, just as I had expected to, but I did not accept them. "Can we go see her?" I asked.

"Yes, of course," the doctor replied, leading the way into the emergency room.

Mary Beth and I went into the emergency room and looked down at our precious little girl. By then she had been disconnected from most of the tubes and wires running to machines, but the doctors and nurses were still in the room working around her. She had a bruise on her forehead and a "strawberry" on her chin, but other than that she looked to be peacefully asleep.

I said to myself as much as to them, "I'm going to pray." The doctors and nurses respectfully stepped aside but remained in the room.

I started to pray aloud. "God, You've done this before. You raised Jesus from the dead . . . You have the power . . ." I just knew that God was going to fix this. He *had* to . . . I *had* to! We believed in Him; we believed He could do miracles, so I was intent on pounding on His door, just as I had on the car door on the way to the hospital.

I prayed that way for nearly five minutes. Finally, I felt Mary Beth's hand on my back. "Sweetheart," I heard her say softly as she leaned into me and hugged me tightly. "We've got to let her go," she whispered. "She's already gone. She's with Jesus, so it's okay to let her go."

I looked deep into the eyes of my precious, brokenhearted wife. I knew these were the last words she ever wanted to hear herself say. "Do you really think so?" I asked. "You feel sure?" I knew deep in my heart that she was right, but everything inside me wanted to fight against it.

She squeezed me tighter. "Yes, I think so," she said sadly, the tears streaming down her face. Mary Beth would later question whether we had given up too soon, but she was right. I simply did not want to accept it and wasn't ready. I was holding on to hope against hope that God would raise Maria from the dead, but it was time to let her go to Jesus. In truth, she already had.

Time no longer existed for us. I don't know how long we stayed right there, but in some real way, I felt like the veil between heaven and earth, between this life and the next, was being pulled back. Part of both of us wanted so badly to crawl into the bed beside Maria and go with her. But we knew we had five other children waiting for us on this side of the veil.

In my heart and mind, I continued to pray, "If this is the answer, God, what now? There has to be purpose in this. God, if You are *not* going to raise Maria and answer that prayer, I have to know You are doing something here, You are answering some prayer. God, You *have* to let me know . . . You *have* to give me something right now . . . Please! I'm Your son, and this is so screwed up. This is so wrong."

I looked around the room at the doctors and nurses. I didn't know anybody there except my wife, but I was overcome with the sense that I needed to say something to the men and women in that room. Nothing made any sense in that moment except to take my next breath and speak the words that came to my lips.

"I know you have experienced this before," I said. "We're standing right at eternity's door . . . the door to heaven. I know you've stood here many times with what you do. I'm prepared to stay here and pray . . . but I think I'm supposed to stop. It's so hard . . . but I think I'm supposed to. And I also think I'm supposed to tell you, to remind you that we're all gonna stand here one day at the door of eternity ourselves. This is what everything in life comes down to . . . this moment right now. And you need to meet my little girl, and you need to meet Jesus, the One who created you.

"I hope you've dealt with that. And if somehow this moment right now could change eternity for you, that would honor my little girl's life . . . that would make this moment matter. Please don't miss this."

I wasn't sure if anything I said even made sense, but in that moment, I knew that eternity was all that mattered. God was pulling back the veil for a moment to let me see just enough to know that it was all true. Heaven was utterly and entirely real, and Maria was alive and well with Jesus.

The doctors and nurses respectfully nodded, though no one said a word. A staff person later told us that one of the doctors in the ER who had worked so desperately to save Maria did not return to work for several days because of the impact of that moment.

Neither Mary Beth nor I wanted to say good-bye to Maria, but we knew we had to—for now, for a little while. Finally, after a few more minutes, I leaned over and gently kissed Maria's forehead. Mary Beth did too, and when she raised up, her entire body was shaking. I held her tightly, and we walked out together to tell our family and friends that Maria was with Jesus.

How does a dad explain such a thing to his children? We huddled up as a family, Emily and Tanner, Caleb and his girlfriend Julia, and Will Franklin—and wept. I whispered as we held desperately to each other, "That is Maria's shell in the emergency room, but her real body is with Jesus now. She's not going to be here with us. It's going to seem unbearably hard, but we are going to hold on to each other and to God's promises. We are absolutely going to see her again, but not on this side of heaven."

As I said those words, I wondered, *How are we going to survive? I know Maria is okay, but how are the rest of the kids going to survive? How are any of us going to survive?*

The moment I said those words I bounced back from that place of intense clarity with Maria—with her shell, her real body being with Jesus—to a black hole of despair. I had to declare again and again, if for no other reason than to remind myself, "The Lord gives and the Lord takes away; blessed be the name of the Lord. God, I'm gonna trust You and Your promises . . . help me remember what You've shown me." Only as I kept my focus on that truth did any clarity or sanity return.

Mary Beth and I went next door, into the larger room where our friends and family members were waiting just off the emergency room. About a hundred people had heard that Maria had been hit by a car and might not survive and had rushed to Vanderbilt to be with us and to pray.

I remembered when our good friend Bill Lee had lost his wife, Carol Ann, for whom he and his family had prayed for days. At the funeral visitation, I approached Bill wondering what I was going to say that might be helpful or appropriate, but I couldn't find the words. Bill's eyes caught mine, and he hugged me. As he held on to my shoulders, he said, "It's true,

Steven. It's all true!" Tears welled in Bill's eyes and then in mine as Bill said, "Keep telling people that it *is* true. God *is* enough. Heaven *is* real. Carol Ann is there. It's all true." At that moment, I couldn't comprehend all that Bill was expressing to me.

Now I understood.

A tug-of-war was going on in my heart and mind and would continue in the days and years ahead, but an incredible clarity came to me in that emergency room. I wasn't working at it or trying to conjure up something that wasn't there. It was so clear. I knew the door of heaven was cracked open just a bit. I couldn't see inside, but there was a light . . . no, more than a light . . . a consuming, comforting, drawing presence. Maria was there with Jesus, right where she wanted to be. She had asked Mary Beth on February 20, "Does God really have a big, big house? I wanna go to God's big house. I wanna live with Jesus in His big house." And I knew—I knew both intellectually and spiritually—that it was true. It was *all* true. Maria was with Jesus.

What we see now only by faith is nonetheless real. Heaven is real and so is life in this world, and right now our daily lives are being lived out on this side of the very thin veil between the two. Yes, we grieve, and that grief can sometimes feel like it's going to crush us—we would come to understand that in the desperate days ahead. But we do *not* grieve as those who have no hope . . . we have the hope of heaven and the promises of God that He will not leave us or forsake us, that He is sovereign and He is good, that He is *with* us and *for* us . . . and that makes all the difference in the real world.

That's why I was able to stop praying, because I knew Maria was home. I knew beyond any doubt in that moment that she was safe in the arms of Jesus. I wanted so badly to push the door wide open and see all the way in, or maybe even run in after her. But I couldn't. I could only stand at the threshold and be comforted by the hope and the promises that I was certain of in that moment. It was all I had . . . and it was enough. A moment between heaven and the real world when God gave me a very brief but life-changing, heart-saving glimpse into eternity.

SEE

Chapter Twenty-eight

Clarity

In the hospital, I experienced moments of incredible clarity even as I was grieving. The clarity was not automatic; nor was it perpetual; it was contingent on declaring the truth. And for me, that was a spiritual tug-of-war. I bounced from moments of intense clarity to a dense darkness and utter chaos. Questions pummeled my mind.

Had Maria been scared when the accident happened? The thought that she had been afraid was honestly more than I could bear. We found comfort in knowing, as we put the pieces together and talked with the doctors, that from the evidence they had they believed Maria had passed from this life into the next in the blink of an eye.

Was she lonely now, missing us and afraid?

I had to trust that she was with Jesus now, as I remembered her prayer on February 20 and how much she had wanted to go see God's big, big house. It wasn't an idea now; it was a reality, and I had to rest in the belief that God is good and Maria was where she wanted most to be—with the One who made her and loved her more than we ever could.

Okay, so by faith I'm trusting that Maria is okay, but how are we going to survive?

How is my wife going to survive this?

How is Will ever going to be able to continue living his life?

Shaoey and Stevey Joy saw the entire accident happen right before their eyes. How are they ever going to get those images out of their minds?

My mind raced, *How am I going to fix this?*

When I dwelled on those questions, it was like a massive dark and heavy wave began to roll over me. I felt myself being sucked into a black hole of despair, falling helplessly out of control, deeper and deeper.

Then somewhere in the corner of my heart, I remembered Job's prayer. "The LORD gave, and the LORD has taken away; blessed be the name of the LORD" (Job 1:21). I knew that if I was going to maintain my sanity and survive this experience, and somehow lead my family through the dark tunnel we had entered, I had to declare the truth of God's Word, whether I felt like it or not—which I didn't. I felt like a drowning man going down for the last time, emitting one final gasp of breath. *Will I use it to curse God and die, or will I use it to praise Him?*

Through my raw throat, I barely whispered, "Blessed be the name of the Lord. He gives and takes away; blessed be the name of the Lord." I slowly said it again, slightly louder. "The Lord gives and the Lord takes away; blessed be the name of the Lord." The more I said it, the more I had oxygen to say it again. "Blessed be the name of the Lord. God, I'm choosing to worship You, even now in this unbearable moment."

The words to Matt Redman's song "Blessed Be Your Name," based on Job's statement, ran through my mind: "My heart will choose to say, 'Lord, blessed be Your name.'"

It was all I could muster, but as I did, the light and the clarity came back. I sensed that we were on holy ground. God's act of drawing back the curtain just enough that I could peer into eternity, to catch a glimpse of His eternal perspective, was a gift He gave to help me survive. I could do nothing to make it open again; there was no magic formula.

In the days ahead, when Will Franklin was in a battle for survival, wondering whether he could make it through another day, it was that gift that allowed me to keep fighting against the enemy for my son and to keep fighting for our family with courage and tenacity. I discovered that my worship of God and my declaration, "God, You are my God, and You are in control; You have defeated the enemy, and I will trust You," was the difference between life and death, between hope and despair.

As dark as our journey through the valley of the shadow of death was, as I worshiped and trusted, I was certain that God was there with us. And the only thing I could imagine being more frightening than going through this darkness with God was being alone in the darkness without God. That would be ultimate hopelessness.

Was it scary? More terrifying than I have words to describe. But I found that as I continued to choose to trust, I could take the next breath; I could take another step.

There was no way we could go home. I could not imagine ever driving up our driveway again. Thankfully, we didn't have to go straight home. Our pastors, friends, and church community surrounded us immediately, helping to take care of us. Jim Houser and Dan Raines from Creative Trust plunged into handling the myriad logistical matters facing us.

Vanderbilt Medical Center had set aside a large room to accommodate the several hundred people who had showed up to pray for Maria and to be there for us. Many of that same group and more soon gathered to pray at Christ Community Church in our hometown of Franklin.

That's where we went too, to meet Stevey Joy and Shaoey, who were with my brother, Herbie, and his wife, Sherri, who pulled in at the church about the same time we did. The girls did not yet know that Maria had gone to heaven. Mary Beth and I now had to tell them before anyone else said anything. We quickly walked to the girls and steered them away from the church to a grassy area, where we knelt down with them under a tree.

Every moment of the last several hours had been unbearable, but this was to be one of the hardest.

Their innocent questions were inevitable. "Where's Maria?" Shaoey wanted to know. "Was she hurt bad?"

"Did they put a Band-Aid on her?" Stevey Joy asked.

Mary Beth choked back her tears and tried to speak. "She was hurt really bad," she said quietly. "She was hurt so bad that Jesus came and took her to heaven, where she will never hurt again."

"It's like Maria has gone on a really long trip," I said. "It's going to seem like a long time before we see her again. But we *will* see her again. We're *all* going to be together again." I was speaking to myself as much as to our daughters. The four of us huddled on the grass and wept together. I didn't want to move. I didn't want life to go any further; I wanted us all to just sit there holding on to each other until Jesus came and took us all to heaven to be with Him and Maria.

As we would soon learn, people didn't know what to say or how to share our grief. Some well-meaning people tried to share Scripture with us or tell of their personal experiences. I listened, but the words seemed to roll right over me. We discovered the best thing anyone could say was the statement one person made: "There are no words . . . I've just come to be with you."

We stayed at the church talking with people for quite a while, and looking back, it's easy to see we were probably operating on autopilot. Eventually, we, along with several close friends and our kids, crashed in the living room at the home of our friends Reggie and Karen Anderson. Nobody said much of anything; we simply wanted to huddle together.

The next few days were a blur of activity that no parent wants to endure. It was such a strange contrast. A day earlier Mary Beth and I had been planning a graduation party and a wedding. Now we had to plan a funeral. We met with a funeral director to choose a casket and a gravesite, and we met with our pastor to plan a memorial service—all in the midst of our questions and grief. I kept thinking and hoping we were in a terrible dream and were going to wake up at any moment.

One of our friends who joined us to meet with the funeral director was a dear friend of Mary Beth's named Terri Coley. When we walked out into the cemetery to pick a location for the burial, Terri noticed that a tiny ladybug had landed on her. "Mary Beth, look at this," she said. We chose that spot as the burial site for Maria's "shell." We used that word as a way to explain to Maria's sisters what we believed about her body, which we were placing in the ground, but it became a powerful reality for me. "If we believe what God says is true," I explained, "Maria is still completely and fully alive. God's Word says that to be absent from the body is to be present with the Lord, so we're sure that all that makes Maria the amazing person she was and is to us is alive and present with Jesus.[1] The shell that was used for her life here on earth is no longer needed by her, and that's what we're placing in the ground, until Jesus returns."

Over and over I prayed the one prayer I had prayed more than any other throughout my lifetime: "God, I believe. Please help my unbelief." My prayers were simple and desperate. "God, I'm going to trust You. I have nothing else."

I thought many times about the disciples of Jesus when He talked about His kingdom coming through suffering and death, and how the crowds went away. Jesus asked His followers, "Are you going to leave too?" And they replied, "Lord, where else would we go? You're the only one who has the words of eternal life" (see John 6:66–68).

I felt something similar. Where else could I go? Along with the disciples, I could say, "I don't understand much. I don't understand Your ways, but I know this much: You are God." Where else could I go? To anger or resentment? To bitterness? Those are all dead ends. Only Jesus has the words of eternal life. He is the Way, the Truth, and the Life.

Things that seemed so significant a few days earlier suddenly faded in importance. I wanted so much to maintain the clear, eternal perspective I felt I had in those earliest days after Maria went to heaven. Why would I ever get frustrated over trivial things ever again? Why would I fuss with my wife or argue about things that won't matter at all in eternity? Even in this dark valley, I had an incredible clarity about what really mattered.

The Christian community surrounded us and upheld us; we felt we were some of the most loved and prayed for people on the planet. Several friends spoke into our lives in special ways. Bible teacher and friend Beth Moore graciously reached out to encourage Mary Beth. "Satan came to the Chapman house to take a fatal blow at your family, but he is not going to win!"

Our good friend Al Andrews said something similar to me. "Satan came to your house, but he chose the wrong house." Greg Laurie, a pastor and friend from California who would lose his own son in an accident a few months later, sent me a note that was a great encouragement to me as he simply reminded me, "Your future with Maria is far greater than your past."

These admonitions put something within me that encouraged me to keep fighting on those days and in those moments when my heart was so heavy I didn't think I could take another step or another breath. Scripture passages I had read many times before took on new and much deeper meaning for me. I especially began to connect with passages that describe the defeat of our spiritual enemy. There was a part of me that was "fighting mad," and I needed to take that fight to the right battlefield. I read Revelation 12:10–11 in a new way: "Now have come the salvation and the power and the kingdom of our God, and the authority of his Messiah. For the accuser of our brothers and sisters, who accuses them before our God day and night, has been hurled down. [I so needed those mental pictures of the enemy being thrown down, tossed aside, and completely defeated!] They triumphed over him by the blood of the Lamb and by the word of their testimony; they did not love their lives so much as to shrink from death" (NIV).

Being able to take all the anger and rage I felt and direct them where they truly belonged, at the real enemy of life and all things good and beautiful, became very important for me. I began to discover verses like Romans 16:20, which says, "The God of peace will soon crush Satan under your feet" (NIV), and Colossians 2:15, which talks about how God has put to open shame the rulers and authorities who are against Him and how He has triumphed over them. I was able to find great comfort in knowing that the enemy who comes to steal, kill, and destroy is not going to have the last word, that he not only has been defeated on the cross but also is going to be brought to great shame and destruction . . . and that God will even let us be involved in the crushing of Satan under our feet! I knew there was an intense battle going on for my heart and for my family, and I desperately needed to keep remembering that the One who is with us and for us is greater than the one who is against us.

The psalms became like oxygen to me. I began to read them in a new light, seeing for the first time how many of the great "worship songs" of David often begin with a cry of desperation and pain. "How long, O LORD? Will you forget me forever? How long will you hide your face from me? How long must I take counsel in my soul and have sorrow in my heart all the day?" (Ps. 13:1–2). Not only was I not alone in asking these questions but it had been the "man after God's own heart," David, who had cried out to God and given voice to the deep wrestling in my soul. But then, along with David in the psalms, I was able to continue my prayer to say by faith, "But I have trusted in your steadfast love; my heart shall rejoice in your salvation. I will sing to the LORD, because he has dealt bountifully with me" (Ps. 13:5–6). I had never been more thankful that God hadn't edited out the pain and the struggle in His Word but had allowed the desperation of the psalmist to be shared to help me find my way through the dark.

Another psalm that became a prayer of hope and encouragement to me and my family was Psalm 34:8: "Taste and see that the LORD is good!" I also discovered Psalm 27, which says, "I remain confident of this: I will see the goodness of the LORD in the land of the living" (v. 13 NIV). Not just in heaven one of these days but here in the real world, in the land of the living.

I prayed, "God, these are Your promises; I am going to declare that these things are true. I can't imagine right now how my family will ever again taste goodness in this life . . . that we will even smile or feel true joy again . . . but I believe we will." I was able to grasp that ultimately in heaven we would taste and see the goodness of God again, but on this side of eternity, it just didn't seem possible, as heavy as our hearts were. *Okay, just let me die and let me go there,* I thought, and there were days when I pondered ways I might get there sooner. But God was faithful to rescue my heart, and every time I lifted my eyes and my heart to Him, just enough clarity and sanity returned to keep me moving forward.

Again and again I would sing, whisper, or sometimes scream at the top of my lungs, "Blessed be the name of the Lord. You give and You take away . . . I believe You are sovereign and in control, and there is so much we will never understand this side of heaven." Through it all, my prayer remained, "I trust You, Father, that You are good, that Your heart toward my family and me is ultimately good, and that just as You promised, somehow, even in this, You are working all things together for Your glory and for our good." These weren't just nice "Christian words" to say; this was me dropping my anchor in the promises and truth of God's Word and holding on for dear life to the only thing I had.

We confirmed the funeral details, a gut-wrenching process in itself, including a visitation time at our church on Friday and the memorial service on Saturday. Late Thursday afternoon Mary Beth said, "I need to go home and get some clothes and other items." Several friends went along with us.

It was a terrifying thought even to approach the driveway leading to our house for the first time after the accident. We recognized we were not ready to go into the house as we normally would, through the back door, close to where the accident had occurred, so we parked in front of the house. We stepped inside, maintaining a somber quietness, almost a holy hush, with friends on both sides of Mary Beth and me just in case we needed help.

The house seemed so terribly silent without Maria. Everything about her personality was loud. The silence was deafening, and as I walked through the hallway, I doubted we'd ever be able to live in this house again.

Each of us quickly grabbed what clothing and personal items we felt we needed. Then we gathered in the family room and formed a circle. It seemed appropriate that we pray while we were there. Caleb and I had prayed together several times at the Andersons', specifically asking God to confirm our faith in some tangible way. "God, You know we trust that Maria is with You and she is okay, even more than okay . . . but could You please just let us *see* something to help us, maybe a dream or even a vision, just something." We weren't even sure what we were asking for, just something we could point to that might bring reassurance.

After the group prayer, I walked through the house, checking to make sure everything was okay but more to retrace my memories of Maria's recent activities. I walked into the dining room and noticed the two little art tables over by the bay window where Maria and Stevey Joy loved to color. Maria had often sat there for hours at a time, coloring and gluing. She especially enjoyed gluing one piece of paper on top of another until she'd made a stack of ten or fifteen layers. Then, if Mary Beth or I didn't intervene, Maria usually covered the whole gooey mess with glitter. Of course, by then, she'd be wearing glue and glitter all over herself as well!

I glanced down at Maria's table, where she had been coloring the day of the accident. There on the table I saw a piece of what looked like notebook paper that had been folded over like a card with some color bleeding through from behind. On the front of the paper, Maria had drawn a picture of her signature flower with six petals. Maria loved drawing flowers, and ordinarily, she filled in each petal with a different color. This flower, however, had only one petal colored, and it was totally filled in—in blue, Maria's favorite color. All the other petals were blank, sketched but not colored in at all. The flower had a green stem with two leaves, and the center of the flower was as orange as the sun.

I turned the paper over to discover that on the back she had drawn a butterfly and had written a word: SEE. As far as I knew, Maria had never before written that word. She had just completed preschool and could write "I love Mom" and "I love Dad" but not much more. But the word SEE was clearly visible on the paper. And the butterfly—a symbol of new life—was the only other drawing on the paper.

As I looked at Maria's drawing, tears welled in my eyes and streamed down my face. Caleb and I had been praying for some tangible evidence that Maria was indeed with Jesus, and it was almost as though Maria had left us a message before she departed this world, and God had allowed me to find it. "SEE," she seemed to say. "I'm okay. I'm in heaven with Jesus, and He really does have a big, big house, just like you said. SEE!"

I also felt like it was a tangible reminder to my family and to me to continue to look at this life with an eternal perspective—to taste and SEE that the Lord *is* good—even when this earthly life seems so hard and sad at the moment, and to remember what 1 Corinthians 13:12 tells us: "We don't yet see things clearly. We're squinting in a fog, peering through a mist. But it won't be long before the weather clears and the sun shines bright! We'll SEE it all then, SEE it all as clearly as God sees us, knowing him directly just as he knows us!" (*Message*, all caps added).

At first, we thought Maria had not finished the drawing. Later, when Mary Beth saw it and was explaining the drawing to someone else, she recognized that Maria had drawn six petals—one for each of the Chapman children. The blue one, representing Maria herself, was filled in, completed. Her life was now complete; she was whole. The others were unfinished, still waiting for their color and yet to be filled in completely in heaven. It was a powerful encouragement to us, and that flower would become a very special symbol to each of us on the journey ahead.

We saved that piece of paper and later framed it. Today Maria's artwork hangs in our home.

We braced ourselves as best we could for the long, grueling hours ahead, including what were sure to be emotionally heavy times in the receiving line at church on Friday evening and the memorial service the following day. We had no idea what to expect, but thousands of people showed up to express their condolences. Mary Beth and I greeted people well into the evening.

Our entire family sat in the front row with our hands raised high in the air as Matt Redman led us in the song "Blessed Be the Name of the

Lord" during the memorial service. My friend Michael W. Smith also led us in worship, as again and again we declared together our trust and hope in God's promises.

Caleb expressed what so many people in the sanctuary were feeling: grief over the loss of Maria and concern for Will Franklin's well-being. Caleb told the congregation, "You know, I feel that as Dad held Maria, as she took some of her last breaths, I held my brother . . ."

Caleb paused, momentarily overcome by his emotions. Standing beside him at the podium, I wrapped my arms around him as he continued to speak. Caleb fought back the tears as he said, "We prayed for healing for Maria, but God healed her in a way that we didn't like. But God is going to heal my brother in a way that I think we're all going to like a lot."

In a spontaneous response, the crowd of people in the church rose to their feet in a standing ovation, expressing their support for Will Franklin, acknowledging the unconditional brotherly love they saw exhibited in Caleb, and conveying their agreement with the hopeful words that Caleb had just spoken. It was a powerful and desperately needed moment.

The following day, in the same church where we had held Maria's memorial service, Caleb graduated from high school. We had actually been homeschooling Caleb during his senior year so he could travel along with me and play guitar in my band. But his classmates, with whom he had traveled the first eleven years of his academic journey, had wanted him to be a part of the graduation ceremony, so they had invited him to sing a song.

The day before, when we had arrived at the church for the memorial service, Will had walked in barefoot, asking if it was okay for him not to wear shoes. He had been struggling with wearing shoes since the day of the accident because of the images it brought back to his mind. So everyone in our family removed their shoes, and all those who participated in the service did the same, both in support of Will and because we knew this was holy ground we were walking on in these moments.

As the students began to file into the church sanctuary for the graduation ceremony, everyone noticed something peculiar—the entire senior class was barefoot! Needless to say, even though we had already cried an ocean of tears in the days before, another river flowed that afternoon. Caleb sang a song he had been writing prior to Maria's going to heaven, "So Long," in which he asked the poignant question, "Why have I waited for so long to be singing you this song?" He had originally written it to be sung to his friends as they went their separate ways on the journeys ahead of them. But it took on an even deeper meaning that day as a powerful reminder to all of us that if there was something we wanted to say, or love that we wanted to express, not to put it off, to do it now.

> So this is the way it goes, we still feel like boys and girls
> Chasing around the hands of time
> I've imagined what I could be, and imagined what I would see
> But I never imagined our good-bye
> And why have I waited for so long to be singing you this song
> I thought that time was all I had
> I have so much left to say but time has faded now
> So take care so long good-bye
> And if our paths don't cross this life, in heaven it will be
> That there's no pain or death . . . just life . . . oh the day that that will be
> So take care, so long, good-bye.

Following Maria's memorial service, life seemed to be on hold. For a while, none of us even wanted to leave the Andersons' home. It became our safe haven and our hideout. When anyone did venture out, we moved together almost as a hive. Certainly, part of that related to our care for Will Franklin. We knew we needed to stay close to him, to continually remind him of our love and God's love. For the first few days, somebody remained with him virtually around the clock. With the help of Pastor

Scotty Smith and other friends, we began arranging what would become a team of professional counselors for all of our children, and we especially wanted to keep Will surrounded with love.

As the husband and dad, I knew I had to be strong, yet I didn't feel strong. I didn't have any more answers than anybody else. And of all the things I'd ever encountered in my life that I felt I had to fix, this was the ultimate "unfixable." I could only pray over and over again, asking God for strength and wisdom and continuing to trust and worship Him.

We stayed with the Andersons for a few more days and then made the short but oh so frightening journey back to our own home. It wasn't easy, and Mary Beth and I both wondered if we could continue living there. It was a gray-sky, overcast day when we returned home, and just as we pulled into the driveway, the bottom dropped out of the sky and it started pouring down rain for about five minutes. Then, almost as quickly, the rain stopped and the sun came out. It was as though God was saying, "I'm weeping with you, but I will also clear the clouds away."

We proceeded past the house and drove up to our barn, where a group of friends and family had prepared a meal for us. We stayed and visited for a while and then drove down from the barn and back up our driveway. Near the play area where Maria had been with Shaoey and Stevey Joy stood a small magnolia tree that had never before bloomed. As we pulled up the driveway, we saw something unusual. There on the magnolia tree was a huge white blossom. But only one.

Coincidence? Maybe. But we chose to take such things as signs that God was showing us He had not forgotten us, that Maria was safely in His care, and that life—although different—would go on.

With Will Franklin on stage.

Chapter Twenty-nine

The Land of the Living

Dealing with our personal matters was difficult enough; dealing with professional issues soon loomed large as well. I didn't know what I was going to do about my career. I just didn't know. Getting back onstage seemed highly unlikely. I especially couldn't imagine going back out and singing songs such as "The Great Adventure," or "Dive," or "Live Out Loud." I knew that a Steven Curtis Chapman concert required the fast, fun songs as well as the slow, more serious songs, and I just wasn't sure it would ever seem appropriate for me to play those upbeat songs again. I was more certain of their messages than ever, but the sadness was so all-consuming.

I could possibly envision me standing in front of an audience and weeping or singing "My Redeemer Is Faithful and True" and crying my eyes out, but who wants to attend a whole concert like that?

For the moment, it was all I could do to keep breathing and taking the next steps in the dark, trying to lead my family. My attitude was, "Relationships are all that matter." Certainly, my family was my priority, but I also had close business relationships, and questions about my concert schedule could not be ignored.

As soon as I came up for air following Maria's memorial service, I knew I had to make some career decisions. While everyone around us had been nothing but supportive and patient, a number of people beyond my extended family depended on me—managers, agents, concert promoters, record label personnel, not to mention the many people who had purchased advance tickets to upcoming concerts. Moreover, for me, my job, ministry, creative work, and business were all woven together. I had publicly declared for years that our faith was our anchor in the time of storms. This wasn't the first time I had experienced difficult times. My audiences had lived with me through our kids' surgeries, my parents' divorce, and Mary Beth's struggles with depression and had walked with us through the adoption process and our work with Show Hope. So dealing with real-life issues was nothing new for us.

And yet I was struggling with the thought of picking up a guitar and singing a concert again. In a real way, I wondered, *Will anything ever matter again the way it did before?*

It wasn't that what I had done previously was insignificant; it was simply that my world had shifted on its axis and I viewed things through a different lens. I wondered, too, if I could ever leave Mary Beth alone again to go out on tour. I knew the courage it was taking my wife just to get out of bed every day and take the next step. I knew the incredible weight she was carrying as a mom to her five children, who were all suffering in different ways. If I was gone for a weekend or an entire tour, that would put even more weight on her shoulders, and we were having enough trouble carrying the load together, much less being apart and attempting to function. And as a dad, I wrestled with being away from my children at all during this time, although Caleb and Will Franklin had been touring with me as a part of my band on my last tour.

Fortunately, I had finished the *This Moment* tour, featuring the song "Cinderella," and I did not have another tour scheduled yet, but I had concerts that had already been booked for as early as the weekend following the funeral. What were we going to do about them? At first, I simply told Jim Houser, "Cancel everything." He was already ahead of me and had done so for the next several weeks.

Most of the concert promoters who had booked me were tremendously understanding and gracious, despite the contractual agreements in place. Jim worked with Michael W. Smith's manager, Chaz Corzine, and for a number of dates that were too close to cancel and I could not fulfill, Michael graciously offered to fill in for me. Not only did Michael perform the dates with his own production staff and band, but he also donated the proceeds from the concerts to Show Hope.

Initially, we had people all around us almost constantly, and we revisited Maria's life again and again. Once we came home, a great deal of Mary Beth's and my time went toward getting our kids into counseling and just being there for them. Meanwhile, Geoff and Jan Moore, Reggie and Karen Anderson, and other friends stayed close to us. We spent few evenings alone, thanks to loving friends. But after a while, we were on our own more and more.

Mary Beth and I had lived much of our lives in the music business, but I never wanted to assume that things had to continue. After every tour, I asked, "Okay, is this it? Do I need to stop? How can I best love my family? God, what do you want me to do?" We had even toyed with the idea of moving to China and living there for six months of the year. We had taken our entire family to China for a month at a time during the summers, and the change of pace was astounding. Mary Beth especially enjoyed being away from the tyranny of the calendar and not having to worry about my schedule. We all drew closer without the demands and pressures of the next album and the next tour.

Even before Maria's passing, we had been thinking about making some changes, so perhaps now was the time. After about a month, however, I started asking, "What is the next step? If it is a step away from what I've done, okay. If not, what is it?"

I had already realized that a significant part of our healing came from declaring the truth of God's Word and His promises. "This is what we believe. This is what we have always believed, and if it was true then, it is true today as well." So how was I to do that? I realized I would have to keep choosing to declare the truth, sometimes taking two steps forward and three steps backward, sometimes dropping twenty steps backward. I had to choose to declare God's truth even on days when Mary Beth said, "You can believe that. But I'm just not sure I believe it today."

I had to choose to believe even on those days when I went upstairs to my soundproof writing and recording studio and screamed as loud as I could, "God, how am I supposed to do this? You have to rescue us! You have to give me wisdom; You have to give me strength to keep walking forward." Some days I yelled so loudly and for so long that I no longer had a voice to yell.

Many times I cried out like David in the psalms. I felt like I was wrestling with God. It wasn't a matter of trying to be "spiritual" or simply saying the right things; it was survival.

"Why are you cast down, O my soul, and why are you in turmoil within me? Hope in God; for I shall again praise him, my salvation and my God" (Ps. 42:5). As I read this psalm, I had a mental image of David pounding on his chest saying, "Come on, heart, come on, soul, don't give in to this despair! Remember what is true. God is for you and with you. Trust Him; hope in Him; praise Him."

Mary Beth's dad had shared with us what he had experienced when he first heard the news of the accident. Jim told us, "When I first started praying for Maria, I saw Jesus put His arms around her and take her up." Jim was not given to visions and such things, so for him to make such a statement gave Mary Beth and me comfort, especially when I was battling those questions about whether Maria was scared or if she had suffered. Another friend, Christina Burke, sketched out what she saw as she prayed for us. It was an image of an angelic-type figure with wings wrapped around a little girl.

Thinking about that moment raised all the usual "Where was God?" questions—Where was God when Maria ran toward her brother's car? What was He doing? What did His face look like when this happened? Certainly,

I believed that God was there at that moment, that He wasn't taken by surprise by any of the things that happened. "I still don't get that," Mary Beth said. "If He was there, why didn't He cause one small detail to change. Will could have come in a few seconds earlier or later, or God could have changed Maria's direction." I had no good answers for her.

Two or three weeks after we were home, I was thinking about how Job shaved his head as an act of mourning. Even standing in front of a mirror and fixing my hair seemed trivial and superficial now, so one day while everyone was gone from the house, I took clippers and went out to the spot where Maria had been lying in the driveway. I got down on my knees and shaved off all the hair on my head.

When Mary Beth came home, she looked at me quizzically but not with surprise or revulsion. I tried to explain, "I didn't want to mess with my hair anymore. Why waste time with something as trivial as my hair? It kinda felt like a Job moment."

I continued to grapple with whether to go back out on the road. Do I wait six months? Should I wait a year? Maybe I should never even consider a return to performing concerts. There were no rule books about this sort of thing. Yet something was stirring within me.

The more I thought about it, the more I wanted to go to war against the enemy, knowing that Satan had already been defeated by Jesus on the cross and that there will be a day when the God of peace will crush him under our feet. As a man—as a husband and as a father—that motivated me to get back out on the battlefield. I could fight for my family, and for other people's families, because I knew that God had a plan for ultimate victory, and I was involved. I felt I needed to stand up and declare truths such as "God is God and I am not" that I had written years earlier. As I thought about it, I realized I even needed to sing songs like "The Great Adventure," because even though my understanding had been incomplete, I had written way back then that we would travel over mountains and through some valleys. Yes, the Wild Mouse had turned into the Screamin' Eagle, but the truth was the same. It was true then, and it was equally true now. Certainly, I now had more questions, but I was more convinced of God's truth than ever before.

I talked with my pastor and other counselors. "I feel like I need to stand up and declare these truths publicly." They concurred.

I talked with Mary Beth, and while we knew we were still in a fragile place and would be for a long time, she understood and agreed for me to go. Caleb and Will Franklin were still a part of my band, and I had a sense of the importance of the three of us Chapman men onstage together declaring what we knew was true.

Finally, after another month went by, I called Jim Houser and said, "I think it's time; I need to go back to work." I knew I had some outdoor festival dates coming up in mid-July in Michigan and Wisconsin. "I think I need to do those dates."

We had little time to rehearse a new show, so I decided to do the same set of songs I had done on our last tour—except for one song: "Cinderella."

Prior to the concert, I told the band, "Guys, I don't think I can do 'Cinderella'; that will just be off-limits; that one's not gonna happen . . . and may never happen, so just leave that spot blank on your set sheets." We gathered in a circle backstage to pray as we always did before every concert. I looked around the circle and saw friends and brothers who had stood with me in the hellish fury of the last several months. My best friend, Geoff Moore, was there.

"I feel like I just need to be beside you for this," he had said.

My road manager and friend, David Trask, who had been the first one up the driveway the day of the accident and had seldom left our side since, was also there. My bass player, Brent Milligan, and keyboardist, Brian Green, both dear friends, were there. And on either side of me stood two of the most amazing and courageous men on the planet, my sons, Will Franklin and Caleb. I knew this was going to be a powerful night; I just had no clue how it was going to work or how far I would get through the set before I broke down.

I needn't have worried. As soon as we walked out onstage, people began applauding. Some were weeping; most were cheering us on. It was as though just showing up was already a victory. The applause lasted for several minutes.

I wanted to speak to the audience before performing any songs. "I don't know how far we will get," I said. "I don't know how this will go. But this is what we are choosing."

I began by singing "Blessed Be Your Name." My voice was not strong, and I squeaked and cried my way through it. But we made it through the song. I said, "If that is true, then these other things are true too. Let's go!" And we launched into our normal concert set.

I looked to my right, where Caleb stood playing guitar, and we smiled at each other. Behind me, Will was on the drums, playing every beat as if he was driving a stake deep in the ground, anchoring down to what is true. I couldn't have been more proud of my sons.

The concert went incredibly well, thanks to the audience's gracious support. Then we got to the spot in our concert set where I normally sang the song "Cinderella." The guys in the band stopped and waited to see what I was going to do.

At that moment, I said to the audience, "You know what, I wasn't sure I would ever sing this song again . . . and I'm not sure how well I will get through it tonight, but . . . tonight as I've sung these songs, I have become even more certain of the truth of God's promises . . . and the truth is I am going to dance again with my little girl."

A hush fell over the huge crowd, almost as though they anticipated that this was going to be a holy experience.

"This song from the beginning was about showing up in the moment," I said, "savoring the opportunity, because I knew these moments weren't going to last forever."

Everyone on the hillside seemed to know that I was talking about "Cinderella," even though I had not yet mentioned the song title.

"This was never a song about eternity. It was about here and now, in the real world. But now, for me, this song is going to be a song that reminds me to show up in these moments because we have only a little bit of time in the here and now to show up in each other's stories on this side of heaven. And this matters. There's a reason why God has us here right now.

"But there is a day coming when He will make everything new; He is going to wipe every tear from our eyes. The story isn't over; the dance is not over." I told the audience about Greg Laurie's note, which said, "Your future with Maria is far greater than your past."

"And this is not a fairy tale or wishful thinking," I said. "It's what Paul said in Scripture. If our hope is merely for this life, if this is all we have, then we are to be pitied . . . we're foolish. If everything in our life is simply to make things better or more comfortable in this present world, then when some unthinkable tragedy happens, we are destroyed. But if our hope is for eternity, and this life is getting us ready for that, if we really believe it, then I can sing this song 'Cinderella' because I have an eternity to dance with my little girl."

I began playing the introduction, and then I sang "Cinderella," crying and squeaking my way through it. A few times I became overwhelmed with emotion and just had to let the band play, joining back in when I could. I finally made it to the last chorus, and when I came to the end of the section where I had originally written, "'Cause all too soon the clock will strike midnight and I know she'll be gone," I spontaneously changed the words to "the clock will strike midnight, but I know . . . the truth is . . . the dance will go on." And with that change the song took on even greater significance; I've sung it that way ever since.

From there we went into "Yours." It seemed especially fitting to declare on this first night back, "It's all Yours, God. I'm Yours. There's no place in my journey that is not Yours." I had rewritten the song after Maria went to heaven, adding a third verse, and had actually released that song to radio as my response to so many who had prayed for our family. That night I sang the new verse for the first time as well.

> I've walked the valley of death's shadow
> So deep and dark that I could barely breathe
> I've had to let go of more than I could bear
> And I've questioned everything that I believe
> But still even here in this great darkness
> There's a comfort and a hope that comes breaking through
> As I can say even in death or in life, God, we belong to You
> We are Yours, God.

It was truly a triumphal moment, not because of my performance, which was fragile at best, but because just by showing up, just by being out there, Caleb and Will and I—as well as our entire family, our management team, and everyone associated with my career—were saying, "We believe. We will not allow the enemy to have the last word. Our God is great and He is good, and we will trust in Him."

Meanwhile, back at home, Mary Beth and I continued to take small steps forward as best we could. Maria's flower and the word SEE, which she had left for us, continued to be reminders and an encouragement to us as we shared the story with others. So much so that Mary Beth began talking about wanting to carry those reminders with her all the time . . . with a tattoo. This time I didn't argue even a little bit but said, "I know, let's do that together."

Mary Beth got a small tattoo on the outside of her wrist incorporating Maria's six-petal flower and a butterfly, and on the inside, she got the word SEE and Psalm 34:8, referencing the Scripture passage, "Taste and see that the LORD is good."

On my left shoulder, I had tattooed an almost exact re-creation of her flower and SEE in her handwriting. Others in the family wanted to join in. Caleb created a version of Maria's artwork and had it tattooed on the inside of his arm, and Will asked to have an M tattooed over his heart. We agreed. Eventually, Will would add a portion of prophetic Scripture: "Come, let us return to the LORD. He has torn us to pieces but he will heal us; he has injured us but he will bind up our wounds" (Hosea 6:1 NIV). Emily also got a tattoo, as did other spouses in the future.

Within a few weeks after the first concerts back, we received an invitation to tell our story on CNN's *Larry King Live*. The producers wanted our entire family to appear on the show.

While we saw this as a potentially great opportunity to declare our faith, I wasn't sure we were ready for such an interview. That would be a lot of exposure for our still very fragile and vulnerable family. Mary Beth and I went to Will Franklin and asked, "What do you think we ought to do?" We had made a decision early on that it would be important to let Will guide us as to how public we would be with our story while it was still so fresh.

Will replied, "If it is a way that we can share what we believe and honor Maria's life, then I think we should do it." We didn't want to stick a spiritual Band-Aid on the deep wounds we had incurred. Our prayer was that we could simply be honest in expressing our pain, our anger, and yet our hope. As a family, we discussed the fact that we felt like God had given us a sacred trust. Our pain and our story were things God had entrusted to us, and we wanted to steward them well. In doing so, we would be able to honor Maria's life and honor the hope and faith that would keep us moving forward. This was an important part of our healing.

In his inimitable interviewing style, Larry King was respectful but curious. He had pointed questions for Mary Beth and me regarding the moments immediately after the accident. "You didn't lose your faith or question?" he asked me.

"I was crying out to my Father," I replied. "I was crying out to the God I know as my heavenly Father." Larry looked at me skeptically but kindly.

In what, to me, were the most sensitive and strongest sections of the interview, Emily, Caleb, and Will joined us on the set. Larry had questions for each of them, and they answered with tremendous transparency yet with great faith. That's not easy to do under the glare of television lights and cameras, and Mary Beth and I were so proud of them. During a commercial break, as we were talking with Larry off camera, he made the comment, "You're an incredible family . . . I wish I could have a faith like yours."

Caleb responded, "Well, Mr. King, actually you can. All you have to do is ask for it; God will give faith to anyone who asks." It was amazing!

We fielded emailed questions from the audience during the show, and one seemed especially poignant. "Have you gotten mad at God because of this?" someone asked. Larry pitched the question to Mary Beth. "Have you asked God why *your* family, why Maria?"

"Yes," Mary Beth replied. "I've been mad, I've been sad, I've jumped up and down, I've crawled under my bed, I've gone in my closet. You name it, and I've done it. I know that I won't understand this side of eternity. Why Maria? Why Will? So to answer that question, yeah, I've been really angry."

"Never at Will?" Larry asked.

"Never," Mary Beth said without hesitation.

Another viewer asked the toughest question of all. "Why would a good and loving God allow the kind of pain your family is enduring?" Larry directed that question to me.

I acknowledged my anger and my questions. I said there was so much about this I certainly didn't understand. But I tried to explain, "My anger has been aimed at the one who comes to rob, kill, and destroy . . . Satan, but if you have ever read the book of Job, you know that God allows evil . . . I believe God was there. I believe He had tears in his eyes."

Around that same time, we did an interview with Robin Roberts on ABC's *Good Morning America*. Our prayer was that we would be completely honest and real but also be able to let those watching see what it looks like to grieve with hope.

Mary Beth said, as she had on several previous occasions, "I don't care whose lives are touched by the story and whose lives are changed or what good comes of it . . . at the heart of a mom, I just want my little girl back. But because I know that she is completely whole . . . because of my faith I know that she is completely whole and completely okay, and I'm going to see her again . . . as a mom, I have to shift that grief."

Shifting our grief was almost mandatory as the summer gave way to fall, and suddenly, Emily and Tanner's wedding was upon us. As they had originally planned, the wedding took place on October 4, outdoors on our property. The couple still wanted the song "Sisters" to play as the wedding party entered, and "Emily's Smile," the song I had been writing for Emily the day Maria went to heaven, played as I walked Emily from our house, through the grass, to the area near the pond where the guests had gathered. The entire celebration was a testimony of the couple's faith as well as that of our family and friends.

Of course, along with the excitement and joy of the day, there was a heavy weight of sadness that we couldn't ignore, so we chose to embrace it. We all missed what would certainly have been the loudest voice in the crowd—Maria's—so Stevey Joy carried a small lantern as she preceded Emily down the aisle. Inside the lantern was a beautiful monarch butterfly in honor of Maria, the missing flower girl. When Stevey reached the front, Tanner helped her open the lantern, and after a brief pause, the butterfly fluttered off into the sky.

In many ways, Emily and Tanner's wedding was an incredible day of redemption as much as a celebration of their love. After I barely made it through the father-daughter dance with Emily at the reception while Caleb sang "Cinderella" (just try to imagine how hard it was for me not to do the ugly cry), the band started playing Earth, Wind & Fire cover songs and everybody hit the dance floor. At one point, I looked out and saw my uncle Barry, who is usually very reserved, cutting a rug with his daughter, my cousin Beth!

In the middle of all the family and friends celebrating, I saw Stevey Joy and all her little cousins and friends, many who were also adopted from

Walking Emily down the aisle.

China, having the time of their lives in a circle, jumping up and down to the beat of the music. Tears filled my eyes again, but this time they were tears of joy as I was overwhelmed with the sense that I was getting another little glimpse of heaven. The pure joy I saw at this wedding celebration couldn't help but make me think about the wedding feasts referenced in passages in Luke and Revelation. I even had the thought, *Maybe this is why Jesus loved weddings when He was on earth, even performing His first miracle at one . . . maybe they reminded Him of home.* The veil between heaven and earth seemed very thin that evening, and I could imagine Maria right in the middle of the celebration in this world and in the one that's coming when our whole family is together again in the presence of Jesus.

We had no sooner calmed down from Emily and Tanner's wedding when Caleb and his childhood sweetheart, Julia Anderson, announced that they, too, planned to be married—and they were the following May 10, within days of Maria's birthday and the first anniversary of Maria's homegoing. It was another amazing celebration, the dance floor was full, and again I had a sense that I was getting a little glimpse of what was just on the other side of the veil, where Maria was waiting for us . . . where I would hear Maria say those words again, "I love it when my whole family is together."

Da

Recording "Beauty Will Rise" in a hotel room with Brent Milligan.

Chapter Thirty

Waiting and Watching for Beauty to Rise

Although I could not have imagined doing so during Maria's visitation and memorial service, I began to turn to my faithful friend, music, to process what I was thinking and feeling. Music became a way to voice my laments, questions, fears, and hopes. I wasn't trying to write songs and certainly wasn't trying to write an album; I was just doing what I had done since I was a kid in high school, trying to put what was stirring around in my heart on a page and in a song. And never had there been so much stirring around in my heart. The themes of waiting and longing in particular constantly found their way into my thoughts and were expressed in songs I was writing.

A few years earlier, John Mayes, a guitar maker from Oklahoma, had sent me a beautiful handmade guitar, which I had played on only a few occasions. I have amassed a somewhat embarrassingly large number of guitars through the years, and many of them have special significance to me. For some reason, my Mayes guitar was the one I reached for as I began to write the songs that stirred inside me. It just seemed to have the story in it. Somehow that guitar had a quiet, sad tone and provided just the right melancholy quality; it almost seemed the guitar itself was weeping with me as I played.

One day as I sat on my front porch thinking about all the implications of Maria's word SEE, which she had left for us, I began to list the things I can't wait to SEE.

I can't wait to see that smile of Maria's that's so big it actually causes her almond-shaped eyes to almost disappear. I can't wait to hear her sing the songs she was singing at her preschool graduation the week before she went to be with Jesus . . . and maybe even the new songs she is learning in heaven!

I can't wait for my wife's heart to be whole again and totally healed forever, never to have to deal with the sadness of being separated from her little girl, or any sadness for that matter ever again. I can't wait to hear the sound of Maria playing with her sisters again, or the sound of her mom laughing at her silliness. And I especially long for that day when my son Will Franklin can sweep his little sister up in his arms again and know, not just by faith but by seeing with his own eyes, that Maria is okay and all is well.

The truth is waiting has never been something I've been very good at or very fond of. Years earlier, I had written a song called "Wait" with songwriter/artist Margaret Becker for my *Real Life Conversations* album. Even then I had struggled with the idea of waiting and the great value that God says comes from it. But I've discovered that in the Bible, the words *wait* and *trust* are the flipsides of the same coin. They go together, and waiting for what God has said will come to pass is not a matter of wondering *if* it will happen but when. So because Jesus assured us that He is preparing a place for us to be with Him, we can be certain that heaven is our future home. And the biblical idea of waiting is not passive; it is actively anticipating that what God said He would do He will do. So to write "Just Have to Wait" was not an ambiguous hope or wishful thinking that we will see Maria again; we *know* we will see Maria again in a little while. But for now, all I *can* do is wait in expectation. In other words, I *only* have to wait for what God has promised to come to fruition . . . it's *only* a matter of time . . . I *just* have to wait for it. There was a tremendous amount of encouragement and comfort for me in this simple truth, and I had to write a song about it.

Another song came as I sat at our kitchen table pondering heaven again, as I often did in those early days after Maria left earth. I was having one of those heart-to-heart talks with God. My side went something like this: "God, You know how much I'm aching and longing to be in heaven, and if You know everything, then You also know I'm struggling with something. I know I'm supposed to want to see Your face more than anything else, and I can say I do, but if I'm completely honest, what I'm longing for most of all right now is to SEE my little girl . . . to see her face and hear her voice and get a kiss from her that smells like the maple syrup she had on her pancakes for breakfast. I'm sorry this is what I'm longing for the most, but, God, You know my heart, and I might as well be honest with You."

As I began to pour out my heart to God, as we're invited to do in Psalm 62:8, and write the song "Heaven Is the Face," it was as if my honesty about my real-world longings and pain opened a door. I was able to get another glimpse of heaven and connect deeply with my longing to be with the One who is in the process of making all things new.

> But in my mind's eye I can SEE a place
> Where your glory fills every empty space
> All the cancer is gone, every mouth is fed
> And there's no one left in the orphan's bed
> Every lonely heart finds its one true love
> There are no more good-byes and no more "not enough"
> And there's no more enemy.

The entire process of writing songs for what would eventually become the album *Beauty Will Rise* was an incredible journey into understanding how unafraid God is of our honesty, how He welcomes us to bring everything we have inside of us—all the confusion, anger, sadness, and hurt—and lay it all before Him. I asked Him the scary, not-to-be-asked questions in a song called "Questions" and was able to acknowledge, "This is not how it should be, but this is how it is, and our God is in control" in a song titled

"God Is in Control." In the song "Beauty Will Rise," I used a pounding rhythm and a bit of a confusing time signature for the verse that talks about the effects of the day "the world went wrong," but then the song becomes more purposeful and sure in the chorus as I declare, "Out of these ashes beauty will rise, we will dance among the ruins, we will see it with our own eyes!" By confessing and honoring the cold darkness we felt in our winter of grief, I was able to begin to acknowledge the first signs of spring that were showing in the song "Spring Is Coming."

I found in those moments that God really was saying, "Come to me, all you who are weary and burdened" (Matt. 11:28 NIV) and bring with you all that burdens you or weighs you down . . . lay it all before Me . . . I can take it . . . I want to take it!" In those precious, life-giving, heart-saving moments, I sensed my heavenly Father, the God of all comfort, drawing me closer to Himself.

Even as the songs were coming, I was still reluctant to say I was making an album. I didn't get together with my usual advisors to seek their wisdom, insights, or opinions about these songs. It just felt like I was treading on sacred ground and didn't want to become concerned with the usual elements that go into the production of an album, like picking singles for radio play or any of that. This was a completely different sort of project—I didn't really even like calling it a "project"—and I wasn't worried about whether it would be commercially viable or not. In fact, I was pretty sure these songs would be so weighty that people would find them hard to listen to. Other than Mary Beth, the only other person I let hear any of the songs was Jim Houser. The two of them understood all too well what I was trying to express.

Later that fall, the tour that my management team had been working on the day of Maria's homegoing—with Michael W. Smith and me—finally came to fruition. We called the concert series the United Tour. Although I still felt fragile, I was looking forward to the tour. Michael and his team had been incredibly helpful and supportive in filling dates for me, and now, for the first time in our careers, we would be working a series of concert dates together. Michael had reached out to encourage me after the accident, and our friendship had grown much deeper, so I was looking forward to just getting to be with a friend who I knew cared about my family and me.

On the other hand, I wasn't sure if I could or should leave Mary Beth. Would that be okay? Beyond that, would she ever be okay with me being onstage again? It was one thing for me to stand onstage and declare, "This is what we believe; this is what is true; God has been with us and for us," but was it inconsistent for me to stand onstage and sing, "Blessed be the name of the Lord" if Mary Beth was sitting in the front row thinking, *I'm just not there yet*?

I had no doubt where Mary Beth would land; she believed as strongly as I did that Maria was in heaven and that we'd see her again. But her mother's heart ached to have her daughter back, and she was understandably fearful of giving the impression that everything was back to normal and we were moving on with life, even though the details of everyday living demanded that we begin to do so eventually.

In a wonderfully tender and loving way, God orchestrated events and allowed me to take baby steps back into the music world by reestablishing the tour with Michael W. Smith. Since we had been talking about doing a tour together prior to Maria's passing, a lot of the logistical work was already done, so we didn't have to reinvent everything. I had done a few isolated festival concerts during the late summer of 2008, and they had gone well, so that, too, encouraged me to think I could do the full tour with Michael.

Michael and I had known each other for years, and although he and I lived in the same town, our kids went to the same school, and we saw each other at a lot of events, we weren't really close friends. Our individual record companies had actually fostered a friendly creative competition between us in some ways.

But during the United Tour, our friendship grew deep. One of the first things Michael expressed to me was, "Steven, right now my ministry is to you. If we do this tour together, you don't have to do any radio or TV interviews or any of the meet and greets. I'll do whatever we need to do." That was an incredible gift to me because I knew that trying to talk with people every night at the concert meet and greets could start to feel like I

Rick Diamond

Prepping for a show with Michael W. Smith.

was standing in line again at Maria's memorial. Multitudes of folks who had experienced heartbreaking loss of their own—loss of a child or a spouse or a sibling or a parent—wanted to share their stories with me. And I wanted to listen to every one of them and be able to comfort and encourage them, but I knew I couldn't wisely carry any more grief than I was already bearing.

Michael said, "You don't have to carry that. I'll carry it for you." And he did. We opened the concert every night with me sitting onstage at the piano singing "Blessed Be Your Name." Michael then came out and joined me and we sang together, Michael on the guitar and me at the piano . . . which threw everybody off a little. Many nights I thought, *What in the world am I doing sitting at a piano when Michael W. Smith is onstage?*

Working with Michael provided me the opportunity simply to do whatever I could. Some nights I could sing; others I struggled to fight back the tears. Some nights I just stood and sobbed onstage. Regardless, every night Michael was there as my brother, leading in the worship, ministering not only to the audience but also to me. I could declare the truth with him or let him declare it for me as we sang "How Great Is Our God."

It was a powerful time for me, "driving a stake in the ground" night after night, at every concert, letting the enemy know that he not only didn't win but also was already defeated.

For me, the best metaphor to describe my life at that time was that of dropping an anchor in the middle of a storm-tossed sea. I'd feel settled and safe for a moment, and then the tsunami of emotion and grief would hit again. Wave after wave threatened to knock me off my feet, so I had to keep dropping the anchor into something solid again and again. For me, that rock-solid place was the Word of God and His promises. Everything else was swirling or sinking.

Brent Milligan, a friend who had played bass guitar on Michael's tours for years and on a number of tours with me, had also played on or produced albums for artists as diverse as the Back Street Boys, Audio Adrenaline, TobyMac, and Rebecca St. James. Brent's music had the honest tone I wanted to pour into the songs I was writing, and because of our deep friendship I knew he was the right man for the job of helping me tell my story musically. Brent was on the United Tour, playing bass again for Michael, so I talked to him about helping me put some of the songs I'd been writing onto an album.

"I want these songs to reflect what I'm feeling in a raw, natural sound. This record shouldn't even be made in a studio," I said. "It should be made on the journey. I want to make it on the road, in hotel rooms, in dressing rooms, wherever we have the opportunity."

Brent agreed, so rather than going into the studio, we took some equipment with us on the road during the United Tour and recorded in all sorts of odd places—in hotel rooms, in the lobby of a theater in Indianapolis, and even in a shower stall in the men's locker room at the University of Kentucky's famed Rupp Arena! We recorded some unusual sounds, some on purpose and some accidentally. On more than a few occasions, we'd be recording in a hotel room and be right in the middle of a soft, intimate guitar part when the housekeeper would come knocking on the door or, worse yet, interrupt us with the roar of an industrial vacuum cleaner out in the hallway!

I had the luxury of being out of my recording contracts, so there were no deadlines or expectations. Brent and I recorded at our own pace while on tour and then worked on the songs in his studio or mine whenever we were at home.

On some of the songs, we were simply trying to get a "scratch vocal" down, a guide vocal I could replace at a later date. But the emotion and the feeling of the songs were so raw and real that we decided to keep the scratch vocal and build the recording around it. One such song was "Heaven Is the Face."

Brent and I set up some microphones in my hotel room in Holland, Michigan. I sang the lyrics with such intensity and honesty that we decided to use the recording, even though my voice was raw. In many ways, that song set the tone for the entire album.

Another recording session took us to a lake where, in the early days after the accident, Will Franklin had spent a lot of time wrestling with God and being loved on by family and friends. I wanted to capture some part of the song "Spring Is Coming" there, because it felt like holy ground and a place where God had met us in profound ways. It would also be the site where Caleb and Julia would be married. So Brent and I traveled to the lake with a microphone and a laptop to record the acoustic guitar track for "Spring Is Coming." It was springtime in Tennessee, and there were birds occasionally chirping in the trees. A few days later, when I was singing the vocal for the song, as I sang a line that says, "Hear the birds start to sing," as if on cue, at precisely the right moment, a bird chimed in on the previously recorded guitar track, singing its song as loudly as it could. I had to smile as once again I sensed that God was sending us another little reminder through His creation that He is with us and for us.

By the end of the United Tour, Brent and I had recorded a group of songs that I felt comfortable playing for some record company executives. Although it was a very different sort of album for me, the team at Sparrow caught the vision for the project. The lamentations were pure, honest, and raw and the natural title for the album stemmed from the song "Beauty Will Rise," a truth I believe with all my heart: God has promised and is even now in the process of carrying out His promise to make all things new . . . to redeem and restore every broken place and thing in our lives as we trust Him. I am convinced that even out of the most broken places in our lives and the ashes of grief and sadness, He will bring some of the most breathtaking beauty. I believe God is going to fulfill His promise to turn all our mourning into dancing (Ps. 30:11), and in fact, we will dance on top of the ruins of what was intended for evil by the enemy. God restores and redeems completely and absolutely, and nothing will be wasted in the process . . . not a single tear, or grief, or pain.

I not only needed to write that; I also needed to hear it, and to hear my own voice declaring it! I believed what I was writing and singing with all my heart, but I could not have imagined how God would give me a clearly discernible, visible confirmation of beauty rising from the ashes.

Playing with the babies at Maria's Big House of Hope in China.

Chapter Thirty-one

Maria's Big House of Hope

In the months following Maria's passing, every "first" seemed to bring with it the deep ache and heavy weight of sadness all over again—the first day of school for Stevey Joy, which would also have been Maria's first day of kindergarten; the first Thanksgiving and Christmas without Maria; our first family spring break trip to Vero Beach without our Maria; the first Easter—the celebration of our Savior's resurrection and the anniversary of my meeting Maria in China for the first time, both of which seemed tightly bound together now as we anticipated seeing Maria in heaven with Jesus. And of course, Maria's birthday and the day of her homegoing brought bittersweet thoughts, memories, and emotions.

Adding to our deep sense of loss were all the unanswered questions we continued to wrestle with. "Lord, this was a child You sent us to China to get so we could bring her back to America and give her a home and make her a part of our family. She had a heart problem, and as far as we could tell, You healed her heart. Was she with us only long enough to put her trust in You?" We grappled with the concept that God had given Maria to us so we could introduce her to Jesus, so we could all spend eternity together.

But perhaps nothing brought together the bitter and the sweet more profoundly for us than our first trip back to China to celebrate the grand opening of Maria's Big House of Hope.

Mary Beth and I had been helping other couples experience the miracle of adoption through the work of Show Hope for nearly a decade, and we were amazed to see all that God had done and was doing. We had also made several trips to China and were seeing some incredible doors of opportunity open there as well.

During one of our trips to China, we met Dr. Joyce Hill and her husband, Robin. Joyce had been born in Singapore, and Robin was a British businessman working among English-speaking expatriates living in China. Joyce had semiretired from her medical career, and Robin was nearing the time to retire as well. Then they visited an orphanage, and their hearts were broken by the enormous needs.

"I'm a doctor," Joyce said. "Maybe I can help some of these children."

Their attitude was, "We are in China, so we must respect their laws regarding how we express our faith, but if we get a chance to take care of a child, we are going to care for that child as if he or she were our own. What did God do for us? God adopted us, called us His own, put the robe of righteousness on us, and welcomed us to His table. He didn't create a second-class citizenry for His adopted kids and give them the leftovers. He gave His best. We may not be able to affect large numbers of children, but we can go deep with a few. And by doing that, we can model what Jesus did for us, one life at a time, in a way that could be far more effective than anything we say." That was Joyce and Robin's philosophy, and Mary Beth and I agreed wholeheartedly.

The Hills made a proposal: "What if we create a care center specifically designed and outfitted to offer life-giving care to children with severe medical needs?"

The government saw the merit in the Hills' proposal and allowed them to create a special care center within the established state-run orphanage system known as the Children's Welfare Institute.

Joyce and Robin pioneered the program that increased the caregiver-to-child ratio and greatly improved the aesthetic appeal of the facility as well.

The facility was immaculately clean, had painted cartoon-type characters on the walls, and most importantly, provided round-the-clock medical treatment and intensive care. As Mary Beth and I walked through their facility, we couldn't believe the beauty and the dignity we saw in the way these children were being cared for, and we wanted to be a part of it.

When Mary Beth and I talked with the Hills, we posed a question: "If we could use my music platform to help you in some way, what would you dream of doing and how could we help more children in China?"

Joyce's and Robin's eyes brightened. "The government in the Henan Province said, 'We will allow you to use a piece of land if you would like to build a facility here,'" Joyce said. Robin explained that the Chinese government would provide the land and would participate in bringing the children to the facility if we built the care center. But Joyce and Robin had limited resources and little access to the broader Christian community. Mary Beth and I traveled out to the Henan Province with Joyce and Robin. We viewed the property and shot a brief video describing the open doors of opportunity we had to have a Christian impact in China. We took that video home and began inviting people to join us in the work.

A few weeks before Maria's passing, a massive earthquake—7.9 on the Richter scale—hit China. The enormous numbers affected by the quake were mind-boggling: more than 87,000 people were killed or missing; more than 370,000 people were injured; 4,800,000 were left homeless. In the weeks and months immediately following Maria's passing, praying for the Chinese people who were digging out of the rubble gave me somewhere to go in my thoughts and prayers beyond only crying out to God for my family and myself in our grief. It was a powerful reminder to me that we were not alone in our suffering and pain, and I shed many tears of empathy for those families. "God, I know the pain we feel at losing our little girl; please help these people in China who have lost sons and daughters by the thousands," I prayed. The Chinese landscape was devastated, as was the landscape of our own lives, and nothing would ever be the same.

At the time of Maria's accident, Show Hope was making slow but certain progress in raising funds to build the care center. When Maria went to heaven, many people wanted to express their love and support for us in tangible ways, so we set up Maria's Miracle Fund and pointed them toward Show Hope and the opportunity to help other orphans, much like Maria, in China. Our family was overwhelmed by a tremendous outpouring of love from people around the world.

The Maria's Miracle Fund amassed an astounding $800,000 designated toward building our first Show Hope Care Center in China. With that money and the funds we had already raised, we were able to complete the construction of a six-story facility in Luoyang City in the Henan Province, one of the poorest provinces in China.

The government of China had initiated the Blue Sky campaign to improve the conditions of the state-run orphanages. As an acknowledgment of the government's positive approach, Robin Hill, who was overseeing the building project, had planned for a small section at the top-center portion of the building to be painted to look like a blue sky with white clouds. Something got lost in the translation, however, and Robin returned a few weeks later to discover that the Chinese workers had painted the *entire* six-story, sixty-thousand-square-foot building blue with white clouds. In the middle of Luoyang, where most of the other buildings are brackish gray, it looked like something right out of a Disney movie. When our family saw it, we thought the building looked fantastic. The "fluke" paint job was a perfect reflection of Maria's presence there—it was almost as if she was saying, "If we're going to do this, we're going to do it loud . . . and make it fun!"

As we prepared to travel back to China for the dedication and grand opening of Maria's Big House of Hope—the name Mary Beth had suggested we give the care center in honor of Maria and her prayer about going to live in God's big house—I felt strongly that I also wanted to visit the areas where the earthquake had obliterated so much of normal life. It seemed like it was to be a part of our journey of healing somehow. I wanted to stand in the middle of where the earthquake had hit, close to where the devastation was the worst, and weep with those people in their heartbreaking loss and tell them about the loss of our little girl who had been born in China.

I also wanted to tell the Chinese people about the hope we have as a family that we will see Maria again because of Jesus. I wanted to tell them how we had survived, that we are alive because of the grace of our God, that we have hope that the story is not over, that out of this sad tragedy our God will yet bring something beautiful.

All of our family as well as several of our close friends, including Jan and Geoff Moore and Karen and Reggie Anderson, accompanied us on this trip to help us honor Maria and declare God's message of hope.

On July 2, after a quick breakfast at McDonald's, we went to Maria's Big House of Hope to have our grand opening and ribbon-cutting ceremony. In addition to the Show Hope friends, numerous local officials and even some officials from the Chinese government gathered for the occasion.

I had written the song "Yours" during my London trip, but after Maria passed away, I wondered, *Can I still sing, "God, it is all Yours; even my children are Yours. Even when You take what is Yours"—and really mean it?*

It is one thing to commit our material possessions to God, or even our careers, but what about our children? Can we really trust Him with everything, even when it means letting go of all the dreams and plans we had for one of our own children? It's one thing to say, "It is all Yours" or "I surrender all," as long as I can still keep my hand on it. But what about when a most treasured part of my life is lost? What then? Will I trust Him there, with that, at that point?

Out in front of the building at the official opening ceremony of Maria's Big House of Hope, I sang the song "Yours," which seemed especially appropriate that day. While technically, the Chinese government owns the land and the building, we knew that the facility really belongs to our God. It is all His and all for His glory! I sang the song with the Chinese government officials in attendance at the grand opening. Near the end of the song, I felt a strong conviction that I was to add a few lyrics and declare publicly, "This place is Yours . . . these children are Yours . . . all of China is Yours, God!"

I wasn't sure how the government officials might respond, and at that point, I wasn't concerned about it. I just sang what I knew to be true and trusted God to take care of the rest. The government officials didn't stand up and applaud, but they didn't seem too upset either.

That afternoon our group of about twenty people walked through every room on every floor of Maria's Big House of Hope as I led the parade with a guitar, singing worship songs, stopping at several points as various people prayed for each child who would eventually be in that place and temporarily know it as home. We went from room to room, praying, speaking blessings over the rooms, and singing God's praises. It was an incredibly powerful time.

The next morning I was walking down the street outside our hotel in the city of Luoyang (a city of about seven million people) and was stunned to see a picture of Maria's Big House of Hope on the front page of one of the city's most prominent newspapers. Along the busy sidewalks every few blocks were large Plexiglas cases where the daily newspaper was displayed for passersby to stop and read. There, for everyone who walked the streets of Luoyang to see, was our story in the headlines. The reporter had quoted all the lyrics to the song "Yours," translated into Mandarin, and had told the story of Maria's Big House of Hope as well as our story of losing Maria.

I couldn't believe it! In a place where I wasn't really able to preach the gospel, God had provided an opportunity for me to share a message of the hope of the gospel and the love of God with a multitude of Chinese people in their own language on the front page of their local newspaper. I remembered the prayers I had prayed on our way home from our first trip to China to adopt Shaoey. I had asked God to give me an opportunity to one day take my music and the message of His love as a gift back to the people of China to thank them for the gift they'd given our family. God had clearly answered that prayer in an incredible way.

We had contacted friends who were helping people deal with the aftermath of the earthquake's devastation, ministering in some of the hardest hit areas, where many of the people were still living in makeshift shelters. Some cities we could not enter because the destruction had been so complete and either it was unsafe or there were no longer any survivors living there.

On July 5, we flew from Luoyang to Chengdu, China, which was the closest major city to the epicenter of the earthquake. The next morning our group loaded onto a bus and began our journey into the heart of the earthquake zone, where so much devastation had taken place a year earlier and just days before we had experienced our own personal "earthquake" of losing Maria. We made it to a little village in the Sichuan Province where we set up for a concert for the entire village that evening.

That afternoon the rains began to fall. It continued raining into the evening, yet hundreds from the village came out to watch and listen while Caleb, Will Franklin, Chris Chesbro, and I played and sang songs declaring our trust in the faithfulness and goodness of our God and our belief in His promises and His love. Before the night was over, the entire team, including my family members and Geoff Moore and his family, ended up onstage together, weeping and worshiping in the rain.

We stayed the night and tried unsuccessfully to get a little sleep in temporary shelters that had been set up by rescue and rebuilding crews. The next morning I explored the streets of the devastated city, deeply saddened to view the rubble yet encouraged to see evidence of rebuilding. It was such a picture of what our family was experiencing—the dust and the rubble and the ruins, but then in the middle of it all, the beginning of something new.

We went outside the city to where there was a memorial marker in the midst of the rubble. The photographer with us took a photo of me there, and we used that picture on the back of the *Beauty Will Rise* album. We

Dale

took another shot of me standing on a rock ledge that projected out over a riverbed far below, where in the background could be seen some of the many homes that had collapsed or had been destroyed completely. With my guitar in front of me, strapped over my shoulder, I raised my hands and, just as I had done many times in the last year, declared God's praise in the midst of the destruction all around me. The photo seemed like a perfect metaphor for how my family and I felt as we purposed to declare God's goodness and faithfulness despite all the rubble surrounding our lives. We used that picture for the cover of *Beauty Will Rise.*

It was a beautiful, brutal, amazing, and agonizing trip. Beyond the overwhelming emotional turmoil, Mary Beth was battling physical challenges as well; her blood pressure shot sky high, her feet and ankles began to swell, and neither of us was able to get much sleep. She was emotionally torn up between the tangible goodness of God in providing Maria's Big House of Hope and all the why questions—why did it have to come about this way?

It was such a struggle for us that I wondered if we had done the right thing by making the trip. Looking back from my perspective now, I know it was indeed a part of our healing to be able to empathize with and intercede for the people of China who had suffered such loss.

One of the amazing benefits we hadn't planned for with Maria's Big House of Hope was the way it would impact the standard of care for children who are orphaned throughout China. In the Chinese culture, where the impact of the one-child policy continues to be felt, many medically and physically "less than perfect" children are placed in the state welfare institutions. Consequently, our focus from the beginning was providing specialized care for the children who were perceived as "broken" because of their special needs. Our philosophy was and is that these children are unique, priceless treasures who deserve to be treated with great dignity.

Interestingly, over time, the directors of the state systems came to tour Maria's Big House of Hope, and it seems the care center began to reshape the way they think about caring for these very special children.

Today at Maria's Big House of Hope, we have about 140 beds, and we now have several other similar facilities in various parts of China. We employ local people at the care centers, so we are not only helping the children but also benefitting the community.

As I walk inside the entryway, seeing the large framed photo of Maria hanging alongside a picture of her flower and her handwritten SEE still sends me on an emotional roller coaster every time. It is a stark reminder of how the facility came to be built so quickly and so well, yet it always makes me sad too. Seeing the beautiful children in every room, however, reminds me again that God does not waste our pain. Although Maria was never a resident of the care center, everyone who comes there is told about her, so it feels as though her presence permeates the property.

People in the area have learned that there is something special about Maria's Big House of Hope. On one occasion, some visitors associated with Show Hope were trying to find their way back to the facility, and they weren't certain of the address, so they described it to their taxi driver. "It's a big blue building with white clouds painted on it," they said.

"Oh yes," the taxi driver said. "The house where God lives."

And he couldn't have been more right!

Kristin Sweeting

Chapter Thirty-two

Step by Step

If this were a Hollywood movie, or a fairy tale, I'd love to be able to say, "And then they lived happily ever after." But by now you know me better than that. Despite the fact that our family was taking baby steps forward, that Show Hope continued to thrive, and that I was writing songs and singing again, we were far from ready to stand up on a rock and proclaim, "Here is how we survived tragedy and how you can do the same."

Quite the contrary, we were making our way through each day as best we could. The grief settled over us like dark, gray clouds heavy with rain. Grief devastates many marriages. We'd heard that 95 percent of marriages don't survive after the death of a child, and at first, that was hard for us to understand. *How is that even possible?* I wondered. After all, in the beginning of our journey following the loss of Maria, our attitude was, "We need each other more than ever." We could not even imagine allowing Maria's homegoing to heaven to become something the enemy could use to destroy us.

Similar to how a person might feel after a major surgery while still taking medication to hold the pain at bay, I felt as though God had initially given us a strong anesthetic, temporarily dulling the full effects of our grief. For a while, it felt like we were living with a necessary numbness that allowed us to keep breathing. We knew we were hurting, but the most intense pain was mercifully being kept at bay.

There comes a day, however, when the patient is discharged from the hospital, they are weaned off the strong drugs, and they begin the journey back to real life, to the "new normal," as Mary Beth called it. That's usually when the worst of the pain begins to be felt.

Mary Beth and I were trying desperately to bear each other's grief, but neither of us was capable of doing so. We could hardly bear the load together, much less individually. My wife is the type of person who is going to be direct and honest about the pain and our processes for dealing with it, so it was no secret around our home that we were in bad shape. Our friends picked up on the tension, but worse yet, so did our kids.

As months passed, the darkness moved in even closer, and it began to take a toll on us. Mary Beth's and my marriage was strong, and we were deeply committed to each other, but we wondered if we could survive. There were actually days when I prayed, "Lord, there's no way I am not going to finish this journey because I love my wife, and I really believe that she loves me . . . but I don't know how we're going to take the next steps . . . I'm really wondering if it would be best for You to take me on home now . . ." And I was desperately serious.

We spent long hours with counselors trying to help our kids process their grief. I had our pastor's phone number on speed dial. Because Shaoey and Stevey Joy had been eyewitnesses to the tragedy, we arranged trauma therapy for them. We stayed close to Will Franklin.

Back home from China, I lay in our own bed, staring at the ceiling in the night. I reached over to hold Mary Beth's hand, and I could tell she was somewhere between crying and seething with anger. "I know God is in all of this," she said, "but I just want my little girl back. I want to turn back the hands of time. I know some people have been helped and some people have been saved, but I really don't care about that right now. And I'm probably going to hell for saying that, but I have a mother's heart. I want Maria back."

It was like a knife in my chest to see her in so much pain, and I knew I had to stand against the enemy who was trying to destroy us, so I tried to gently encourage her to remember what we knew to be true—that God is still God, that He loves us, that His plans for us are for good. But given her depth of pain and my past mistakes of making her feel spiritually inferior at times, Mary Beth would often interpret my attempts to encourage her as judgmental overtones, and we plunged into the abyss of discouragement. I became afraid to say anything for fear of saying the wrong thing, but I also felt a strong conviction that I needed to keep speaking the truth, even if just to hear myself say it. We both felt intensely lonely, and we desperately needed help.

We made it through Maria's birthday, the first anniversary of her homegoing, and Caleb and Julia's wedding all in the month of May. Previously, we had wanted to mark the month of May off our calendars, but now we had something to celebrate each year during the same season.

By the fall of 2009, after we had returned from the grand opening of Maria's Big House of Hope in China, Mary Beth and I knew we needed more than just an hour-per-week counseling session that barely scraped the surface. Our pastor, Scotty Smith, suggested we do something more intensive, a counseling encounter where we could draw away from the everyday routines of life and focus for a prolonged period of time on our condition.

My friend Tim Burke recommended that we talk with Larry Crabb, a highly regarded Christian counselor and someone who had walked closely with Tim through some difficult things. I had read Larry's book *Silence of Adam* years earlier as well as several of his more recent works. Maybe the "professional" could help us, and as desperate as we were, I was ready to go wherever and do whatever was necessary. One of the challenges I have with counseling is my tendency to go in with unrealistic expectations. Each time Mary Beth and I would begin the counseling process with someone, I would feel a sense of hope rising up in me that maybe this person was going to finally have the answer or be able to tell us what we were doing wrong, and how to start doing it right. Even though I knew better, I couldn't help but think, *Maybe this will finally be the fix we need.*

Caleb and Julia's wedding, May 2009.

Tim put me in touch with Larry, who lives near Red Rocks, Colorado. Larry knew a bit about our experiences, our public platform, and our struggles, so Mary Beth and I arranged to visit with him for several days in late August 2009. We quickly discovered that Larry was the type of counselor who did not mince words or pull punches. That was refreshing to us, as we really wanted to "get fixed."

"We desperately need help," I said. "Tell me what to do. Cut me open, give me a lobotomy, a heart transplant, or something so I can think straight; do whatever you need to do. I want this to be better. I want my wife to be healthier. Tell me what to do, or tell my wife what to do."

Larry smiled, but he didn't offer any easy fixes, or any difficult fixes for that matter. He listened to Mary Beth and to me, provided some insights, and allowed us to talk about some of the deep concerns we carried, and that was helpful—but Mary Beth wanted change. "How are we going to change?" she asked. "I don't want to go back to the way we were before."

That had been our ongoing struggle.

For me, I tried to express my unconditional commitment over the years through my songs. Mary Beth always seemed to appreciate the songs I wrote for her, but the songs didn't solve our problems. Mary Beth's sense of security revolved around the predictability of her life when growing up. Her trust issues were not about my faithfulness to her while I was on the road. Her question was, "Can I trust that I am important to you? I hate feeling like we are flying through life by the seat of our pants. Time, schedules, and predictability are important to me, and when those things feel unstable, it's hard to trust that I am important to you."

I immediately tried to fix things. I had to save the day or I would feel like a failure, but there was little I could do to help Mary Beth trust that she was more important than my career or my creative work. If she wanted time and predictability, I wanted to provide them, so I tried to figure out a way to do so, but it was impossible with my type of career and calling.

Over and over I wrestled with the same questions: What counselor can fix me? Can somebody help me learn better time management? Or can a counselor help Mary Beth change her expectations or help her better understand how my creativity works, that it comes in waves? What can we do if that is not how God made me? I would even pray, "God, I know this is a ridiculous question, but are You sure You knew what You were doing when You brought us together? How are we supposed to make this work?"

While Mary Beth's need was for predictable time, my need was for affirmation and respect, to know that she believed in me. I longed to hear the words, "I believe in you; I trust you; you are taking good care of me."

Added to that emotional mix was the spiritual truth that there were needs within both my wife and me that no human being could meet. Only God could provide that peace and security.

In her effort to be completely honest, at times Mary Beth might say to me, "I love you and I'm not going anywhere, but I really don't like you right now. You say you love me and you write songs for me, but I don't believe you because we're still doing the same things. We still haven't finished redecorating the house; we haven't cleaned out the basement like you said we would. We're just too busy."

When she said those kinds of things, it triggered one of two responses: I'd try to fix the situation by making her feel better, or I'd tiptoe around her so I wouldn't make her mad.

Larry hit me right between the eyes about that. "When you do that, Steven, you are making Mary Beth feel like a snake in the grass. You can't blame her for that. You've given her that sort of power over you that she doesn't really want."

"Really?" Part of me wanted to punch him in the mouth, but I also knew there was some truth to what he was saying.

"What does it mean for you to be the man God created you to be?" Larry asked. "What does it mean for you to love your wife on good days and bad days and not try to keep all the plates spinning?" Larry looked at me sternly and said, "Mary Beth needs to know that you are confident that God has called you to be who you are."

I appreciated what Larry was saying, and I realized there were no easy answers. Advice on a book to read, getting a predictable job, five steps to take—that's what I was hoping for. But he didn't offer those solutions. He couldn't.

Through the years, no counselor that Mary Beth and I went to ever suggested I stop doing what I felt called by God to do. In his or her own way, each said, "I really don't believe that's the answer. That will not fix what is broken. You need to be sensitive; you need to communicate; you need to be wise about giving up unnecessary opportunities, or getting involved in things that take excessive time away from your family, but that has to be done in any career. Every husband and wife has to determine where to draw those lines in their relationship."

Ultimately we came back each time to what we knew to be the bottom line, as Ephesians 4:2 puts it: "Be completely humble and gentle; be patient, bearing with one another in love" (NIV). The Bible makes it clear that we will never master the art of the perfect relationship, especially marriage, this side of heaven. Instead, it calls us to humbly, patiently, and gently care for and bear with each other, with love as our final goal.

Mary Beth used to joke when she was speaking to women's groups, "I really wanted to marry an accountant," which to her meant someone with a seemingly safe and predictable routine of life. Ironically, after working closely with the accountants helping Show Hope, Mary Beth said to me, "You're right! I would have been crazy had I married an accountant!"

I was hoping Larry might say something to Mary Beth like, "This is not all your husband's fault. It is a broken system; that's life, and yes, you will disappoint each other, but you still have so much to celebrate in your marriage. Your husband is doing what God has called him to do, and you two are in this thing together."

Larry did that in some ways, but the bottom line for Mary Beth remained: she wanted predictability. And having suddenly lost Maria only added to the pain and grief of living with the unpredictability and randomness of life. "I'm mad at God," Mary Beth said, "and you're the person I'm closest to, so I'm going to take it out on you."

When she did, I'd sometimes try to fix it by reminding her of Scripture. For that, Larry gently rebuked me. "Steven, when you say such things, all she hears is you preaching at her. So can you just listen and love her? She simply needs you to sit with her in the middle of this."

Larry was equally direct with Mary Beth. "You can be hard to live with," he told her.

Mary Beth agreed. She admitted to Larry, "I can be a hard person . . . I get scared and lonely and angry, and I can be hard to live with . . . but my husband has loved me well."

"Your peace and contentment aren't going to come from Steven," Larry reminded her. "And although you protest about him being so busy, part of you has enjoyed what he does. And you have been able to do things because of his career that you might not otherwise have been able to do, so there are blessings that you can acknowledge. You've had a lot of fun and a lot of joy because of your husband's creative success. You've traveled the world; you have the blessings of Show Hope. There's a lot you can and should celebrate."

Larry's bottom line for both of us brought us full circle: you have to trust God. You can't fill each longing in each other's head or heart, and you can't fix each other.

During our sessions with Larry, Mary Beth and I experienced some great moments of feeling connected and hopeful. Our spirits were temporarily lifted. On the flight home from Denver, however, we got into a discussion about going back to real life, and before long, it felt as though the plane was nose-diving toward the ground.

We came away from our time with Larry clinging to the good things we had learned yet ultimately disappointed. We had gone to the "master" for five days, hoping he could perform heart and brain surgery, that he could fix us. He couldn't. Instead, he could only remind us, "This is a journey, and you're going to have to keep taking the next step forward."

It was the fall of 2009, and October 13 was our twenty-fifth wedding anniversary. I had made plans for us to go to Hawaii, but we were both pretty nervous about being alone for a week given all that seemed so broken between us. But we went. There I was in the most beautiful place on earth, with the person I loved more than anyone else on earth, trying to celebrate twenty-five years of life together, and yet we both felt so desperately lonely and sad. I stood at the ocean one evening and thought about swimming out as far as I could until I had no strength to make it back. I knew it was a crazy thought and wouldn't fix anything, but I just wanted to stop hurting.

About three days into our trip, it was as though God pushed back the dark clouds for a few days and gave us a window of sweetness and tenderness together. We wept together and even laughed together in ways we hadn't in a while. We remembered how desperately in love we were and how much we wanted to stay close to each other. Even though we returned to find much of the same heaviness we had left with, it felt like God had given us a moment to taste and SEE His goodness and to have some winds of hope blown into our sails at a time when we desperately needed it.

Mary Beth had been journaling some of her thoughts and feelings and sharing them in blogs on the internet. There had been such a great response to the raw honesty in her words that she had been approached about writing a book. While writing a book wasn't anything she aspired to or imagined she would ever do, as we prayed about it together, she began to sense that perhaps sharing her story would be an important part of the grieving and healing process for her. She began writing her book at the beginning of 2010, and while the process seemed to be cathartic for her in some powerful ways, it also served to intensify the pain and the struggles and sent us reeling again. It seemed as if her attempt to steward the story in a way to encourage others and declare our trust and faith in God's sovereignty and faithfulness had again alerted the enemy to attack us. In the process of trying to tell her story along with fighting the battles we were facing, our pastor, Scotty Smith, suggested we talk with another professional, his good friend Dan Allender.

Dan suggested that Mary Beth and I each spend a few days individually with him and then spend some time together as a couple. We visited with Dan in March 2010 and then again in June 2010.

During our intensive counseling sessions, we talked about our struggles, frustrations, and the sadness that permeated our lives. From those sessions, I realized more than ever that we were in a spiritual battle. Dan said something like, "Satan is screaming lies over us all day long. And God whispers the truth in a still, small voice. So often the voice we listen to most is the one we hear the loudest."

It was as if the enemy was ruthlessly planting destructive thoughts and ideas in our minds about each other and ourselves and attempting to exploit our vulnerabilities. Dan helped us remember that Scripture clearly tells us, "The thief comes only to steal and kill and destroy" (John 10:10), and he encouraged us to be aware of what voice we were listening to.

As Dan helped us talk and pray through what he saw us battling, he spoke about something he called "a spirit of ruin."

"It seems that the enemy is constantly screaming at you both that it is all in ruins, and you're defeated. Yet even with the loss of Maria and all that you have already come through after this tragic loss, you are fighting to be together, and there is a beautiful fragrance of God in that, so the enemy screams at you even louder and attempts to find any area of weakness to use against you. He is so relentless. You just can't seem to get a break."

I didn't say much, but I nodded my head as the tears streamed down my face. *Yeah, that's right*, I thought.

As much as I wanted to solve everything, I had to keep remembering that I was not solely responsible for my wife's emotional well-being. Certainly, as the husband and father in our family, my role is to be a servant leader. My desire as a follower of Jesus has been to love my wife the way Scripture calls me to in Ephesians 5:25: "Husbands, love your wives, as Christ loved the church and gave himself up for her." But even at my very best, I can't meet the deepest needs in Mary Beth or in our children; only God can do that. And in the same way, only God can meet the deepest needs of my heart.

For me, one of those deepest needs was to hear words of encouragement and affirmation. I think every man wants to hear his wife and children say, "Thank you for all you do to take care of us. We need you and we believe in you." Those kinds of words will keep most of us going; we'll throw ourselves into overcoming any obstacle simply to obtain that sort of admiration. But to make hearing those words my goal in life was foolish.

Something I've come to realize is that Mary Beth's and my failings are a part of our story. The places where I have allowed my foolish, self-righteousness to create insecurity in her are real; her failure to be the encourager I have desired is real too. Out of that, we have both been forced to trust God, knowing that we love each other, that we honor each other, but that we are not able to fix each other, to reshape the other person into our own image.

Although our counselors couldn't wave a magic wand over us and make everything better, Mary Beth and I were grateful to spend time in the darkest of our days with some of the wisest, most respected counselors in Christian counseling—the guys who literally wrote the book on much of what Christian counselors use in their work with individuals and couples. We saw that as one more of the many ways God proved to be with us and for us on our journey. We had to keep trusting Him and taking the next step.

> If there's an ocean in front of you
> You know what you've got to do
> Take another step and another step
> Maybe He'll turn the water into land
> And maybe He'll take your hand and say,
> "Let's take a walk on the waves
> Will you trust Me either way
> And take another step?"
>
> "Take Another Step"

Kurt Heinecke

With Stevey Joy, Mary Beth, and Shaoey at the K-LOVE awards.

Chapter Thirty-three

Together

In 2010, Mary Beth's book, *Choosing to SEE*, was published. As important and right as we believed it was for her to write the book, watching her wrestle her way through telling her story while we were trying to find our way through our grief was almost unbearable at times. There were many days we asked the question, "Are we doing the right thing and will we survive this?" But at the same time, it seemed clear that for Mary Beth, being able to tell the story and see the incredible impact it had in other people's lives was a vital part of her healing.

Upon release of the book, we found ourselves facing another opportunity that seemed very important and very frightening at the same time. Mary Beth was asked if she'd be willing to share her journey from stage, both as a part of Women of Faith conferences as well as on a tour with me. She had made me promise years earlier that I'd never "make her" go onstage except maybe to wave a quick hello. Of course, the idea of me "making" Mary Beth Chapman do anything she didn't want to do was a bit humorous, but I had promised I'd never put any expectations on her to do that. As my manager, Jim Houser, presented these ideas to us, I was surprised when she said, "I really feel like this is something I'm supposed to do . . . just for a short season."

We had already come to the realization that a ruthless enemy seemed to be using every weapon he had to try to destroy us as a couple and as a family. Many times in our darkest moments, I had spoken . . . sometimes even screamed in desperation . . . what we both knew was true. There *is* an enemy who wants to destroy us! But we are *not* the enemy of each other.

As the tour got closer, the battle seemed to intensify. Several times I decided to pull the plug on the whole thing, but then after praying and talking with our friends and counselors, I chose to keep moving forward. Now there were contracts signed, tickets sold, plans that couldn't be undone, and we were in terrible shape. I made a desperate call to a good friend and wise counselor. I said, "I don't know if we can do this. How can we stand onstage as broken as we are? In good conscience, I'm not sure we'll be presenting something truthful."

For years, I had always been honest with the people who attended my concerts. Some nights before I sang "I Will Be Here," I would tell the audience, "I'm sorry my voice is a little rough tonight. They say you're never supposed to apologize from stage, but you guys are not fans; you're family. So the truth is the reason my voice is so scratchy is because before I left home, my wife and I were arguing and yelling at each other."

Rather than rejecting me for my lack of spirituality, many people breathed a sigh of relief. "Hey, me too," I heard from struggling believers again and again. So I knew from years of experience that sharing honestly from my own places of weakness could be a great encouragement. But this was different . . . it felt like we were going to break apart at any moment, and we were going to go onstage and talk about how God was holding us together. I was really struggling to reconcile the situation in my heart and mind.

I told our friend, "This whole thing could fall apart on us right out there for the world to see. It may be that we'll be out onstage and blow up . . . when Mary Beth will pull the plug and say, 'That's it. I can't do this anymore. You don't get it. You don't get me. I'm done.'"

My gut feeling was, "We don't need to be doing a tour; we need to go away somewhere to have a six-month-long counseling session . . . or a six-year session . . . so we can fix this!" I worried, "We can't do this if it is not fixed, at least a little bit, and this is *definitely* not fixed!"

I was at the place where I basically said, "Okay, God, if that's what You want to do, to have us stand in front of the world as broken as we are, and maybe even have everything fall apart with everybody watching, then it's in Your hands . . . I can't imagine how that's a good thing, but I'm going to trust You with it."

Our friend's response was simple and yet exactly what I needed to hear. She said, "Steven, I'm so sorry and I don't have the answers for you, but here's what I know . . . I know you and your wife love God and you love each other. And the truth is right now you're together. That's all you need to say when you stand onstage: 'We're together. By the grace of God, we're together. Today.' You don't have to pretend. You don't have to say you have it all figured out. All you need to say is, 'We're here; we're busted up, we're broken, we're hurting, but we're here, together."

We could do that, if nothing else . . . and that would be enough.

Mary Beth and I took each other's hands and said, "Let's go do this—*together*." Although it was scary, we did the speaking engagements, the tour dates, the television and radio interviews . . . all on purpose, with counselors weighing in and helping us each step of the way. At every concert, people thanked Mary Beth for her honesty.

And everywhere we went God used our brokenness to give people hope and to remind them that no matter what they had experienced, the story wasn't over yet. God is for us and with us every step of the journey, even when we can't see Him or feel Him. He does know the plans He has for us, and He really is working everything together for good, if we'll trust Him, even with our pain.

Still, there were nights when we weren't sure we were going to make it onstage because of the sadness or madness going on behind the scenes. But by God's grace, I watched in amazement every night as my beautiful, brokenhearted bride stood courageously in front of people doing something she had never wanted to do to talk about a journey she had never ever wanted to take. And standing onstage with us were our two sons, Caleb playing guitar and Will Franklin playing drums. Night after night we stood up together to say and sing, "The enemy has been defeated . . . Our Redeemer is faithful and true . . . and out of these ashes beauty is rising!"

On the last night of the tour, after she had finished speaking to the audience, Mary Beth leaned over to me onstage, kissed me on the cheek, and whispered in my ear, "Can I please go home now?" I smiled and nodded.

We were able to do the tour only because, even with all our unanswered questions, we believe the story isn't over yet . . . we're not home yet, but we are going home! There is a day coming when God is going to wipe every tear from our eyes and take us to a place where all the sad things will come untrue. That's what we were made for, and that's what we are longing for.

I think that's part of why I want so badly to fix things. It's connected to an ache deep in the soul. We were created to live in the Garden of Eden, where everything worked beautifully and perfectly . . . where everything was "fixed." So we have a longing within us for this life to be made right and a frustration when things go wrong.

I don't want my wife to feel frustrated because there's never enough time. I don't want things to be broken in my relationships with her and our kids. We were made for things to work. But sometimes they don't.

And that's where the tension increases.

As C. S. Lewis pointed out, "If we find ourselves with a desire that nothing in this world can satisfy, the most probable explanation is that we were made for another world."[1]

And the solution for the ache isn't to kill the longing or to try to dumb it down or numb it down. I believe we need to feel it—even the pain that comes with it—and let it remind us of who we truly are, what we were made for, and what is to come . . . when all our longings and hopes will be completely and absolutely fulfilled by the glory and the presence of our

God. Every broken thing will be restored, and every relationship will be as we long for it to be. That really will be heaven! It is real . . . it is coming . . . but not yet.

The Fix-it Kid is now Fix-it PopPops and still unable to fix everything that needs fixing. Thankfully, Mr. Fix-it has realized that some things won't be fixed this side of heaven. If everything were fixable, there would be no more orphans; yet if there were no children in need of a family, my wife would never have comprehended how much God unconditionally loves her, how much she matters to Him, and how He has adopted us into His eternal family. Yes, some things are unfixable, so we live with the tension—and ask God for more grace to continue to trust Him.

Recently, our daughter Emily, now the mother of three beautiful children, wrote a sweet letter to me in response to a question I had asked her about the unfixable moments in our family's life and the title of this book. Her response surprised me.

> *Dad, thanks for stopping by today. I love you lots and I'm proud of you and all you are doing these days. Just wanted to follow up and reiterate, I really like the book title—a clever and poignant twist to a song title that many will recognize. It really summarizes where you have been on your journey here in the real world hoping for heaven.*
>
> *I am proud of you and will be the first in line to purchase the book.*
>
> *After you shared a bit, I got to thinking about some brainstorming I did once about a book if I were ever to write one. And I was reflecting on yours and Mom's parenting and the greatest gifts you and Mom have given me.*
>
> *One of the best things, ironically, I believe that you gave me was your inability to fix it. Really, it was a kind and gentle introduction to a harsh world that eventually every child has to grow up in and out from under their parents' wings and cope with. If you could have fixed it all, why would I have needed to turn to God? You always led us to the throne of grace, especially when you couldn't fix it.*

And that, that is indeed a great gift, because on these really hard momma days, when I feel like I am failing, the enemy is throwing all his darts, Tanner and I are at odds, and the trauma never leaves, and then somehow I have to raise kids and have hope to look for the kingdom coming in what can feel like a hellhole at times, I remember what you taught us. Maybe I can't fix it, but I know the One who can.

And so at the feet of Jesus I will lay my burdens down.

Thankful for you. Love you lots,

Emily

Reading those words coming from the heart of my daughter was a priceless gift reminding me that God really is taking all things, even the unfixable things, and masterfully, lovingly working them together for our good and for His glory.

Mary Beth and I still struggle and have to keep taking one step at a time. We still don't have life figured out, but God has met us in those unfixable places in our lives . . . the ultimate unfixable being our experience of losing Maria and all that has come with it. Like Jacob in the Old Testament, after wrestling with God, we walk with a limp. Some days it's still hard just to keep breathing. The rogue waves of grief still come crashing sometimes without any warning. Mary Beth still deals with depression, so that means I do too. And so does our entire family. But we love each other and are committed to God and to each other, so we keep showing up for each other.

Living with the brokenness is not easy . . . sometimes it seems impossible. Some people get mad and run away, look for an escape or another person or their drug of choice, or they make life a living hell for everyone around them. But when we do that, we can forfeit something amazing that God has for us. And where can we run anyhow? In Mary Beth's and my journey, and especially since Maria went to heaven, we are convinced that our determination to stay the course and trust God for the strength to take

Shaun Menary

Me marrying Will Franklin and Jillian, an amazing day of healing and joy!

the next step is what has allowed us to experience a depth and a richness that we wouldn't have known any other way.

We shudder to think what might have happened had we not held on to each other through all the turmoil. We would have missed some of the greatest moments of our life together.

For instance, it was only a few years later when Mary Beth and I stood with our arms around each other . . . *together* . . . at the cradle of baby Eiley, our first grandchild born to our daughter Emily and son-in-law, Tanner. Looking at that beautiful new life through our tears, we realized not only that we had survived but also that God was bringing us new "firsts" to celebrate.

Then in 2013, I would be honored to officiate at the wedding of Will Franklin and his lovely bride, Jillian. Since I am not an ordained minister, I served under the authority of a local pastor, but I presided over the entire ceremony, presented Will's and Jillian's vows, and pronounced the couple husband and wife. My tears that day were tears of joy, as I knew not only that Will was going to survive but also that God had given him a priceless treasure, an angel named Jillian to walk beside him, hold his hand, and even write and sing songs to encourage him on their journey through life together.

Our family continues to heal, and God continues to give us new beginnings. God has been faithful to us, and we believe that what He raises from the ashes will be greater than anything we've yet imagined.

Mary Beth's and my twenty-eighth anniversary was a particularly important one for me for several reasons, so as I had done on a few occasions before, I wrote a song to Mary Beth. I recorded the song "Together" on *The Glorious Unfolding* album.

> Here we stand and here we are
> With all our wounds and battle scars
> From all the storms and all the wars we've weathered together
> We had no way of knowing when
> We started way back there and then

How the road would twist and turn and bend
We just knew we belonged together
And if it wasn't for God's mercy and His grace
There's no way we would be standing in this place
But because He has been faithful
Every step along the way
Here we are together.

Camille Blinn

With the love of my life . . . together!

Chapter Thirty-four

New Beginnings

Ever since the accident, the question of whether we could or should stay in our house had been growing like a storm cloud over us. At first, we were so concerned with trying to care for our kids and rebuild our lives around the "new normal" that our living situation was put on the back burner. But as the months passed and the numbness began to fade, I noticed a growing uneasiness in Mary Beth about staying in our house. Driving up the driveway to the place where the accident had taken place began to bring back terrible images and memories. Every day as we walked up the steps from the garage into the house, we crossed over the very spot where I had tried to perform CPR on my own little girl. And while the house was full of happy memories as well, even those seemed to be overshadowed by the constant reminder of who and what was missing.

We returned home after our tour together as Christmas of 2010 was approaching, and one afternoon while we were sitting in the living room trying to discuss what to do about our house, the dam of sadness and anger broke again. There was yelling and screaming and crying like many times before, but this time we ended up exhausted in each other's arms weeping together, and I heard my wife whisper, "I just feel so stuck . . . I can't live here, but I can't leave here." We had discussed selling the house and moving, but this land felt like holy ground because of all that had happened here, good and bad. The idea of leaving it felt somehow like leaving Maria behind, and that was unbearable. We had looked at the possibility of doing a major renovation to our house so that it would feel completely different. But through her tears that afternoon she said, "I know it makes no sense, but what I really want to do is tear this house down and build a new house . . . make a new start right here on this spot."

Everything inside me wanted to give my wife what she was asking for, but the "responsible guy" voice in my head began to speak to me. "There is no way you could justify doing that . . . tearing down a perfectly good house. That would cost a lot of money, actually waste a lot of money, and you know what kind of good that money could do in places like China in your work with orphaned children. And what in the world would people think if you did something so wasteful and extravagant as tearing down a house that still has good years left in it. Good stewardship would have you sell this house, take that money, invest it wisely, and buy another house." On and on the voice in my head tried to counsel me to do the wise and responsible thing. But the more I prayed about how to care for my wife in this area, the more I couldn't escape the idea.

One day as I was praying and wrestling with the whole crazy notion of tearing down our house to build a new one, I felt God answered me in a very clear and surprising way. Usually, I have found that the answers to my prayers are slow revelations, becoming clear only as I walk forward in a certain direction, sometimes being redirected as I try to listen for that voice saying, "This is the way, walk in it," as Isaiah 30:21 talks about. But on a few occasions, God has graciously given me a very clear and direct answer, not audibly but in an undeniable voice nonetheless. Thankfully, this was one of those occasions when I think God knew I needed something very tangible. If I were to put it in a conversation, it would sound something like this.

"Father, here I am again asking You for wisdom about what to do about our home. Mary Beth still really wants to tear our house down and build a new house, and as much as I want to do that for her and our family, it just seems so wasteful and extravagant." (Those seemed to be the two words I kept struggling with . . . *wasteful* and *extravagant*.)

"Steven, can I remind you of something . . . you keep using those two words *wasteful* and *extravagant* . . . don't you realize that the way I love you is often very wasteful and always very extravagant? I've heard you say and sing over and over again how you will trust Me when I give and when I take away . . . how you trust that I am good and My love for you is great. You have trusted Me in the taking, now will you trust Me in the giving? If I want to love you and your family in a way that might seem wasteful and extravagant to you, can you trust Me . . . even with that?"

What? I couldn't believe it. I was undone, and the tears streamed down my cheeks.

My family and I had held on to the words of Psalm 34:8 like a lifeline to hope in the darkest days. "Oh, taste and SEE that the LORD is good! Blessed is the man who takes refuge in him!" Obviously, we knew a new house was just a temporary thing, but now it was clear that God wanted to use this temporary, finite thing to show us His infinite goodness in a very tangible way.

Christmas Day was approaching, so I decided that rather than tell Mary Beth about my "conversation with God," I would surprise her on Christmas. I also knew that she would probably be skeptical and wonder whether I would change my mind or "need more time to think about it," as I usually did with every decision. So I bought two books about how to design a new house. I also called an architect who came highly recommended and set up an appointment for the first of the New Year. Then I wrote Mary Beth a note telling her about how I felt like God had made it clear that it was the right thing for us to tear down the house and rebuild and how I had already set up an appointment with an architect for her to begin designing a new home. I wrapped up the note with the books and put them under the Christmas tree.

While much of 2010 had seemed like "the year from hell," as our family gathered for what would be the last Christmas in our house, we were more thankful than ever to be celebrating the truth of Christmas, that God really is with us! We read the Christmas story and remembered again how God came from heaven to enter into our very real world of pain and suffering, even being born in a dirty, smelly stable instead of a palace to let us know He was coming to be with us in our brokenness.

His love for us has always been wasteful and extravagant.

Mary Beth opened her gift from me, and the hugs, kisses, and tears ensued.

"Oh, taste and SEE that the LORD is good."

We began a back-to-basics crusade in our house, getting rid of stuff. Like many families, we had acquired a bunch of material things that we no longer used or needed, so even before we decided to build a new home, Mary Beth had begun to purge our attic and closets, getting rid of everything she could. I often told the kids, "Get up and move every few minutes or you might get thrown away." Simple living was nothing new for Mary Beth; she had always been wired that way, but after Maria's passing, her desire for it had intensified. We began to realize that even the purging process was part of the grieving and healing that God knew we needed. It gave Mary Beth the reason she needed to approach the almost unbearable but necessary task of cleaning out Maria and Stevey Joy's room and closets. By the time we had cleared out the house in preparation for the demolition, we'd all gained an even greater perspective about holding loosely to the *stuff* in our lives.

When we got all of our furniture and belongings out of the old house, I realized it wasn't just a house; it had been the focal point of our family for more than two decades. It was the place where our kids had enjoyed most of their good memories, where they had experienced their initial life moments, parties, prayers, laughter, music . . . and yes, tears. I descended the stairs, thinking I was going to have some emotional struggles dealing with thoughts of all the happy memories over the previous twenty years of our kids coming down the steps at Christmas. I stopped and looked back up the stairs, and it hit me: There's no life in this house. It is wood and drywall. The life is in the people. The memories will live on within the people. Later, when I came back into the house, without all the furniture and our family members gone, it was just a building.

August 16, 2011, was to be the day we would begin the teardown process. The day before the wrecking crew arrived we all gathered at the house for one final walk-through and a chance to pray, cry, laugh, and remember. (Actually, much to my wife's frustration, I was still cleaning out my closet as well.)

By now we'd stripped everything out of the house that could be used, and Habitat for Humanity had made several trips to salvage anything they could reuse. That was helpful to me because even with all I had experienced, a part of me was still struggling with whether we were doing the right thing.

Finally, the family gathered in what was left of the master bedroom. Besides being the "love den," as my wife and I called it just to make our kids uncomfortable, this was the place where we'd spent many sleepless nights, especially in the last two years, wondering how and if we would make it. Just above where the headboard of our bed used to be we spray painted the words, "The enemy has been defeated!" We gathered the family in front of the wall for a picture, and we all did our best "rock face" in honor of Maria, who was known for her rendition of "I Love Rock 'n' Roll," sung while making her famous "rock face". . . something her mom and brothers had taught her of course. A large print of the picture we took that day hangs in our new home today as a powerful reminder to us.

Even though I knew God had made it clear to me about tearing down the house, I continued to wonder if we were doing the right thing. They don't call me the king of second-guessing for nothing. I woke up the morning of August 16 in a full panic, knowing that a demolition crew would soon be driving up the driveway to my house to destroy it. Had I really heard from God the way I thought I had?

As I try to do every morning, I opened my favorite devotional, *Daily Light*, to the page of the morning reading for that day.

August 16 Morning Reading:

> The house that is to be built for the LORD must be exceedingly magnificent.
>
> 1 Chronicles 22:5

The Enemy has been
DEFEATED!

I know there may be some who would call this a coincidence or offer a number of explanations as to what that verse may or may not mean. But I can tell you without a doubt, I believe God not only orchestrated that verse to be right where it was when I needed it but also had a big smile on His face as I read it.

We drove to the house and watched as the burly, yellow backhoe-type wrecking machine began to take its first ferocious bites out of our house. I walked over to put my arm around Mary Beth and noticed tears in her eyes.

I asked, "Sweetheart, are you all right? Are you sure you're okay watching this?"

Mary Beth looked back at me and said, "These tears aren't about this house at all. I'm not feeling regret about tearing down the house, or any second-guessing.

"I realize that what I am watching physically happen to our house is what we went through on May 21, 2008, as a family. It was a destructive force that came through and violently tore apart everything normal about our lives." She waved her hand toward our front porch. "I need to see this torn down," she said, "because I'm getting a tangible, visual picture, and it helps me to put our grief into context. So now we can start again and build a new normal."

I knew Mary Beth was right, but my emotions overwhelmed me. With the machines demolishing our house behind us and the dust rising in the air, I turned away from Mary Beth with tears in my eyes to find a good place to fall apart, and as I walked a few steps away, I experienced something rare.

As you know by now from reading my story, I'm very careful about using phrases like "God spoke to me" or "I heard God say this or that." But on this day, I heard His voice in a very real and startling way. It wasn't a sermon or a song. It was simply a word: "Good."

One word, loud and clear, over the growl and the sounds of glass breaking and wood splintering in the jaws of the wrecking machine. "Good."

I looked up, and in a broken voice, I said out loud, "God, is that You? Did You just say, 'Good'? Seriously? You're calling this *good*?"

I realized that up to that point I had been thinking of this whole process as something God was more or less tolerating . . . but instead, it was clear to me in that moment that He wanted me to hear Him say, "This isn't merely okay. It is not something I am merely putting up with. I am not turning my head away in disappointment that you have chosen to do something as crazy as tear down your house. This is *good. I* am good. I want you to do this *good thing* . . . trust Me and embrace the process."

Again, I was amazed by the thought that God would love us in such an extravagant way. Not only was Mary Beth able to find healing in the thought and planning of a new home but watching our old house being torn down was also helping her process her grief. And God wasn't finished amazing us yet.

Emily and Tanner had moved to Belfast, Ireland, in 2009 to attend a small Bible college for a year. They enjoyed the culture of Ireland, the slower lifestyle, and the relational atmosphere so much that they decided to stay for another two years and continue their education. They had come home to Tennessee to visit us for Easter of 2011. In the same way that Christmas had become much more significant to us after Maria's passing, Easter and the reality that our Savior had conquered death and risen from the grave had taken on an infinitely deeper meaning as well. As our family gathered around the dining room table to celebrate with an Easter Sunday feast, Emily announced that another new beginning was on the way. She was pregnant and due in November!

Emily and Tanner had returned home again to Tennessee for the summer, but a couple of days after the house demolition began, they returned to Belfast, where they would finish school and Emily would give birth. Mary Beth went with them to help Emily settle in and get her nursery ready. I stayed behind with the demolition project, and each day I sent her photos and updates of the progress.

Near the end of the demolition, when the wrecking crew was taking a break, with the dust still rising from the devastation, I walked around the house taking pictures using the camera on my phone. By that time, most of the structure had been destroyed except the front steps area. I shot some pictures without any elaborate lens or special effects.

I copied the photos onto my computer, and as I prepared to send some of the final photos of the teardown to Mary Beth, suddenly I got chills. One photo showed our front steps leading up to where our house had stood. The dust was rising above the ruins, and in the midst of the devastation was a rainbow of colors from the sun shining through. I looked more carefully. *What is that?* I wondered. I thought I saw the shape of the letter E written in the dust hovering a few feet above the ground. *What?* I looked again, and on the left side of the E was an S, and on the right was another E. I gasped. There, clearly discernible in the swirling, rising dust, were the letters forming the word SEE!

I could hardly believe my eyes. As I've often teased, I grew up Southern Baptist, so I don't go around looking for physical signs, but this sure seemed like one to me. I knew I had taken the photo on my phone, with no special effects on the camera. Whatever the camera had seen, that's what the picture was. But could it really be what I thought it was? Did it actually say SEE in the dust? Or was it simply my imagination?

I sent the picture to Mary Beth without any explanation and said, "I'm going to send this to you, and just tell me if you see anything."

Mary Beth responded without hesitation, "Oh my goodness! I see Maria's SEE written in the dust rising!"

"Yeah, that's what I see too," I said, "but I wanted to make sure I wasn't just imagining things or seeing something that I desperately wanted to see."

Similar to an optical illusion, the word was easy to discern once I saw it. Everyone in the family saw it too and couldn't believe it. Not only were we amazed to spot the word SEE above the remains of our former home, but the rainbow shining through the dust also seemed like a reminder of

The picture I took as our house was being demolished with SEE rising in the dust

God's new beginnings. To us, it was as though God was speaking life to us. I felt God was saying, "I'll write it in a cloud of dust if you need Me to, because I'm going to keep reminding you. SEE My hand in this; SEE that I am with you and for you, and I'm bringing beauty out of the ashes in ways you can't imagine."

The Chappy Campers.

Chapter Thirty-five

A Glorious Unfolding

We wondered where we should live during the building process. Should we rent an apartment as we had done years earlier? Our contractor had indicated that the building project was going to take about a year—which inevitably meant almost a year and a half.

On our property, just beyond where our house stood, we had a barn I used for band rehearsals. The barn is basically a gymnasium with a kitchen area and two bathrooms with showers. The only thing we didn't have was a comfortable sleeping area.

Together, Mary Beth and I began to concoct another crazy idea. I said, "What if we turn the barn into an indoor campground?"

"Yeah!" she answered. "We can get a camper and pull it right into the barn and live in there while the house is being built. That way we can be close by so we can oversee the construction project, and we'll have everything we need."

The more we talked about it, the more Mary Beth's eyes brightened. She had grown up camping with her family, and she loved it. Emily and the boys had already moved out of the house and were on their own, and we had only Shaoey and Stevey Joy at home, so the camper was doable.

Mary Beth loved the idea. We bought a two-bedroom, thirty-foot camper that we could resell after we were done with it and pulled it inside the barn.

The camper had a master bedroom at one end and bunk beds for the girls at the other, with a living area in between.

We did our cooking in the barn's kitchen, so we didn't use anything in the camper except the sleeping area. I had spent half of my life riding in a tour bus, and I had learned how to live in a small space, so that part of it came naturally to me.

Mary Beth said, "Okay, if we're going to do this, I want to have fun with it. I want to make the barn look like a campground." She had green Astroturf installed on the floor so it looked as though the camper was situated on grass. We set our outdoor chairs in a circle in front of the camper around a fire pit with canisters for an outdoor campfire—so at night, we could sit around our artificial campfire right there in the barn. I even piped in cricket sounds over speakers some nights to complete the experience. We had our own trailer park set up in our barn for more than a year and a half, and we made some great memories.

During that time, my managers visited us and suggested that the scene in the barn looked like a television set for a reality show. We actually thought of doing a show called *The Chappy Campers*, in which the audience could follow us through a year of indoor camping, but I quickly decided that was a terrible idea.

We moved in to the new house in January 2013. Our new home is in the same location as the old house, but it was designed differently with lots of open space, particularly good for little Chapmans (and Richardses) to play in. Although Emily is married to Tanner, and Caleb is married to Julia, and Will is married to Jillian, our house is far from empty. In fact, there is a great deal of new life happening within the walls of our home these days. In addition to Shaoey and Stevey Joy, we presently have four grandchildren filling our lives with much laughter, new memories, and endless photo opportunities: Julia and Caleb's son, Noble Day Chapman; and Emily and Tanner's three daughters, Della Rosamond, Verity Lou, and Eiley Eliza Richards. Nowadays, the kids call Mary Beth Grammy and me

PopPops. Yes, the Lord gives and the Lord takes away, but He promises to care for us and walk with us every step of the way between heaven and the real world. He has certainly done that for our family. God is faithful to His Word, and we truly have been able to SEE the goodness of the Lord in the land of the living!

In the old house, the driveway wrapped around and the entrance to the garage was behind the house. In the new layout, the garage is on the side, and where the driveway once curved around the old house, where the accident happened, we built a new recording studio. Although none of us will ever forget, we no longer encounter the physical reminders every day.

Instead, in the very location where the enemy tried to destroy our family, God allowed me to build a recording studio, a facility where I can continue to create new music that honors Him and celebrates the hope that has sustained us. You'll find me there on any given day, and my sons, Caleb and Will Franklin, are often making music in that studio with me and with their own band, Colony House. Will's wife, Jillian, creates some of her beautiful music there as well. New songs, new music arises where once the thief came to steal, kill, and destroy. Already, I've recorded *The Glorious Unfolding* and my first ever album of worship music, *Worship and Believe*, in the new studio. It seems appropriate that "blessed be the name of the Lord" is a message heard often within the studio walls.

Having the old house obliterated was symbolic of so much for us. The whole process was an important turning point for our entire family, but especially for Mary Beth and me. In many ways, it marked a new beginning of a new journey.

While we were in the process of designing the new house, Mary Beth and I made a trip to the Grammy Awards in Los Angeles when *Beauty Will Rise* received a nomination. It was the morning of the awards ceremony, and Mary Beth and I were lying in bed talking about our journey of the last three years. She said, "I feel like I've been wandering around in a dark, dense forest looking for Maria, and every time I get to the edge I can't bring myself to step out into the sunlight because I'm afraid I'm leaving Maria behind in the forest. But I think I finally understand that Maria is not in there, that she's out ahead of me, and it's time for me to take my first steps out to begin the journey toward her and Jesus."

Of course, we still have plenty of days when the weight of grief comes and knocks the breath out of us again. Tears come freely without warning or even any explanation sometimes. We know there's a day coming when every tear will be wiped from our eyes—just not yet.

We understand that we really are in between heaven and the real world, living day to day with the sure hope of heaven before us. And we also know how important it is for us to show up in the here and now, where God has us today. This life is so short, and there is much good to be done and much love to be shown in these few days we have on this side of the veil.

So we make it our prayer to live with our eyes wide open to SEE what's right in front of us and with our eyes looking forward in anticipation of SEEING Jesus and Maria—with all her ladybug dots glued on for good!

My story has been amazing so far, certainly beyond anything I could've ever imagined as a boy in Paducah . . . and each day as I watch more of it unfold, I'm more and more convinced—this really is just the beginning of the beginning.

> This is going to be a glorious unfolding
> Just you wait and SEE and you will be amazed
> You've just got to believe the story is so far from over
> So hold on to every promise God has made to us
> And watch this glorious unfolding.

nd

On stage at the Ryman with Caleb, Herbie, and my dad.

Acknowledgments

Mary Beth for her love every step of the way.

Emily and Tanner, Caleb and Julia, Will Franklin and Jilly Jane, Shaoey, Stevey Joy, and Maria for inspiring the most beautiful parts of my story and for believing in me through the process of sharing it.

Eiley, Della, Verity, and Noble for bringing so much joy and beauty to the most recent chapters of my unfolding story.

Dan Raines, Jim Houser, Jeanie Kasserman, Mark Mattingly, and Rachel Pinkerton for your support, service, and friendship through the years.

Ken Abraham for walking alongside me in the process of helping me tell my story. Without your gifts of listening and encouraging, I'm not sure how this story would've ever been told.

Andrea Doering and Twila Bennett for believing in me and cheering me all the way through the finish line. Your commitment to honor Mary Beth, me, and my family and the story God has entrusted to us has been an incredible gift.

All the folks at Revell for your support.

Our Show Hope family for some of the most amazing chapters of Mary Beth's and my story.

My mom and dad for loving and leading me through the early years and giving me their blessing to share honestly so that others might be encouraged and helped.

My brother Herb for taking me on the helicopter ride so I could tell the story years later, but mostly for inspiring me and cheering me on all these years. I couldn't have asked for a better big brother.

All the family and friends who have journeyed with Mary Beth and me through the many chapters of our story. Whether or not you are mentioned in the pages of this book, we are who and where we are because of each of you.

To each and every person I've had the privilege of working with through the years who has helped me share the music God has given in ways I never could've imagined, I'm grateful.

To all who have been on this "Great Adventure" with me through listening to my music, coming to my concerts, praying for my family and me, singing along in your car or in your shower (or maybe even on stage with me somewhere), and now reading my story, thank you.

Finally, to the Author and Finisher of the story He started writing when He breathed life into me, the One who has been faithful every step of the journey, and the One who promises that the best is yet to come . . . to Him be all glory, honor, and praise.

Notes

Chapter 14 Breakdown

1. Mary Beth has written about her journey with painful but beautiful honesty in her book, *Choosing to SEE*. It is an amazing book, and I'm so proud of how she has shared her difficult story.

Chapter 19 God Follower

1. Elisabeth Elliot, *Through Gates of Splendor* (Wheaton, IL: Tyndale, 1956), 172.

Chapter 24 Cinderella

1. Kuyper's full quote is, "There is not a square inch in the whole domain of our human existence over which Christ, who is Sovereign over all, does not cry, Mine!" James D. Bratt, *Abraham Kuyper: Modern Calvinist, Christian Democrat* (Grand Rapids: Wm. B. Eerdmans Publishing Company, 2013), 12.

Chapter 28 Clarity

1. 2 Corinthians 5:8 KJV.

Chapter 33 Together

1. C. S. Lewis, *Mere Christianity* (New York: Macmillan, 1952), 20

Permissions

"Beauty Will Rise," words and music by Steven Curtis Chapman. © 2010 One Blue Petal Music (BMI) / Primary Wave Brian (BMI). All rights administered by BMG Rights Management (US) LLC. Used by permission. All rights reserved.

BMG Platinum Songs (BMI), subpublishing on behalf of BMG Rights Management (UK) Ltd. (PRS), administers 100.00% for the WORLD on behalf of Steven Curtis Chapman / One Blue Petal Music (BMI) / Primary Wave Brian (BMI).

"Heaven Is The Face," words and music by Steven Curtis Chapman. © 2009 One Blue Petal Music (BMI) / Primary Wave Brian (BMI). All rights administered by BMG Rights Management (US) LLC. Used by permission. All rights reserved.

BMG Platinum Songs (BMI), subpublishing on behalf of BMG Rights Management (UK) Ltd. (PRS), administers 100.00% for the WORLD on behalf of Steven Curtis Chapman / One Blue Petal Music (BMI) / Primary Wave Brian (BMI).

"Take Another Step," words and music by Steven Curtis Chapman. © 2013 One Blue Petal Music (BMI) / Primary Wave Brian (BMI). All rights administered by BMG Rights Management (US) LLC. Used by permission. All rights reserved.

BMG Platinum Songs (BMI), subpublishing on behalf of BMG Rights Management (UK) Ltd. (PRS), administers 100.00% for the WORLD on behalf of Steven Curtis Chapman / One Blue Petal Music (BMI) / Primary Wave Brian (BMI).

"Glorious Unfolding," words and music by Steven Curtis Chapman. © 2013 One Blue Petal Music (BMI) / Primary Wave Brian (BMI). All rights administered by BMG Rights Management (US) LLC. Used by permission. All rights reserved.

BMG Platinum Songs (BMI), subpublishing on behalf of BMG Rights Management (UK) Ltd. (PRS), administers 100.00% for the WORLD on behalf of Steven Curtis Chapman / One Blue Petal Music (BMI) / Primary Wave Brian (BMI).

"Remembering You," words and music by Steven Curtis Chapman and Caleb Chapman. © 2005 Sparrow Song (BMI) (adm. at CapitolCMGPublishing.com) / Primary Wave Brian (BMI) (adm. by BMG Rights Management (US) LLC.) Used by permission. All rights reserved.

BMG Platinum Songs (BMI), subpublishing on behalf of BMG Rights Management (UK) Ltd. (PRS), administers 56.25% for the WORLD on behalf of Steven Curtis Chapman / Primary Wave Brian (BMI).

"Yours," words and music by Steven Curtis Chapman and Jonas Myron. © 2007 Atlas Mountain Songs (BMI), Sparrow Song (BMI) (adm. at CapitolCMGPublishing.com) / Primary Wave Brian (BMI) (adm. by BMG Rights Management (US) LLC.). Used by permission. All rights reserved.

BMG Platinum Songs (BMI), subpublishing on behalf of BMG Rights Management (UK) Ltd. (PRS), administers 75.00% for the WORLD on behalf of Steven Curtis Chapman / Primary Wave Brian (BMI).

"Maria," words and music by Steven Curtis Chapman, James Isaac Elliott, and Mary Beth Chapman. © 1992 Sparrow Song (BMI) (adm. at CapitolCMGPublishing.com) / Primary Wave Brian (BMI) / Cabinetmaker Music (ASCAP) / MBSee Music (BMI) (adm. by Wixen Music Publishing). Used by permission. All rights reserved.

BMG Platinum Songs (BMI), subpublishing on behalf of BMG Rights Management (UK) Ltd. (PRS), administers 37.5% for the WORLD on behalf of Steven Curtis Chapman / Primary Wave Brian (BMI).

BMG Gold Songs (ASCAP) administers 12.50% for the WORLD on behalf of James Isaac Elliott / Cabinetmaker Music (ASCAP).

"Be Still And Know," words and music by Steven Curtis Chapman. © 1999 Sparrow Song (BMI) (adm. at CapitolCMGPublishing.com) / Primary Wave Brian (BMI) (adm. by BMG Rights Management (US) LLC). Used by permission. All rights reserved.

BMG Platinum Songs (BMI), subpublishing on behalf of BMG Rights Management (UK) Ltd. (PRS), administers 50.00% for the WORLD on behalf of Steven Curtis Chapman / Primary Wave Brian (BMI).

"Well Done," words and music by Steven Curtis Chapman. © 1978 Chappy Campers Music (BMI). All rights administered by BMG Rights Management (US) LLC. Used by permission. All rights reserved.

BMG Platinum Songs (BMI), subpublishing on behalf of BMG Rights Management (UK) Ltd. (PRS), administers 100.00% for the WORLD on behalf of Steven Curtis Chapman / Chappy Campers Music (BMI).

"Together," words and music by Steven Curtis Chapman. © 2013 Primary Wave Brian (BMI) / One Blue Petal Music (BMI). All rights administered by BMG Rights Management (US) LLC. Used by permission. All rights reserved.

BMG Platinum Songs (BMI), subpublishing on behalf of BMG Rights Management (UK) Ltd. (PRS), administers 100.00% for the WORLD on behalf of Steven Curtis Chapman / Primary Wave Brian (BMI) / One Blue Petal Music (BMI).

"So Long," words and Music by Caleb Chapman. Used by permission. All rights reserved.

"Hiding Place," words and music by Steven Curtis Chapman and Jerry Salley. © 1987 Sparrow Song (BMI), Greg Nelson Music (BMI), Universal Music—Brentwood Benson Songs (BMI),

Steven Curtis Chapman is a Christian music icon with over eleven million records sold, fifty-eight Dove Awards, five Grammys, an American Music Award, and forty-eight career number one radio singles. He's been featured on *Good Morning America*, CNN, MSNBC, *CBS Sunday Morning*, *Fox & Friends*, *The Today Show*, *The Tonight Show*, and in *People*, *Billboard*, *Parents* magazine, and countless others. He and his wife, Mary Beth, have six children and live in Nashville, Tennessee.

Ken Abraham is the *New York Times* bestselling author of many books, including *Against All Odds* with Chuck Norris and *Let's Roll* with Lisa Beamer. His work has been featured on *20/20*, *Dateline*, *Larry King Live*, *Good Morning America*, *The CBS Morning Show*, *The Today Show*, and many more. At present, Ken has more than ten million books in print. Learn more at www.kenabrahambooks.com.

WORSHIP
AND
BELIEVE
STEVEN CURTIS CHAPMAN

FEATURING
ONE TRUE GOD,
MORE THAN
CONQUERORS

"

Not everyone is called to adopt, but everyone is called to do something.

"

Mary Beth Chapman